LA PASIONARIA

LA PASIONARIA

The Spanish Firebrand

Robert Low

HUTCHINSON
London

This edition first published in 1992 by
Hutchinson

Random House UK Ltd
20 Vauxhall Bridge Road, London SW1V 2SA

Random House Australia (Pty) Ltd
20 Alfred Street, Milsons Point, Sydney, NSW 2061, Australia

Random House New Zealand Ltd
18 Poland Road, Glenfield, Auckland 10, New Zealand

Random House South Africa (Pty) Ltd
PO Box 337, Bergvlei, 2012, South Africa

A CIP catalogue record for this book
is available from the British Library

ISBN 0 09 174572 1

Set in Bembo by Deltatype Ltd, Ellesmere Port
Printed and bound in Great Britain by
Mackays of Chatham PLC, Chatham, Kent

CONTENTS

ACKNOWLEDGEMENTS

I am indebted to the following libraries or archives. In Spain: the archives of the Spanish Communist Party; the National Library, Madrid; the Hemeroteca Municipal (Municipal Newspaper Library), Madrid; archives of the newspapers *El País* and *ABC*; the Archivo Histórico Nacional (Sección Guerra Civil), Salamanca. In Britain: the British Library, the London Library, Canning House Library, the Marx Memorial Library, the *Morning Star* and the Public Record Office. In Moscow: the archives of the Communist Party of the Soviet Union.

I wish to thank La Pasionaria's daughter Amaya Ruiz Ibárruri and granddaughter Dolores ('Lola') Sergueieva Ruiz for their help; Ian Gibson, for his kindness in collecting research material and his unfailing encouragement; Richard Cohen, with whom I planned this book and who maintained his interest and advice after he had left Hutchinson; Neil Belton and Karen Holden for taking over the project and being so helpful and efficient; Jill Sutcliffe, for her impeccable copy-editing; Mary Kenny, whose column in the *Sunday Telegraph* first set me thinking about writing this book; and above all my wife Angela Levin, for her constant support, tolerance of my absences abroad for research purposes, and patience while I was writing.

I also wish to thank the following for their help: Rafael Alberti; Bill Alexander; Santiago Alvarez; Tamara Andreyevna; Tony Atienza; Pilar Bonet; Irene Falcón; William Forrest; Mark Frankland; Vladimir Gabrilovitch; Olga Lepeshinskaya; Enrique Líster; Father José María de Llanos; Robin Lustig; Anastasio Monge Barredo; Svetlana Rosenthal; Tomás Tueros; Stella Volkenstein; Sebastián Zapiraín.

Finally, I am very grateful to the following for their kind permission to reproduce the photographs displayed in the plate section: Fundación Dolores Ibárruri, Madrid (FDI); Archives of the Communist Party of the Soviet Union, Moscow (ACP); Sebastián Zapiraín (SZ).

R.L.

INTRODUCTION

On 12 November 1989, a frail old Spanish lady of 93, named Dolores Ibárruri, died peacefully in a Madrid hospital. If anyone could be called a twentieth-century legend, it was she. Indeed, it was the mythical quality of her life that had been its chief fascination for so many people, to whom she would always be better known simply as La Pasionaria.

Born into the humblest sector of Spanish society at the end of the nineteenth century, she emerged from the drudgery and rigours of life as a poverty-stricken young wife and mother to become a revolutionary leader and symbol. She soared up in the 1930s and blazed through that turbulent decade like some sort of revolutionary comet, adored by the Left, reviled by the Right, an object of fascination to all. She was the most notable figure to be thrown up by that appalling fratricidal conflict, the Spanish Civil War, along with General Franco, her greatest enemy and the ultimate victor. Their mutual detestation was to last for forty years. She was by any standards one of the most impressive orators of the century, a natural coiner of slogans that passed instantly into the language.

She was even immortalised in fiction, by the greatest contemporary chronicler of the Spanish Civil War, Ernest Hemingway. In *For Whom The Bell Tolls*, a gathering of republican leaders in the Hotel Gaylord in Madrid is talking of fighting near Segovia. A 'puffy-eyed' *Izvestia* correspondent tells Karkov, a Russian officer:

> Dolores brought the news herself. She was here with the news and was in such a state of radiant exultation as I have never seen. The truth of the news shone from her face. That great face . . . If you could have heard her . . . The news itself shone from her with a light that was not of her world. In her voice you could tell the truth of what she said. I am putting it in an article for *Izvestia*. It was one of the greatest moments of the war to me when I heard the report in that great voice where pity, compassion and

1

truth are blended. Goodness and truth shine from her as from a true saint of the people. Not for nothing is she called La Pasionaria.[1]

Hemingway, who was in Spain as a war correspondent, saw plenty of La Pasionaria and succinctly described the adulation she inspired. But he also spotted the cynical reaction to her of the Soviet military and political 'advisers' who were effectively running the republican war effort by mid-1937. For Karkov's answer to his effusive compatriot is a dry: 'Not for nothing . . . You better write it for *Izvestia* now, before you forget that last beautiful lead.'[2]

La Pasionaria was also a feminist heroine, a woman who succeeded in a particularly masculine-dominated society (the very word 'machismo' is, after all, Spanish). Although she never allowed herself to be categorised as primarily interested in women's issues, she was deeply concerned with the problems of Spanish women and children and was a leading figure in a variety of women's organisations.

Nobody was indifferent to her. Dressed always in black, she was seen either as a Mother Courage to the family of the poor and dispossessed, or an Evil Enchantress who represented the forces of death and destruction, depending on your point of view. At the height of her fame, with the collapse of the Spanish republican cause, she was suddenly whisked from the stage and placed in a sort of cold storage in the Soviet Union. Trapped first by the Second World War and then by the impotence of exile, she was to emerge after nearly four decades to return in modest triumph to her native country, still a legend but already a figure of history whom time had overtaken. But for all that, there were still those who thought that only with La Pasionaria's return could the Spanish Civil War finally be said to be over.

Dolores Ibárruri's life exactly matched that of the communist movement, to which she was so profoundly attached. She was one of the first members of the Spanish Communist Party (PCE) in 1921. She became a member of its central committee in 1931, a communist deputy to the Spanish parliament in 1936, and general secretary of the Party in 1942, a post she held until 1959 when she was kicked upstairs to be its president.

She was a devotee of Stalin, loyally supporting the monolithic dictator throughout his long reign. She did not change her allegiance even after the Soviet Communist Party itself started to recognise the extent of Stalin's crimes and to distance itself from him, and she never yielded to the persuasive charms of Eurocommunism which were to attract so many of her comrades in the 1970s and after.

2

It was entirely fitting that she and the Communist Party all over its former strongholds in Eastern Europe should pass away more or less simultaneously at the end of 1989. She had, by her own account, thrilled to the news of the bolshevik revolution in Russia in 1917, when she was living in abject poverty in a Basque mining village. She witnessed the birth a few years later of the Spanish Party. She captivated a thousand Party rallies, sat through countless interminable Politburo meetings, and exhorted young men to fight and die for the cause.

She lived in the Soviet Union for nearly forty years, proposed an endless stream of fraternal greetings to her comrades in arms at stage-managed congresses throughout the communist bloc, travelled the communist world tirelessly toeing the Party line and promising its eventual triumph. True, she did break ranks with the Kremlin after the Soviet invasion of Czechoslovakia in 1968 and delivered a protest on behalf of the still-exiled Spanish Communist Party but she never considered leaving the Party in which she had spent most of her turbulent life.

The prize of political power in Spain was always to elude her, though she had the satisfaction of outliving Franco, of seeing democracy restored in Spain for the first time since 1936 and of finally being allowed to return to her homeland in 1977. But although she enjoyed the remarkable feat of winning re-election to the Cortes, the Spanish parliament, for the same region, Asturias, which she had represented more than 40 years earlier, the communist triumph she had always longed for never materialised. By 1982, the Spanish Communist Party had been decisively rejected by the voters and then split into three squabbling, ineffectual rumps. It was a pattern that within a decade would be repeated throughout Europe, both East and West. Her own political life had been crowned not with triumph but with absolute failure.

And yet, by the time she died, La Pasionaria had achieved a triumph of sorts. She had been canonised after a fashion. She would always be a secular saint, to hard Left and soft progressives alike, for her role in the 1930s. But by the end she had been accepted back by a new Spain, free of the hang-ups of the past, to be accorded a measure of respect and indeed reverence by many of her compatriots who had no time for her political philosophy but who could recognise a sort of greatness in her refusal to give up the struggle, her dignified and graceful ageing into a symbol of national reconciliation.

3

There was general recognition too that Dolores Ibárruri was a tragic figure, not only politically but personally. Of the six children she bore, only one survived beyond early adulthood. Four died in early childhood because of the desperately poor conditions into which they were born, including two of the triplets she bore in 1923. Her only son, Rubén, whom she adored, died at the age of 21, fighting for the Red Army in the defence of Stalingrad. Her marriage ended in failure; her only known love affair, with a man 20 years younger, exposed her to ridicule at the height of the Civil War, and also came to nothing. She had to endure the misery of exile for half her long lifetime, never a day of which, she frequently said, passed without her thinking of her beloved Spain.

Little wonder that she would sometimes muse in old age on what might have become of her if she had married a different man instead of Julián Ruiz, the young Basque miner who converted her to socialism. She would dismiss talk of her as a legend and a myth. In exile, she was notoriously reluctant to give press interviews and back in Spain continued to wonder why journalists should be so interested in the story of 'an ordinary Spanish working–class woman'. But she knew she was nothing of the sort.

CHAPTER ONE

A BASQUE CHILDHOOD

The Spain into which Dolores Ibárruri was born on 9 December 1895 was emerging from a period of relative calm, stability and prosperity into an era of change, turbulence and uncertainty. Since the great days of the Spanish empire, the country had been in decline for three centuries. The industrial, social and political advances which transformed Europe in the eighteenth and nineteenth centuries made little mark on Spain outside a few cities. Travellers in Spain in the nineteenth century were fascinated and often delighted by the very primitiveness they found, particularly in the countryside. They found a country which seemed to look back towards the Middle Ages rather than forward to the modern industrial era. Indeed that timeless quality was in evidence well into the twentieth century and continued to be a factor that attracted people escaping from the pressures and conformity of contemporary Western society.

From the mid-1860s, however, Spain had entered upon an industrial revolution – a century after its northern neighbours – but it was a revolution none the less. It was based in the northern regions of Catalonia and the Basque country, which bordered on France and which prospered accordingly. These developments were accompanied by political stability under the restored monarchy, first of Alfonso XII and then, after a spell of regency, of his son Alfonso XIII. Government swung between conservatives and liberal administrations who observed a gentlemen's agreement to allow each other to take turns to govern.

But the progress that had been made in certain areas since the 1860s could not hide the fact that at the turn of the century Spain was still one of the poorest countries in Europe. It suffered from a rigidly stratified social structure with an idle landowning class, a small but growing middle class which contained a high proportion of liberal/republican sympathisers, a significant (and highly politicised) artisan class, a comparatively small working class mostly to be found in the big industrial centres around Barcelona, capital of Catalonia, and Bilbao, the Basque capital, and a huge underclass of peasantry, whose living and working conditions were appalling, particularly in the central province of Castille, in Estremadura, bordering on Portugal, and in the largest and least developed province, Andalusia. Here lay the greatest injustice and scope for social unrest.

The gross inequalities in Spanish society had led to a rapid growth of socialist or revolutionary political movements among the working and labouring classes, who felt totally excluded from the political process. The two biggest of these were the Socialist Party, founded by Madrid printers in 1879, and the anarchists, who found the harsh soil of Spain fertile ground for their uncompromising creed. Unknown in Spain before the proselytising visit of the Italian Giuseppe Fanelli in 1868, anarchism flourished in Spain as nowhere else in Europe. By 1882 it had an estimated 50,000 adherents, 30,000 in Andalusia and the majority of the others in Catalonia. These two regions remained the great centres of anarchism in Spain. The socialists espoused reformism rather than revolution right up to the mid-1930s, and even then it was only one wing of the Party which opted for the extremist path. The socialists and anarchists became great working-class movements, each with their own trade union organisation: the General Workers' Union (UGT) of the socialists, and the National Confederation of Labour (CNT) of the anarchists.

The Spanish Communist Party, to which La Pasionaria belonged, was founded only in 1921, after a split in the socialist ranks, and it attracted little popular support in its first 15 years of existence. It was only at the onset of the Civil War in 1936, because of their discipline and organisation, particularly in resisting Franco's forces during the siege of Madrid, that the communists experienced the most extraordinary explosion in popularity and membership which made them almost overnight the driving force of the Spanish Left.

Many other factors contributed to produce a potent and unstable brew. Regionalism was a recurring theme in Spanish history with the Basques and the Catalans to the fore in seeking greater autonomy or outright independence from Madrid and Castille. Both had their own language and culture, and their economic growth in the latter half of the nineteenth century increased the separatist impulse. Religion was also a force that could never be left out of the reckoning. The Catholic Church exercised a strongly conservative influence, but its identification with the powerful rather than the dispossessed had earned it widespread loathing among the poorest sectors. Although almost every Spaniard was baptised a Catholic, the figures for those who attended church had gone into a steep decline. But the most powerful force in the country remained the army, which by European standards was huge. It was also ramshackle, corrupt and top-heavy with officers. Throughout the nineteenth century it had constantly intervened in politics, with a succession of officers declaring 'pronunciamientos' – uprisings – and taking power.

Since the restoration of the monarchy in 1874, the army had kept to the sidelines at home, while abroad it was the means by which Spain hung on to the last vestiges of its mighty empire, on which once the sun had never set. But in 1898 that empire effectively came to an end. The brief and (for Spain) utterly disastrous Spanish-American war of that year ended in total defeat, with Spain ceding her last major colonies, Cuba, Puerto Rico and the Philippines. It proved to be a watershed. From then on, the army's only sphere of operations outside mainland Spain was North Africa, first in its garrison towns of Ceuta and Melilla, then in the colony of Spanish Morocco, the northern coastal region of that country facing Spain which was carved out in 1912 while France grabbed the richer spoils to the south. The colony served as a useful training (or dumping) ground for the Spanish army, whose comportment there against a series of native uprisings was less than glorious until the mid-1920s, when a more professional approach than had been seen for two decades finally subdued the tribesmen.

Moroccan disasters usually had repercussions on the mainland, contributing to disillusionment with the monarchy (Alfonso XIII was particularly identified with the humiliating defeat at Annual in 1921 at the hands of Abd el Krim, the leader of the Rif rebels) and to popular reluctance to send ordinary working people off to die in pointless colonial wars. But Morocco was to be the proving ground for the generation of professional officers, including Colonel Francisco Franco, who rose against the republic in 1936 to precipitate the Civil War.

The loss of Cuba in 1898 was seen in Spain as a humiliation, but it was more than that. It set in train a national process of heart-searching and self-examination. One result was an explosion of literary and artistic creativity centred on the so-called 'Generation of 1898', a gifted group of writers, poets and artists who articulated the intelligentsia's concern that their country, like Great Britain half a century or so later, had lost an empire but not yet found a role with which to replace it. But whereas Britain was a stable and mature democracy which was to survive the dismantling of its empire with relative equanimity, Spain was the opposite. It lurched uneasily into the twentieth century without the political or social structures to withstand the immense underground tensions and strains that were building up.

Several of these factors played a part in shaping Dolores Ibárruri. She was a Basque, whose family were almost all employed in the iron mines which were crucial to the region's relative prosperity. She was, until the age of 20, a devout Catholic. Although she came to espouse communism with the same fervour, a respect and affection for her former religion never left her and was a recurring theme throughout her long life. During the Civil War she twice intervened to save communities of Catholic nuns from potential mistreatment; from the 1950s onwards, she constantly appealed to the progressive wing of the Catholic Church to work with the communists for social and political change; and at the end of her life she was regularly visited by just such progressive priests and nuns, who delighted in her company. It is interesting that the Basque country was the only part of Spain in which Catholic trade unions made any headway in the first two decades of the twentieth century, becoming a significant factor in the political scene. When the Civil War broke out, the Basque clergy was heavily for the republic.

But there was another dimension to La Pasionaria's relationship with Catholicism: this was the quasi-religious reverence with which she was regarded by ordinary people, especially during the Civil War. Observer after observer noted this phenomenon. She had the ability to turn mass rallies into something akin to an evangelical prayer meeting: people would treat her as a secular saint. They reached out to touch her as they would a religious leader, they wrote to her in expressly religious language, asking her to intercede with authority on their behalf, as they would pray to a patron saint for a favour. Writers who watched her in action compared her to Joan of Arc or St Teresa of Avila. It was a natural thing to happen in such a deeply Catholic country. The faith was so profoundly rooted in ordinary people that even when they rejected it superficially they merely transferred their piety from, say, the Virgin Mary to the cult of Saint Dolores, La Pasionaria. Conversely, some of her fiercest opposition came from

8

the most fanatically Catholic elements of the Spanish Right, who fostered the image of her as a vampire who sucked the blood from priests' necks, as one famous article in a French fascist newspaper *Le Gringoire* had it.[1]

La Pasionaria was intensely proud of her Basque roots and links with the iron mining industry. One of the outcomes of the September Revolution of 1868 was a free trade policy, which included an open door to foreign capital to develop Spain's plentiful natural resources. British, French, Belgian and German companies moved in to invest in the Basque provinces' iron and copper mines, exporting via the port of Bilbao most of the ore to their own countries to be processed. The period from the early 1870s to the end of the century was one of boom for the region, one of the results being a big influx of men and women (including La Pasionaria's mother, Dolores Gómez) from other parts of Spain in search of the many new jobs that were created.

The Basque boom peaked in 1899 when 8 million tons of iron ore were exported and Britain alone invested more than £7 million in the industry.[2] But even though they were in comparative decline after that, the iron mines and the steel industry that grew up alongside continued to be one of Spain's most important sources of wealth.

Though wages might be better than could be earned elsewhere, social conditions were not. The mine-owning companies had little concept of social welfare for their employees, who worked long hours in often dangerous conditions, returning at night to cramped, overcrowded and insanitary homes, or more often than not bunk-houses owned by the mines. They were also forced to buy their food and living essentials from company stores. The owners' response to the miners' attempts to gain better conditions was normally primitive: troublemakers would be sacked (such was the frequent fate of La Pasionaria's husband Julián Ruiz) and strikes broken up by blackleg labour (of which there was an almost limitless supply) imported from outside. It was a natural breeding ground for revolutionary political activity, and resentment against the foreign owners, whose representatives lived in conditions of comparative luxury, was intense.

Until the 1890s the miners' actions to gain better pay and conditions were fragmented and disorganised. But the Socialist Party in particular was steadily gaining adherents among the Basques and in 1890 the miners' grievances exploded in their first general strike. It was sparked off when the British company Orconera dismissed five men who were active political organisers, and it quickly spread across the whole

9

region. Troops and civil guards were sent in to suppress the strike but they were unable to do so. The miners fought like tigers, sabotaging their own workplaces and using with great effect dynamite stolen from the mines to disrupt the authorities' activities. The mine-owners eventually capitulated and conceded a shorter working day (it was reduced to an average of ten hours a day), better accommodation and an end to their stores' monopoly.[3]

The miners' victory was the start of 15 years of unrest, marked by a succession of general and individual strikes. The bitterest of these came in 1903 and lasted from spring to autumn. Again the miners refused to give in and again they came out on top, with the government inquiry supporting their demands for more money and individual freedom. A feature of these prolonged disputes was the vigorous support the miners received from their wives, who went out into the streets to confront the soldiers sent in to attack their husbands. La Pasionaria was heir to a tradition of tough, disciplined women who were not afraid of political action.

But the essential nature of the Basque people was independent, conservative and Catholic. They had lost their ancient 'fueros' (laws) in 1839 after the unsuccessful first Carlist rising (1833-40) in which they enthusiastically backed the cause of Don Carlos of Bourbon and his claim to the throne of Spain. The Carlists rose a second time from 1870 to 1876, again unsuccessfully. La Pasionaria's father, Antonio Ibárruri, fought for them in this campaign. The Carlists were a deeply conservative and Catholic movement with strong roots among the relatively prosperous peasant farmers in the north, particularly the Basque provinces of Navarre and Aragon. They were brave, reckless, bloodthirsty and expert in the art of guerrilla warfare. They supported the reintroduction of the Inquisition and bitterly opposed both the imposition of King Amadeo of the House of Savoy in 1868 and the republic which followed it two years later. Even after they were defeated, the Carlists remained something of a force to be reckoned with and were devoted supporters of Franco and the nationalists in the Spanish Civil War. La Pasionaria's father was typical of the breed, hard-working and brave.

His daughter inherited her father's qualities. Although her experience of life was to cause her to transfer her allegiance to first the Socialist Party and then the communists, she remained a conservative figure in her personal habits and tastes throughout her life, for example abhorring women who smoked, drank or wore trousers. Her own preference was for severe black clothing, typical of the Catholic tradition from which she sprang. However she never learnt the Basque language; she knew only a few words of that difficult tongue.

When she was well into her eighties Dolores Ibárruri still remembered her childhood with the utmost clarity. She could still sing the songs – in tune and word perfect – that she and her schoolmates had sung for King Alfonso XII when he visited the Basque country.[4] The chapters describing her childhood and upbringing in the first volume of her autobiography *El Unico Camino* (translated into English as *They Shall Not Pass*) are easily the freshest and most vivid of a book that thereafter is little more than a crude defence of Communist Party tactics before and during the Spanish Civil War. In it, she wrote of the 'painful memories of a sad childhood and an adolescence that was not relieved by hope'. But there is enough fond detail in her descriptions of growing up in a Basque mining village to suggest that her childhood, though undoubtedly harsh, had its lighter moments.

Dolores Ibárruri Gómez was born in the iron-mining village of Gallarta, in Vizcaya, one of the three provinces that make up Euskadi, the Basque region of Spain. Modern Gallarta is a neat, well looked after town half an hour from Bilbao by train. A single-line railway winds through the shipbuilding and industrial belt which runs along the River Nervion out of the city. Nowadays the short journey provides a graphic picture of the decline of the great industries of the Basque country. In the 1970s and 1980s, recession and modernisation took an enormous toll. The view from the train is largely one of rusty docks and industrial dereliction; the walls are plastered with political propaganda, most of it supporting various Basque nationalist parties. Of support for the Communist Party there is little sign. The tiny station at Gallarta is overshadowed by the workings of a still operational iron mine.

The town itself is hilly and largely composed of pleasant blocks of flats, many of them built in Franco's time. The only sign of eccentricity is a large and ugly monument celebrating, of all things, the bicycle. There is no monument to Gallarta's most famous daughter. There is, however, a little park named after her. There is little or no trace of the village where Dolores grew up; the most obvious link with the past is an enormous crater, 100 metres deep, on the outskirts of town, all that remains of an iron mine. Unfenced, abandoned, it might be on the moon. Above it sits a new industrial estate designed to accommodate small factory units. They are the old and new faces of Basque industry.

Dolores's first name is inscribed in the civil register as Isidora, which came as something of a surprise to her when she discovered it on returning to Spain in 1977. She went so far as to take action to change it officially to Dolores, the name by which she was always known. She was the eighth child of Antonio Ibárruri, a miner, and Dolores Gómez. Her parents had a total of 11 children, three of whom died in infancy.

La Pasionaria's early life was dominated by the mines. Her paternal grandfather died in a mining acccident, her father worked in the mines all his life, and most of his sons followed him. She married a miner and spent the first 36 years of her life in the mining region of Vizcaya.

Her father was known as Antonio el Artillero (literally Antonio the Gunner, meaning dynamiter). In the open-cast iron mines his job was to set off the explosive charges that blasted the rock from the mountainsides. He was virtually illiterate; his daughter Dolores had a natural facility for reading and writing and would read newspapers and books aloud to him in the evenings.

La Pasionaria's mother was not a Basque. She emigrated to the Basque country in search of work. She came from the beautiful old city of Soria, in the heart of Castille, which was to be immortalised in the poetry of Antonio Machado, Spain's greatest twentieth-century poet after Federico García Lorca, and a staunch republican in the Civil War. Dolores Gómez was tall, beautiful and, like her husband, a devout Catholic. (La Pasionaria inherited her mother's looks and her father's toughness.) She too had gone to work in the mines as a teenager – she collected the pieces of rock and carried them in baskets to the railway wagons. She married Antonio at the age of 17. She was a literate woman who liked to read the newspapers and keep up with the news – but according to her daughter she was not at all interested in politics. After their marriage, she devoted herself to her home and the care of her growing family, whom Antonio somehow managed to feed on his miner's wages.

La Pasionaria described the conditions in which her father worked in his later years:

I see my father, an old man, cleaning up the wastes washed down the embankments by the rain or by the water from the ore tanks. He worked with a small group of old miners like himself, who stood in a sea of mud with their trousers rolled above their knees, shovelling the mire, which contained small pieces of ore, onto screens. When they came out of the water they could hardly put their shoes on. They were trembling with cold, exhausted. But they couldn't give up that painful job. As old men they had no alternative.[5]

Such were the conditions older miners had to put up with instead of enjoying a comfortable retirement. In his prime Antonio's work as an explosives expert gave him skilled status. By the time little Dolores was going to school, two of her brothers were working – one in the mines, the other as a baker. Three pay packets meant that Antonio Ibárruri's household was among the better-off among the working class of Gallarta. La Pasionaria admitted in later life that the conditions in which she was raised were not nearly as bad as those she was to endure after she herself married and started a family.[6] But her husband, unlike her father, was unskilled and frequently out of work for political reasons.

The young Dolores was a bright and fiery girl with a mind of her own: 'I was always extremely combative from young. I always rebelled against injustice as a girl, including when my mother beat me unjustly and I would protest with all my soul. I was never a little angel. I was a typical miner's daughter, rebellious but nothing more.'[7] There was injustice aplenty to rebel against. The mine-owners, many of them foreign, were notoriously harsh employers and the miners' working conditions were frightful. One of La Pasionaria's contemporaries recalled hundreds of deaths and injuries in the mines around Gallarta. The injured were taken to the Miners' Hospital in the town of Triano where 'they didn't carry out operations, just amputated their arms or legs, and carried out the first trepans because of the number of miners whose heads had been destroyed.' The mine-owners would pass through the village in black carriages pulled by five beautiful horses, 'with their servants staring at us as if we were animals'. If one of the horses ever had to be put down, the miners would go up to the owner's house to beg for the meat.[8]

Dolores's childhood may have had none of the comforts to which modern children are accustomed, but it was one which encouraged individuality, imagination and self-reliance from an early age.

Our happiest times were the school holidays. Our mothers left us completely to our own devices. We would go to the far end of the town . . . we would make excursions to the nearby mountains . . . from which we would catch sight of the bay of Biscay in the distance. And we would dream, dream . . . We dreamed of Argentina and of Mexico, of fabulous Eldorado; we recalled the names of navigators and discoverers . . . we loved the immensity of the sea.

We climbed the hills to pick berries and madronas in summer and to gather chestnuts in autumn. Accustomed to a hard life, we were not afraid to take risks. We – both boys and girls – raced through the mine sites; we leapt onto moving freight wagons; we slid down the steepest slopes; we hung from aerial tramcar cables; we crawled through tunnels; we explored the mine drifts and the railway trestles. We possessed no toys, but any of us could have written an anthology of children's songs and games.[9]

It was a childhood in which Catholicism and superstition – the latter liberally encouraged by the former – were dominating influences. For instance, it was customary for mothers to sew little bags containing images of the Saints, in particular that of Saint Peter Zariquete, the patron saint of sorcery, into the clothes of new-born babies. The children would continue to wear them as they grew up. Young Dolores followed her faith enthusiastically. She was devoted to the Virgin Mary and would pray to her regularly. She joined a group called the Apostolate of the Adoration and in village processions proudly wore a scapulary, a cloth garment resembling a monk's habit, adorned with a Sacred Heart of Jesus on the front and a cross on the back. She went to communion at Mass every Sunday and was frequently chosen by her schoolteacher to prepare the altar. She had no doubt that she had a vocation, which she never questioned.[10] She appears to have thrown herself into it with the same enthusiasm with which she was to embrace communism as a young woman. It was always all or nothing for her.

Above it all lay the shadow of the mine. It dominated everything in Gallarta, as in a hundred other Basque mining villages. In a newspaper article written in 1936, La Pasionaria gave a graphic illustration:

I lived in a workers' quarter, beside the mine: so near that when the red flags and the three blasts on the cornet announced the explosions of dynamite, nobody was left on the street because on it, with a deadly impetus, landed the rocks torn from the heart of the mountain.[11]

One of her brothers, working in the mines, was killed by a falling rock after just such an explosion.[12]

Housing for the mining families of Gallarta was primitive. A typical house would be made of mud bricks and wood; the animals – pigs, perhaps a cow or two – would live on the ground floor; the family's quarters were on the first floor. The miners and their families depended on hand-outs from the mine-owners to bolster their meagre wages. Yet a contemporary of Dolores remembers that there was pride among the poverty: the children wore patched clothes but were clean and presentable.[13] But there was one thing which had the power to suspend the mine's activities: the weather. Vizcaya's climate is as wet as Manchester's; Dolores was fond of recalling that it used to rain 160 days a year, which meant that work stopped in the mines, all of them open-cast. No work, no pay, was the rule, which meant further hardship for the miners and their families.

School, and in particular a devoted teacher, gave Dolores her best memories of childhood. The love of reading and learning kindled within the poor little Basque girl was to stay with her always. Her first school was the kindergarten for miners' children, which took them off their mothers' hands for the sum of one peseta a day. It was situated on the floor above the town prison. The children could look through the holes in the floorboards and see the prisoners below, some of them miners jailed after disputes with their bosses. There was precious little class solidarity between them and the children above their heads, who would urinate or pour jugs of water through the cracks on to the prisoners. They would respond by shouting or hurling their shoes up at the ceiling, much to the children's delight.[14]

At the age of seven or so, the children moved on to the boys' or girls' elementary school. In the first volume of her autobiography, published when she was 71, La Pasionaria was dismissive of the school, claiming that the children disliked it 'because of the routine teaching, the monotony of the classes and the application by our teachers of the Latin maxim "Letters enter with blood".' But she remembered her main teacher, Antonia Izar de la Fuente, 'with real devotion'. She was clearly a remarkable woman, one of those schoolmistresses who was utterly devoted to her pupils. By one of those ironies of history, Doña Antonia was to be one of the 1,000 who were killed in the German bombing of Guernica, site of the Basques' sacred oak tree, in 1937. It was the first mass bombing of modern history, an event that was to reverberate around the world and will always be remembered as the subject of Picasso's most famous painting. The horror of the attack would become a constant theme in the speeches of Doña Antonia's erstwhile pupil, by then one of the Spanish Civil War's leading figures. In an interview at the age of 88, La Pasionaria recalled:

Doña Antonia was always a marvellous teacher who never drew any distinction between us and the well-dressed daughters of the mine-owners, the daughters of those who exploited our fathers. There was a great difference between them and us: they were just waiting to leave that school to go to a much better one in the capital; we knew that we were never going to have the possibility of going to another school, and we learnt as much as we could, which was not a little.[15]

In this and other interviews given in old age, La Pasionaria painted a much happier picture of her schooldays than in her autobiography. One gets the impression that she was much more relaxed and honest about herself when she was chatting to interviewers, back in Spain at last after 38 years of exile, than she was in the book, where she tended to apply the Party line to everything and depict herself as entirely shaped by the class struggle, without much hint of her real personality being allowed to creep in.

Her other source of books and enlightenment was the local Casa del Pueblo (House of the People). The Casas del Pueblo were a remarkable institution, developed early in the century by the Socialist Party as a forum in which ordinary people could meet, discuss politics and, if they wished, improve their rudimentary education. Each one consisted of a café, a lending library and meeting rooms, and they spread rapidly throughout the country. As Hugh Thomas wrote: 'The barracks of the civil guard, the church and the town hall were now accompanied in most of the cities and the whitewashed pueblos of Spain by a fourth building, also, like them, the expression of a centralising idea, but one combining Marxist thought with educa-tion.'[16] In a country with only a handful of public libraries[17] the Casas del Pueblo became an indispensable means of broadening their outlook. For young Dolores, Gallarta's Casa became a second home. In an article on the subject of the anniversary of the Paris Commune in March 1936, she wrote: 'There was a modest Workers' Centre (in Gallarta) where the children loved to go; it was our favourite meeting place. Red flags were lovingly preserved by the miners in showcases. We loved and knew them all.'[18] She devoured the books in the library to satisfy her passion for knowledge.

Politics was lived in the streets and squares of the Basque villages. Dolores was growing up in an era of increasing political and working-class activity. Rival politicians would visit villages like Gallarta and get their message across by means of public meetings. With no other rival attractions, the whole village would turn out to

16

hear what the visitors had to say, and no one was a more enthusiastic spectator than young Dolores. She would then go home and relate to her parents what she had seen and heard. This was an important phase of her political education for it was at these meetings that she subconsciously imbibed the rhetorical skills that were later to make her famous.

The love of knowledge that she acquired at school and in the Casa del Pueblo led her to want to become a teacher herself, a highly ambitious plan for a girl of her background. She did well enough in her final school examinations, taken at 15, to be able to go on to the one-year preparatory course for the local teacher training college. She entered the college but had to withdraw after a year because of the financial strain the course was putting on her parents' slim resources. Her failure to go on to qualify as a teacher may not, however, have been entirely a matter of economics. Years later, living in Moscow, she left her granddaughter (also named Dolores) with the impression that her parents disapproved of the whole notion because girls of her class just did not have those sort of aspirations. At any event, she moved to a dressmaking academy, which was presumably more to her parents' liking.

There were generally two career options for working-class Basque girls at that time: to work in the mines or go into domestic service. Having acquired her dressmaking skills, Dolores opted for the latter and went to work as a servant for a well-off local family for three years. It was a gruelling and poorly paid life: she got up at 6 am and did not get to bed until 2 o'clock the following morning. She had to wash, clean and serve at table; she even had to look after the livestock. Her wage was 20 pesetas a month. Eventually she rebelled against the drudgery and tried to leave, but her parents would not hear of it. She was obliged to stay.[19] She was still a political innocent but it would be surprising if this experience did not contribute to her subsequent espousal of revolutionary communism.

CHAPTER TWO

DOLORES BECOMES LA PASIONARIA

Dolores chose the traditional escape route from her life as a skivvy: she got married, at the age of 20. It was not long before she realised that she had exchanged one form of servitude for a worse one. Her husband was a miner called Julián Ruiz. He was not Dolores's first boyfriend; that honour belonged to a young metalworker named Miguel Echevarría, from the village of Matamoros. She liked him but he appears to have been rather a shy young man and he failed to press his suit with sufficient ardour for the headstrong girl from Gallarta. (In old age she sometimes reminisced about him to her granddaughter Dolores, wondering aloud what her life would have been like had she married him. Sometimes she appeared to regret not having done so.) She dropped him, and Julián Ruiz came into her life.

Julián was 20 when Dolores first met him, while she was only 15. He claimed she spotted him first: 'When I first noticed her, she had already noticed me. She was young but I liked her a lot.'[1] They first spoke to each other when Dolores obtained a part-time job at a café in Gallarta. They got on straight away.

Julián was an ardent member of the Socialist Party and heavily involved in political activity in the mines. Possibly because of this, possibly because they thought their daughter could do better for herself, and perhaps through a combination of both, Dolores's parents took against Julián and did everything they could to terminate the budding relationship. Dolores was still very religious and, like all Spanish girls of the time, paid a great deal of attention to what her parents told her. She and Julián only rarely managed to see each other. They told her he was a drunk and a gambler, much to his chagrin. 'The whole village knew I was the hardest worker there,' he said.[2]

Possibly because of blacklisting at the mines, Julián went to work building a road at Aulestia. He missed Dolores badly and eventually wrote proposing marriage to her and urging her to ignore her parents.

Somehow he managed to convince them that he wasn't the bad lot they were making him out to be. Presumably Dolores had made her intentions clear too – and she generally managed to get her own way. The local priest took their side and advised her parents against preaching too much to her, on the grounds that such a stance would rebound against them. They relented, and after a five-year courtship, Dolores and Julián were married on 15 February 1916 in the church of Saint Anthony of Padua, Gallarta. It was the last time Dolores Ibárruri was to enter a church, for a religious service at least. Under Julián's tutelage, she swiftly rejected Catholicism in favour of revolutionary socialism and then communism.

Marriage to Julián Ruiz was the start of Dolores's political education. She freely admitted that if it had not been for him she might never have become a communist at all. He was never reluctant to take the credit for converting his devoutly Catholic young wife to revolutionary politics. According to him, she was 'a girl who had only read novels'. But the reality of life as a miner's wife, combined with Julián's enthusiasm for the cause, gradually turned her into a left-wing zealot. 'I taught her and she soon responded, with her steam-rolling temperament, her zest, her ideas,' Julián reflected in old age. 'If it wasn't for me, she would never have been La Pasionaria. I put in her hands the first books and I opened her eyes. If instead of me she had married someone else with other ideas, for example very Catholic like her family, everything would have been different.'[3]

Although Julián first implanted revolutionary ideals in her, and her natural rebelliousness welcomed them, disillusionment with him and the institution of marriage and the life he brought her also helped to shape Dolores as a political activist. Naturally, in the fashion of the times, she was a virgin when she married, as she indignantly insisted in a newspaper interview nearly 70 years later.[4] She soon realised that she was not the type of woman who would long put up with the indignities that most of her contemporaries took for granted. She was one of those rare working-class women who sought liberation for themselves with little help from elsewhere.

In her autobiography, Dolores was brief to the point of reticence about her marriage: she could not even bring herself to name her husband. 'At 20, seeking liberation from drudgery in other people's homes, I married a miner whom I had met during my first job as a servant.' She made it plain that the marriage was not a success but gave little else away about Julián:

My mother used to say, 'She who hits the bull's-eye in her choice of a husband, cannot err in anything.' To hit the bull's-eye was as difficult as finding a pea that weighed a pound. I did not find such a pea.[5]

One reason Julián was not the required pea was that he was a typical Spanish man of his time as much as he was a revolutionary. To this day, Spanish men are traditionalists around the house. The idea of the New Man had certainly not filtered through to the Basque working class in the first decades of the twentieth century.

Julián was accustomed to spending his evenings in the bar with his friends and did not see any reason to change after marriage, even when he and Dolores were virtually penniless. And he wasn't much up to when he did get home:

> He was very loving, but incapable of doing anything around the house. Only the mine existed for him; of the house the only thing he knew was the table, because he sat down to eat there, and the bed, because that's where he slept.[6]

Their first home, in Julián's native village of Somorrostro, a few miles from Gallarta, was lent to them by an aunt of Julián, who had a bit of money and lived some way away, in Santander. It was customary for newly-married women to have a child as soon as possible and Dolores was soon pregnant. Her first child, a girl named Esther, was born on 29 November 1916, nine-and-a-half months since her wedding. It had not been a happy year. She wrote: 'I had already suffered a year of such bitterness that only love for my baby kept me alive.'[7] Although she had already experienced years of drudgery in service, the sheer poverty of her new life was clearly a revelation to her, compared with the relative comforts of her former home. It is difficult to avoid the conclusion that if her marriage had been more successful she might have got through the rigours of life somehow.

> Believing that mutual attraction and fondness would compensate for and surmount the difficulties of privation, I forgot that where bread is lacking, mutual recrimination is more likely to enter; and sometimes, even *with* bread, it still creeps in.[8]

But perhaps a woman of her ability and ambition, in that place and at that time, would have been unlikely to find a soul-mate from the type of man around her.

It is at this period that she started to follow Julián's promptings and acquaint herself with Marxist literature. She still thought of herself as

20

very much a Catholic, even if she had stopped going to church every Sunday, and it was difficult for her to break with everything she had believed with such fervour. It was not, of course, a society in which Catholic and Marxist thinking could co-exist, as they can for many nowadays; for most devout Catholics, Marxism and socialism were then anathema, and were to remain so for many decades in Spain, as the Civil War was to demonstrate. Dolores gradually became enthusiastic about what she was reading. Socialism was not so much a creed which made sense of life as one which gave men and women like herself the means to aim at a better life for themselves. She devoured all the books she could lay her hands on in Somorrostro's Casa del Pueblo. She admitted to finding much of the local left-wing press hard going because of its leaden style. It was not until she started on Marx and Engels that she felt she was getting somewhere.[9] She could never get enough to read: a woman contemporary remembered her walking slowly up to the mine where Julián worked, carrying his lunchbox, her head buried in a newspaper. It was unusual to see a woman act in such a fashion: she began to be talked about.[10]

The Spanish Communist Party did not yet exist. For those attracted to revolutionary ideas in Spain before 1921, the choice was between the anarchists, who had deeper roots in Spain than anywhere else in Europe, and the socialists. Julián and Dolores belonged to the latter. The general political situation in Spain was one of deepening instability as a series of conservative governments battled to keep the lid on a rising tide of revolutionary violence, while an increasingly disillusioned army moved towards the centre of the political action. In this febrile atmosphere, the socialists had, in 1916, moved from their previously reformist posture to a much more aggressively revolutionary one, with a programme that included abolition of the monarchy and the army, the separation of church and state and the nationalisation of land. It was at this dramatic period that Dolores took the first decisive step from sympathetic onlooker to political activist by following her husband into the Socialist Party. She was never to look back.

The Socialist Party's rhetoric was taken very seriously indeed by its more militant members in the Basque country, who started preparing themselves for the armed insurrection they saw as imminent. A group of miners in Dolores's circle decided to manufacture primitive bombs, using dynamite stolen from the mines. 'I was an eager participant,' said Dolores.[11] Having tested them and found that they produced a satisfactory noise, at least, they stored them and waited for the revolution. The same sort of thing was going on elsewhere, particularly among the Basques and in the tough neighbouring mining region of Asturias. (Around the same time Valentín González, known as El Campesino – the Peasant –, who became a communist folk-hero like La Pasionaria during the Civil War because of his military exploits, used dynamite stolen from an Estremaduran coal-mine for his first guerrilla action, when at the age of 16 he blew up and killed four civil guards.)[12]

The national situation continued to deteriorate, but the summer of 1917 passed without the expected uprising, while the militants grew increasingly restless with the failure of the national socialist leadership to take the plunge. Finally, in August, their hand was forced by a railway workers' strike. A general strike was called to support it, with socialists and anarchists united on the issue. In the Basque country and Asturias, the strike was greeted by the Left, and particularly the miners, as the dawning of the revolution. But the conservative government of Eduardo Dato met the uprising head on and sent in the army: seventy strikers were killed (mainly in Catalonia), the socialist strike-committee was arrested *en masse* and miners like those in Dolores's little group were left in disarray. To get rid of the evidence against them, they disposed of their bombs in a stream; Julián went on the run, hiding in a shepherd's hut. When the civil guard arrived at their home, Dolores refused to tell them where he was. To her fury, Julián gave himself up, on the advice of a socialist leader. He was imprisoned in Bilbao, while Dolores was left alone, with no means of feeding herself or her baby daughter. She just managed to get by, bartering her skills as a seamstress for milk for the baby, and helped by a gift of money from a group of Julián's friends. To visit him in prison, she had to walk the 10 kilometres to Bilbao along a dangerous cliffside path, holding the baby on one arm and a basket on the other. To save money, she refused to get a train for the last five kilometres. She moved back to Gallarta. Being nearer to her family was, however, little help. Although she had a rapprochement with her mother, and her older sister Teresa continued to be loyal, her links with the rest of the family had been severed with her marriage and were never restored. Her fortunes since then must have confirmed their worst fears for her.

But much worse was to come from their wayward daughter as far as Dolores's family was concerned. Events in Spain had been played out against a backdrop of war in Europe and revolution in Russia. The bolshevik revolution of November 1917 had a galvanising effect on the Spanish Left and on Dolores Ibárruri in particular. It is not hard to see why: she was a young socialist whose own rather pathetic involvement in an insurrectionary movement a few months previously had been a disaster: her husband was in jail, she had a baby, no work and no money coming in. When she saw the newspaper headlines announcing the Russian Revolution, she was jubilant:

> Instinctively I knew that something immeasurably great had taken place. My thoughts focused on that far-off country, which, from that moment on, was to be so close to us. Two names were fixed in my consciousness, hammering at my heart and my brain: Russia and Lenin. My former sadness vanished; I no longer felt alone. Our revolution, the revolution which even yesterday we considered to be remote and beyond reach was now a reality for one-sixth of the world.[13]

The following year she acquired, virtually by accident, as these things often happen, the name by which she was to become famous: La Pasionaria. She was asked to write an article for a local miners' newspaper, *El Minero Vizcaino* (*The Vizcayan Miner*). She did so and cast around for a pseudonym (a sensible insurance against reprisals). As it happened to be Passion Week, she thought of the name Pasionaria, meaning passion flower, which according to legend opens to show the Passion and death of Christ.[14] It was a brilliant choice, conveying as it does the sense of passion that characterised Dolores's whole life. The English-speaking world probably thought that the sobriquet meant 'The Passionate One'. The name certainly helped to create and then sustain the myth of the tireless fighter. Dolores Ibárruri might well not have had nearly the same worldwide impact without that simple, striking pseudonym.

CHAPTER THREE

TRAGIC YEARS

The communist triumph in Russia sparked an immediate reaction in Spain. There were strikes and land was occupied, with the anarchists in the vanguard, intoxicated by the notion that the Russian example could be copied in Spain. It was the one European country which offered enough of a disparity between rich and poor, between an embattled bourgeoisie and a fast-growing industrial working class, for that to seem more than a remote prospect. The socialists were split between reformism and revolution.

Matters came to a head in 1920. A majority of the executive of the Socialist Youth movement broke away to form the first Spanish Communist Party (PCE). Among its founder members in the Basque country were Dolores Ibárruri and Julián Ruiz.

La Pasionaria's byline appeared on trenchant articles in *La Bandera Roja* (*The Red Flag*), of Bilbao, pouring scorn on the socialists for their lack of revolutionary fire and their 'collaborationist' tactics with employers. She had a suitably flowery style but some of her sentences went on for up to 100 words, which may have been tough going for her working-class readership. But she had a vivid sense of metaphor and there was no mistaking her message. Should the Socialist Party affiliate to the Comintern? There was intense debate about this within the Party that year. Fernando de los Ríos, a leading socialist intellectual and libertarian (and friend, incidentally, of Lorca) was sent to Russia to investigate the situation there and help the Party decide. He concluded that a vital ingredient was lacking in the new communist paradise. 'Where is liberty?' he enquired of Lenin himself. 'Liberty? What for?' was the reply.[1] The Party nevertheless voted to support Comintern membership, but the debate continued, and at a special congress in April 1920 a majority voted against joining the Third International.

This decision led to a further breakaway by a group of members

24

who formed the Spanish Communist Workers Party (PCOE). From having none, Spain now had two Communist Parties. They were swiftly persuaded by Moscow to merge under the name of the Communist Party of Spain (PCE) in 1921. The Somorrostro group, to which Dolores and Julián belonged, was an active one. In the same year she was elected to the first provincial committee of the Basque Communist Party, the first step in her steady rise to the top of the Party bureaucracy.

The 1920s were hard years for La Pasionaria. Personal tragedy and deprivation forged her then both as a woman and politically. She was largely alone – Julián was in prison much of the time, because of his political activities. When he was out, La Pasionaria would get pregnant; when he was back in prison, she would be left to raise a growing family with scant resources. But she did not confine herself to home and children: she became deeply involved in the affairs of the young Spanish Communist Party and increasingly well-known in the Basque country as that rare being, a highly-politicised working-class woman. Her political work can be seen as remarkable, given the exigencies of her personal life. But any doubts she might have secretly had about the wisdom of her actions were swiftly dispelled by the sheer misery of the life she had to endure.

Her second child and only son, Rubén, was born on 9 January 1920. But in the same year little Esther died, possibly of tuberculosis. Her mother had to borrow money, first to buy medicine, then a coffin. Three years later, in July 1923, she gave birth to triplets, all girls: they were named Amaya, Amagoya and Azucena. Many years later, looking back over her long and eventful life, she described it as 'the greatest happiness I had ever had.'[2] But the happiness did not last long: Amagoya died soon after birth. A neighbour made a coffin out of a crate, and Julián, who was on strike at the time, carried it to the cemetery on his shoulder. There were complications; La Pasionaria had to spend 18 days in bed. The doctor gave his services free, saying that Julián could pay him when he was next in work. The neighbours rallied round. Azucena lived for only two years. She died because her parents could not afford medicine for her. Only Amaya survived. A sixth child, Eva, was born in 1928. She died at the age of two months and was buried beside her three sisters. The anguish of a mother who has lost four children by the age of 33 needs no underlining. La Pasionaria was not given to displays of emotion about her private life but she made no secret of her feelings at that time:

25

Every day, when I took lunch to my husband at the mine, I had to pass the cemetery where they were buried; each time, my heart was torn with anguish . . . It is difficult to measure the amount of grief a mother's heart can contain; it is equally difficult to measure the capacity for resistance to suffering that such hearts can acquire.[3]

For the surviving two children, Rubén and Amaya, life continued to be hard. At times their mother could not feed or clothe them properly. Sometimes she had to take them along to meetings because there was no one with whom she could leave them. At night, she would leave them asleep in bed while she slipped out to get on with her political activities. Once she came out of an evening meeting at the Casa del Pueblo to discover that Rubén, whom she had left asleep in the auditorium, was missing. She was panic-stricken; a search was organised. There was still no sign of the little boy. Eventually he was found fast asleep, curled up among some seating erected for meetings outside the Casa del Pueblo.[4]

The 1920s were no easier for the Communist Party itself. It built up a certain strength in the trade unions but it ploughed a lone furrow, refusing any association or collaboration with the other movements of the Left. Indeed there were bitter struggles with the socialists for control of the unions, frequently ending in bloodshed. The communists regarded themselves as revolutionaries, working to overthrow the bourgeois state and install a régime based on soviets on the Russian model.

The Spanish Communist Party was always deeply loyal to the Soviet Union. It accepted almost all Moscow's dictats without question; indeed, it was this blind loyalty which was to lead future left-wing allies to come to distrust it so deeply and for the country as a whole to hate it so much. Soon after its formation, according to La Pasionaria, the communists started planning an armed insurrection, for which the Basque miners were to be the shock troops. It was the purest fantasy and the whole thing was soon shelved; but the fact that the militants could take it as seriously as they did is an indication of the heady atmosphere of the times.

In fact the government was overthrown in 1923 from the other side of the political spectrum, by the colourful General Miguel Primo de Rivera, captain-general of Catalonia, who led an army coup. Primo de Rivera was 53 when he came to power, but he was by no means the

26

archetypal dictator. Although like Mussolini in Italy he oversaw a massive programme of public works – dams, railways, roads and electrification schemes – he had no particular political philosophy beyond the vague slogan of 'Country, Religion, Monarchy' and there were no political executions during his rule. His greatest achievement was to end, in 1927, the Moroccan War on good terms for Spain, thus ending a long-running drain on national resources and morale. Primo was an extraordinary, larger-than-life figure who worked hard and played hard, being a familiar figure in Madrid's cafés and brothels. After six and a half years, he was brought down in 1930 by the increasingly chaotic state of the public finances (partly caused by his expensive public works), popular dissatisfaction with his autocratic rule, and the withdrawal of the army's support. But he was not without a certain political touch. He had no time for any of the left-wing parties apart from the socialists, whom he cleverly courted and bought off in return for their co-operation on his social legislation. He cracked down on the anarchists and locked up most of the communist leaders; the Party itself he judged too insignificant to be worth the bother of banning but its members were liable to harassment, arrest and prosecution.

At the Party grass roots, the decade was thus one of clandestine activity and persecution. Julián Ruiz was only one of many militants who suffered long periods of imprisonment. La Pasionaria was involved in the usual political activities, distributing leaflets and supporting strikes, and she visited Julián in prison. Tired of this last activity, she assembled a deputation of prisoners' wives to visit uninvited the governor of Vizcaya and demand their husbands' release. He was astonished at their nerve but did not yield to their protest. A contemporary, Sebastián Zapiraín, recalled that she brought the practical qualities of the housewife and mother to Party meetings. 'If she saw one of the comrades with a hole in his sock, she would tell him to take it off and would darn it for him while the meeting went on,' he said. 'She was an excellent cook and would frequently make omelettes for us all. She cooked for us as if we were in a restaurant,' he said. He remembered her as a model wife and mother but still perceived her as an early feminist, a highly unusual stance for a woman, particularly in the deeply Catholic Basque country, where the mother figure was venerated in the home but expected to confine her activities within its walls. Zapiraín thought that La Pasionaria's Catholic upbringing had a lasting influence on her political beliefs. 'She had a certain mystic quality. She came from a very Christian and very political family and she came to the social struggle with those beliefs. It was like an early version of liberation theology.'[5]

She taught miners to read and write, or read the newspapers out loud to them. She was a type of woman Zapiraín certainly had not encountered before. She came to public notice through her involvement through demonstrations, pamphleteering and newspaper articles in a series of miners' strikes in the early 1920s. The cost was high: 'To Catholics she seemed little better than a prostitute,' recalled Zapiraín. 'To Carlists like her father and grandfather, she was little better than a traitor. She would even be denounced by priests from the pulpit as an envoy of the devil.' This kind of image – La Pasionaria as a Red harridan with demonic undertones – was to be used against her throughout her political life, reaching its peak during the Civil War and lingering on long afterwards.

As her ideas developed, she started urging her comrades to involve their wives more in their Party activities and fulminated against those who kept their partners in the background. She got women to distribute propaganda leaflets on the streets, hiding them under the baby in the pushchair.

La Pasionaria had a lasting impact on Sebastián Zapiraín. They continued to be associates through the 1930s and the Civil War. After several years in exile, he and another communist leader, Santiago Alvarez, went back into Franco's Spain secretly in 1945 to work for the by now illegal Communist Party, but they were soon betrayed and captured. They were sentenced to death by a military tribunal but reprieved after an international campaign. Zapiraín served ten years in prison. 'When I was being tortured, I didn't want to be a coward. That was the example of Dolores Ibárruri,' he said.[6]

In 1927, Primo de Rivera summoned a national assembly, in which the political parties were invited to participate. The Moscow line was that the Communist Party should join in, but a conference of the Party in the Basque country decided against, a rare example of the Spanish communists taking an independent line. It wanted to maintain its separateness, rejecting any notion of co-operating with Primo. Instead, the Party unsuccessfully tried to call a general strike in the Basque provinces; La Pasionaria was active in promoting the notion, via meetings and articles. The Party continued to hold itself aloof from every other left-wing movement. But by the end of the decade, with Primo de Rivera's dictatorship crumbling, things began to look up for the Left. At a secret Communist Party conference in Bilbao in 1930, called the Conference of Pamplona, La Pasionaria was elected to the central committee and plans were laid for the more open political period that was clearly approaching. Primo's rule ended ignominiously in the same year, the dictator departing into exile and death in Paris. The pressures that had been bottled up for seven years exploded. With the legalisation of political parties, the Communist Party could break cover and work in the open again. A turbulent period followed, culminating in the elections of April 1931. The result was victory for the parties advocating the abolition of the monarchy and the establishment of a republic. King Alfonso XIII too went into exile.

The election campaign was particularly notable for La Pasionaria. During it, she made her début as a public speaker. It can be argued that she made her biggest political impact as an orator, indeed that she was one of the finest public speakers of the century. She was certainly one of the most powerful. She came in at the very end of the age of oratory; after the Second World War, the public would increasingly be addressed via television and not the platform. La Pasionaria adapted well to radio, making a number of key broadcasts during the Civil War.

She was at first unwilling to speak in public; for all her natural fire, it was a big step for a working-class woman to take. Even when she was famous, she was always extremely nervous before making a speech and often felt like turning tail and fleeing. But once on her feet she was a natural orator. She wrote all her own speeches and delivered them with eloquence and emotion. She had a gift for coming up with a punchy phrase – 'They shall not pass'; 'It is better to die on your feet than to live on your knees'; (to the International Brigades) 'When the olive tree of peace puts forth its leaves again, mingled with the laurels of the Spanish republic's victory – come back!' – which would linger long in the audience's mind and often pass into history. Her physical presence helped: she was a tall and imposing figure who used her arms and hands forcefully to punch home the message. Much of the time she spoke without the aid of a microphone to huge audiences, drawing on those childhood memories of listening to the visiting orators at Gallarta who had so fascinated her.

Her opponents accused her of demagoguery. When they are read in the cold light of day half a century later, many of her speeches do seem little more than a succession of stale communist clichés. But imagine her in the heady atmosphere of Spain in the 1930s, her great decade, the tall Basque woman with the impassioned voice and the revolutionary message, urging defiance in the bullrings and cinemas of a besieged Madrid packed with young men and women who might be fighting in the trenches in a few days' time. Or picture her in the great Vélodrome of Paris, the indoor cycling stadium, where she made many famous speeches appealing to the world to defend the embattled republic, to an audience of rapt French workers and intellectuals to whom the Spanish Civil War was the great cause of the day and for whom she was already a legend. She may have had something of the demagogue about her but she was a speaker nobody ever forgot.

In the late 1920s La Pasionaria and Julián were finding it difficult to pay the rent and were threatened with eviction. Despite their financial problems they reckoned they would be better off buying some land and building their own house. Dolores, always the more decisive of the two, appears to have been the prime mover. They found a small plot outside Somorrostro, and Dolores determined they should have it, despite her husband's protestations that they could not afford it. With the help of a friend, they managed to scrape together enough money to buy the plot from the local municipality. Their daughter Amaya remembers her mother saying it cost '70 duros' or 350 pesetas. On this land they built themselves a little house, using stone from the nearby mountains.

It still stands to this day, a tiny, isolated, whitewashed cottage at the end of a grass track, surrounded by lush green fields in which cattle graze. Behind, the ground rises slowly into pine-forested hills. In front there is a view, across the fields, of Somorrostro in the distance. The main difference between now and the 1920s is that a large petrol refinery dominates the town. In 1990, the house was still occupied by an elderly woman who had lived there for 52 years: the only improvements made since La Pasionaria's and Julián's day were, she said, running water and electricity. The inside of the house remained much as it must have been when it was first built, dark, damp and primitively furnished. In any other country it would long ago have been turned into a museum. Perhaps it is better the way it is.

Amaya thinks the family moved there in 1928 or 1929. 'We could count the stars because the roof was only beams. It had an earth floor.'[7] Amaya was then around six years old and went to the local school in Somorrostro only intermittently. Her brother Rubén went more regularly. They had no leather shoes, only straw sandals which they wore inside wooden clogs. Amaya recalled that when she did go to school, she had to leave the clogs at the classroom door and wear the sandals. Another recollection sheds light on La Pasionaria's ambivalent attitude towards the Catholic Church:

> The first thing we did [at school] was to kneel down in front of the Crucifix and recite the Our Father. I remember that when I returned home Dolores asked me: 'Amaychu, what have you learned today?' I said: 'The Our Father' and she said: 'Our Father, stuck in a basket, from head to foot, eating cherries.' Then I got so confused I didn't learn any more of the Our Father. Dolores was a believer until she was twenty, when she got married. But when it began to clash with life, she said 'This can't be true, a God could not permit such injustice. So when she saw that I was taking the road of religion, she said that I could not, that I had to learn other things. But at the same time I want to tell you that although she wasn't a believer, she didn't believe in God, not at all, but in Somorrostro, married and everything, on the wall at the head of the bed she had [a picture of] Saint Anthony of Padua, who was her saint [ie she was born on his saint's day]. And she always had the greatest respect for believers, I swear to you. If they wanted to believe, let them believe. All that reactionary propaganda of Franco, that she ate priests, is a lie, is utterly false.[8]

Amaya remembers her mother working extremely hard in the house – 'she always had an apron on'. Life was hard and their food poor: potatoes with leeks, sardines (sold by *la sardinera*, a woman selling them from door to door), garlic soup, a classic Spanish peasant dish, and little else. They supplemented this diet with fruit picked by the children from the trees and bushes which grew in abundance all over the area: apples, pears, blackberries. Many Basque miners would have a little patch of land on which they grew a few vegetables. In La Pasionaria's family, it was she who went off to cultivate the potatoes. She made rag dolls for her daughter; Amaya had no 'proper' dolls until she was ten. With the sewing machine she had been given as a wedding present, La Pasionaria would also finish off men's trousers for a nearby tailor's shop, when Julián was out of work or in jail. Amaya recalls her mother's involvement in politics too. 'Our door was always open: comrades came and met in our house, planning strikes, demonstrations, sharing out the work, who was to do the leaflets and so on.' Amaya remembered her father, Julián, being constantly in and out of prison during the 1920s, and visiting him there.[9]

La Pasionaria's reputation was starting to spread outside the Basque country, helped by articles in the national press such as that published by the picture magazine *Estampa* in 1931. Headlined 'Una "terrible" bolchevique – La "leader" comunista Dolores Ibárruri "La Pasionaria" ', the article was an early example of the 'At Home with' genre. She was photographed reading on the balcony of her house, with Rubén and Amaya (10-year-old Rubén looks a strapping lad in long shorts and bare feet, already standing well above his mother's shoulders), with the children of her neighbourhood in Somorrostro, working in the garden, and addressing a political meeting. She looks grim and unsmiling, even in a family atmosphere. Perhaps she knew her life as a Basque housewife was not to last much longer.[10]

CHAPTER FOUR

A NEW LIFE

If 1931 marked a watershed for republican politics in Spain, it was equally one for La Pasionaria. It was the year she left her native Basque country for Madrid, the year in which she effectively separated from her husband and started forging a career as a national politician. The period between 1931 and 1936, when the Civil War began, was one of intense political activity for her, interspersed with frequent spells of imprisonment because of it, and culminating in her election to the Cortes, the Chamber of Deputies, in February 1936.

The Communist Party had marked her out as a most unusual asset: a working-class woman, totally dedicated to the Party, an able journalist and a budding public speaker. Her election to the central committee had brought her abilities to the attention of the Party leaders and, more important, to the Comintern's representatives in Spain, who supervised the Party's activities. Her slavish loyalty to Russia, from which she was hardly ever to deviate, would not have gone unnoticed in Moscow. She was summoned to Madrid to work for the Party newspaper, *Mundo Obrero*, (*Workers' World*) a daily broadsheet. It was the central element in the Party's energetic and skilful propaganda campaign. Its red masthead incorporated the familiar slogan 'Workers of the World Unite' and it relentlessly supported whatever happened to be the Party line of the moment, performing agile U-turns whenever necessary, most notably in 1935 when the Party embraced the idea of a Popular Front alliance with the other left-wing parties which *Mundo Obrero* had hitherto regularly excoriated. Its editor was Vicente Uribe, a half-Castilian, half-Basque former metalworker and now central committee member, whose political life was to be bound up with La Pasionaria's for three decades.

A typical edition of *Mundo Obrero* would contain a long front-page article by Uribe or another Party leader outlining the correct line of the day, on a red-letter day a piece by Georgi Dimitrov, head of the

Comintern, or even, best of all, a message from Stalin himself. Inside there would be long accounts of Party rallies with verbatim reports of the speeches, extensive foreign coverage with particular emphasis on the rise of fascism in Germany and Italy, and glowing features on the Soviet Union – a report on the attractions of life on a collective farm, perhaps, illustrated with photographs of muscular, smiling workers. Only the sports columns seemed free of a political slant. Devotees of the *Daily Worker* and later the *Morning Star* will be familiar with the mixture.

La Pasionaria was employed as an editor and she also wrote frequent articles, whose general theme was a passionate attack on whoever the Party had in its sights at the time. Her speeches would also be reported in full, frequently accompanied by her photograph so she was soon an established figure in the newspaper's pages. She had another task: she was placed in charge of women's activities. This was a field where the Party saw an opportunity for expansion and recruitment.

What about the children? Rubén was now 11, Amaya 8. At first, La Pasionaria left them with her sister Teresa in Sestao, an industrial suburb of Bilbao. It was just as well that she did not at that stage take them with her to the capital because she was arrested and imprisoned for the first time soon after her move. She gave two different accounts of her imprisonment. In her application for delegate's credentials to the Seventh Congress of the Soviet Communist Party in Moscow in 1935, she listed her periods in prison. For the offence of 'hiding people under pursuit', she wrote that she had been sentenced to 18 years imprisonment but served only two months in jail.[1] (This disparity between sentence and time served was not unusual in Spain at that time, when sudden amnesties might be declared, or the political climate might swiftly change). In her first volume of memoirs, however, she wrote that after two months in jail, 'in the first week of January 1932 . . . the case was dropped because of lack of proof, and all charges against me were also dropped.'[2]

She brought Rubén to Madrid where she had returned to work at *Mundo Obrero*. She had still not found a home of her own when she was rearrested, this time for 'insulting the government' at a meeting. They were staying with a family who on hearing of her detention threw Rubén out on to the street. Still only eleven years old and a Basque country boy totally unfamiliar with Madrid, he had to find his way through the city to the women's prison to ask his mother what he should do next. She managed to get friends to look after him and a few weeks later he was taken back to Somorrostro by lorry. It was clearly not a satisfactory situation.

La Pasionaria's first experience of prison came about because, just before she left for Madrid in September 1931, she briefly sheltered a communist who had been wounded in a shoot-out with a rival socialist group and was on the run from the civil guard. She was arrested a few weeks after she had started work in Madrid. She was taken to the women's prison in Quiñones Street, pending transfer back to Bilbao. Her fellow-prisoners were petty criminals and prostitutes, to whom she was a novelty: 'A communist woman in that world, on the outside of society, was something nobody had ever heard of or seen.'[3] She had a (literally) captive audience for her lectures on communism, to the consternation of the nuns who ran the prison and the female director of the workshop, a socialist. At the end of November 1931 she was sent to the Larriñaga prison in Bilbao. Her fellow-passengers on the train, learning that she was a political prisoner, not a common criminal, plied her with fruit and other food. She politely declined their offers of money. In the Bilbao jail, with a group of communists and anarchists, she went on hunger strike for four days.

Her daughter Amaya recalled visiting her once a week with her Aunt Teresa. They would take a basket with fruit, cooked meat and other food and normally would talk to La Pasionaria in the visiting room, through a wire grille. 'I could always hear her coming because of her loud voice,' said Amaya. On one occasion Amaya was allowed by a kindly governor to pass through into the women's section of the prison to kiss her mother. In her sixties, Amaya remembered that day vividly:

It is a memory that has remained with me all my life. There was a big room and in the middle were the cells. They were tiny: all that fitted inside was a bed and a little table. There was no room for chairs. Each prisoner had a cell of her own. Beyond the cells was a room where the prisoners were: they were peeling potatoes. There was a big stewpot and around it there were several benches. The prisoners were peeling the potatoes for supper, for themselves and the male prisoners. My mother said: 'Amaya, come into my cell.' I went in – it was tiny, tiny – she sat me down on her bed, and said 'Now I'm going to show you my work.' She was making me a jersey. She knitted very well. Then she showed me some handkerchiefs she had sewn. I was there for three or four hours. I watched the other prisoners peeling potatoes. When my mother spoke, they all went quiet, listening to what she was saying. My stay coincided with visiting time. I said: 'Mother, can I go with you to the visitors' room?' 'Yes, yes,' she replied, so I went out with her, clutching her hand, and the people on the other side (of the wire) said: 'What's this? Is the little girl inside too?' And I said, 'Yes, yes!', very happy to present myself as a heroine.[4]

As for Julián, he claimed much later that his marriage to La Pasionaria started to disintegrate with the onset of the Civil War in 1936. The reality was that the couple were living apart from 1931 and the gulf between them grew even more rapidly as La Pasionaria's new life developed. Julián was a simple man and accepted the situation with stoicism. La Pasionaria threw herself into her new role with her customary energy. The victims were the children, shuttling back and forth between the Basque country and Madrid and a variety of different guardians of their welfare.

The Spanish Communist Party was not in good shape. Throughout the 1920s it had been beset by schism, reflecting the battle going on in the Soviet Union and elsewhere between Stalin and Trotsky and their followers. The big issue facing the Party in 1932 was its attitude towards the newly-established republic. Should communists support it, as the expression of the democratic wish of the people and an improvement on the monarchy, while working for its replacement by a Marxist-Leninist workers' state on the lines of the USSR? Or should communists reject any collaboration with this bourgeois state and work actively for its overthrow, fomenting agitation and disruption?

Moscow decided on the latter course. Its dictats were transmitted via the Comintern's representatives, a series of exotic revolutionaries from East and West Europe, often parading under *noms de guerre*. The Spanish communist leaders, headed by the Party secretary-general José Bullejos, were increasingly at odds with these representatives, whose high-handed approach and refusal to listen to the Spaniards' point of view gave offence. Bullejos thought the republic should be supported. In March 1932 the Party held its IVth Congress in Seville, the first time in its short history that it could do so openly. Bullejos and the rest of the leadership were confirmed in office; La Pasionaria was re-elected to the central committee. But Moscow was not prepared to leave it at that; it plotted a putsch.

In August, General José Sanjurjo launched an abortive coup attempt with the aim of overthrowing the republic and restoring the monarchy. Bullejos and others came out in defence of the republic. Shortly afterwards he and other Party leaders went to Moscow to argue for their position to be adopted as official policy. The debate was settled behind their backs. The Russians prevented them from returning to Spain for several months. When they stuck to their guns, they were expelled from the Party and when they finally got back home they found a new Politburo had been 'elected' in their absence; in fact, it had been hand-picked by the Comintern's latest representative, Vittorio Codovila, an Italian-Argentinian brought up in South America.

Codovila was one of the most extraordinary of the foreign delegates sent by the Comintern to supervise Party affairs. A plump, bourgeois figure who enjoyed the good things of life, he went under the *nom de guerre* Medina, and was said to be a personal friend of Stalin (though unlike many of Stalin's friends he lived to tell the tale, surviving until 1970.) He was an expert at mass organisation and was to play a vital role in the rapid development of the PCE in the mid-1930s and during the Civil War. He was a key figure in the creation of the International Brigades and in the unification of the Socialist and Communist Party youth movements in 1936, which was designed to be a forerunner of the hoped-for (in Moscow at least) fusion of the Parties at all levels, a tactic which was successfully resisted by the socialists.

The new communist leadership was young and loyal to Moscow. The new general secretary was José (Pepe) Díaz, a former bakery worker from Seville who had entered the Party from the anarcho-syndicalists in 1927. He was an honest and diligent man but he was placed in the job because he would do as Moscow ordered, although he was to start having doubts in the later stages of the Civil War.

La Pasionaria was the oldest member of the Politburo, at 37. She was now among the Party's top leaders, a meteoric rise from the obscurity of Somorrostro. But it was a close thing; she had originally supported the Bullejos line and only narrowly escaped being expelled from the Party along with him. She saved her skin with a humiliating 'self-criticism': asking herself if Bullejos and his friends were solely responsible for the party's 'errors', she wrote: 'With bolshevik frankness, I say No; although the greatest responsibility lies with the group, I, and with me all those who make up the central committee . . . bear a part of the responsibility, for having been weak, for having been cowards, for having lent ourselves to being extras of the sectarian executive committee.'[5] So she betrayed Bullejos, who as secretary of the miners' union in Vizcaya in the 1920s, had encouraged her to join the embryo Communist Party.

She performed her U-turn from prison. The day after she arrived back in Madrid after attending the Seville Congress, she had been arrested for the second time, for 'insulting the government'. She was sentenced to nine years' imprisonment and held until November in the women's prison; her desertion of the Party leaders may not have been unconnected with the fact that, according to her, nobody from the Party came to visit her during the eleven months she was detained. Once again, she was transferred to Bilbao and released the following January, with 10 years of her sentence unspent.

The Russians' motives in picking Díaz, La Pasionaria and the others to take over the PCE were clear. Stalin wanted to pull the strings from Moscow: he and his Comintern advisers could see that Spain offered rich revolutionary prospects. The first pre-requisite was to have complete control over the local Communist Party. From this time on, the Spanish Communist Party was notable for its sub-servience to the Moscow line. The rapid progress of the PCE from the mid-1930s onwards was evidence of the skill Stalin employed in reshaping the Party exactly as he wanted it.

As the Politburo member in charge of women, La Pasionaria was heavily involved in promoting women's issues during this period. In 1933, she helped to set up the Spanish branch of the World Committee of Women against War and Fascism, which was based in Paris. It was the sort of communist front organisation which found a ready echo in the 1930s; it set up a network of branches throughout Spain which attracted intellectuals, republicans and a few socialists until suspicions about the extent of communist influence caused the Republican Union Party to pull out. Irene Falcón, who was to be her secretary for the best part of 50 years, remembers La Pasionaria organising a demonstration in Madrid under the Women against War banner. The immediate cause was a government call-up of reservists to send to Morocco.

We went to Neptune Square [in the centre of Madrid] and then on to Cibeles [a famous eighteenth-century fountain in the shape of the Greek goddess of fertility's chariot situated at the junction of the Paseo del Prado, the Alcalá and the Paseo de la Castellana]. At first we were alone, wondering whether anyone would turn up and hoping that men wouldn't come because they might complicate things. Then women wearing *hats* began to arrive – they looked so middle class. More and more arrived. There were thousands of us. Workers from the tobacco factories started arriving by tram – the drivers let them on free. People stood on chairs in the cafés to applaud as we marched past, with Dolores at the head. We went to the Ministry of Defence, where of course they wouldn't let us in, and then we went off to some poor areas until the police dispersed us with water hoses.[6]

Irene Falcón was a fascinating figure in her own right. She exercised considerable influence over her famous mistress. She was the exact opposite of her: small, bird-like, unassuming, the model of the backroom girl. But she had a reputation for intrigue and manipulation and she espoused La Pasionaria's politics with the same fervour. She was born Irene Levi Rodríguez in the dour and sombre city of Valladolid, of a middle-class Jewish father who died when she was five. She was educated at the German College in Madrid and spoke several languages. At the age of 15 she was employed as a translator by the great Spanish Nobel Prize-winning doctor Santiago Ramón y Cajal; her sister Kety was his secretary (and also eventually held an important position in the Communist Party). At 18, Irene was London correspondent of the newspaper La Voz. She married a Peruvian revolutionary César Falcón, also a journalist, and with him founded an extreme left-wing party, the Revolutionary Anti-Imperialist Party (IRIA), which was absorbed into the Communist Party in 1933. After that, she devoted her life to Communism – and La Pasionaria, from whom she was virtually inseparable, apart from a period in the 1950s when her Czech lover Beadrich Geminder fell foul of Stalin and was shot along with his boss Rudolf Slansky. Irene was dispatched to China from the USSR but was later reunited with La Pasionaria, with whom she stayed until her idol died. Then Irene devoted her life to guarding and burnishing La Pasionaria's memory for posterity.

In the Spanish general election of November 1933, the communists won 200,000 votes but no parliamentary seats. It was, however, an encouraging result for them, particularly as their bitter rivals the socialists lost ground (although, to put these figures in perspective, they received 1.7 million votes). The republican-socialist government was replaced by a centre-right administration. Spain entered a disturbed two-and-a-half years, known as the Bienio Negro (the Black Two Years) which ended in Civil War. The communists threw themselves into vigorous opposition to the new government, while they became increasingly aware that they needed to move away from their isolated position on the Left and seek allies for the dark days ahead. The catalyst for this was Hitler's coming to power in Germany in 1933, which powerfully concentrated the minds of hitherto bickering left-wing forces.

In November 1933 La Pasionaria made her first trip abroad. She travelled to the Soviet Union as a delegate to the XIIIth Plenum of the Communist International. She was ecstatic about what she found there; no Soviet scriptwriter could have bettered her impressions:

> For one who viewed it with her heart, [Moscow] was the most marvellous city in the world. Here socialism was being constructed: the earthly dreams of liberty fought for by generations of slaves, outcasts, serfs and workers, were becoming reality; the Soviet people were marching towards Communism . . . [7]

Perhaps a woman from the Spanish working-class who had suffered as much as La Pasionaria had more excuse for wearing such red-tinted spectacles than the battalions of Western intellectuals who reported back from the USSR in similar vein in the 1930s.

Under the aegis of Women against War, La Pasionaria also travelled to Paris in August 1934 as head of the Spanish delegation to the organisation's first international congress.

The Asturias uprising of October 1934 was a turning point for the Spanish Left and for La Pasionaria personally. It was the event which first made her a nationally and internationally known figure and helped to create her legend. Asturias is the northern coastal province which borders the Basque country to the west. It is a tough, mountainous region, rich in iron and coal, whose miners were among the best organised trades unionists in Spain. It had a long tradition of union activity. Both the socialist UGT and anarchist CNT unions had deep roots there and the communists were starting to make inroads too. In the autumn of 1934 its workers were, at a terrible cost to themselves, the only ones to carry through a revolt that was planned by the socialists to be nothing less than a full-scale Spanish revolution. It was a reaction to the appointment of ministers to the cabinet from the Spanish Confederation of Autonomous Movements of the Right (CEDA).

The socialists' veteran leader Largo Caballero had been moving steadily away from reformism towards revolution and he had by now despaired of making any future progress by conventional political means. In conjunction with some anarchists and other left-wing movements he planned his revolution, but when the signal was given the result was farce – everywhere, that is, except in Asturias, where the final outcome was tragedy. A general strike was called but it received little support in Madrid. In Barcelona the leader of the Esquerra left-wing/republican coalition, Lluís Companys, declared Catalonian independence within a federal Spain but that was snuffed out within a day by the army.

Only in Asturias was the revolution an initial success. Socialists, anarchists and communists joined forces in a prototype Popular Front. The uprising began on 5 October and the miners, well stocked with dynamite from their workplaces, were soon largely in control of the region's main towns, Oviedo and Gijón, plus most of its villages. They added to their weaponry by looting thousands of rifles and machine guns from the province's main arms factory. But their triumph was short-lived. The army was dispatched to put down the uprising and after several days of bitter fighting, which included hand-to-hand combat in the streets, managed to subdue it. The miners fought with incredible skill and bravery against overwhelming odds and in the knowledge that help would not arrive from any quarter. Among the commanders of the army units was General Francisco Franco, whose Moroccan army was sent in by sea to spearhead the action. They behaved with notable savagery against the miners but the authorities' worst atrocities were saved for after their opponents had surrendered. Some 40,000 were arrested and untold numbers were simply executed without trial. The total death toll of the uprising was later estimated at 4,000. Many more were tortured in order to get them to reveal the whereabouts of their arms caches.

The scale of repression, when it leaked out, shocked Spain and spread abroad. The Asturian uprising became a rallying point for supporters of the Spanish Left at home and abroad. In its battle lines and the ferocity with which it was conducted, it was an all too realistic practice run for the Civil War.

La Pasionaria was heavily involved in humanitarian work in its wake, under the aegis of the Women against War committee. She displayed the qualities which characterised her interventions in such matters: impulsiveness and courage. (Her modus operandi was often more typical of the anarchists than of the more disciplined communists.) Her style was to march into a tricky situation and tackle it head-on, demanding immediate action. Her physical presence and hectoring manner tended to disconcert the authorities, generally middle-aged men who were not used to this sort of apparition. She frequently got results in the most unlikely circumstances.

In Asturias, she decided the most helpful relief work would be to evacuate children of dead or imprisoned workers, mainly miners. It was a risky undertaking, because Asturias was under military occupation. La Pasionaria related how, when her car was stopped at one civil guard checkpoint, a guard told them 'they were looking for La Pasionaria, a dangerous communist who was reportedly in the neighbourhood.' When she freely admitted being her, the shocked guard called for reinforcements and she was arrested. Held overnight in Oviedo, she was released the next day and told to leave the region within 24 hours. She boldly said she would go if she was allowed to take 150 children with her. The authorities agreed, probably glad to see the back of her.[8] The children were distributed among sympathetic families around Spain. Some ended up in the Soviet Union, as indeed did La Pasionaria's own children; so eventually did some of the rebellious Asturian workers. La Pasionaria managed to evacuate a further 200 children from Asturias and retained a close emotional link with the region. She was always invoking the name of the Asturian miners in her speeches ('The executioners of October [1934] shall not pass'; 'Remember the heroic women of Asturias') and, in February 1936, was elected to the Cortes as a deputy for the area (and again, astonishingly, in 1977).

Reports of her activities in Asturias filtered abroad; the main conduits were the contacts she had made at the Paris conference of Women against War a few months previously. The combination of revolutionary and Scarlet Pimpernel was irresistible to the foreign press. As one historian put it, 'There began to be created around her the legend which turned her into the Spanish Rosa Luxemburg.'[9]

CHAPTER FIVE

THE ROAD TO CIVIL WAR

In the wake of the Asturian uprising and repression, there was another crackdown on the Communist Party. The Party itself was not declared illegal but its leaders were. In the latter stages of 1934 and the whole of 1935, La Pasionaria had somehow to carry out her increasingly onerous workload in secret. The background was the rapidly worsening political situation in Spain and the whole of Europe.

Fascism was in power in Germany and Italy and on the march elsewhere. The task facing the European Left was how to confront it. In 1934 the French Communist Party urged the Comintern to sponsor the idea of a united Popular Front of all left-wing forces. In its conservative way, the Kremlin was initially reluctant to embrace a notion that stood its previous policy on its head. Maurice Thorez, the general secretary of the French CP, went to Moscow to argue the case. Georgi Dimitrov, the Bulgarian who headed the Comintern, was sympathetic, if Stalin was not.

In Madrid, La Pasionaria found the restrictions of working under cover increasingly irksome. She moved out of the house where the police had her registered and from then on was living illegally. Amaya described their life as 'very hard'. La Pasionaria rented a series of small apartments to keep one step ahead of the police. Amaya later recalled this time:

> The apartments were extremely modest because the Party in those days had no money. They were interior flats (with no windows) with little light, because they were cheaper and relatively small. But because we were living illegally we could not get friendly with the children in the street so that they didn't ask us questions – who we were, where we came from. We changed houses every few months to shake off the police, so we couldn't go to school either.[1]

When their mother had to go out to work Rubén and Amaya were left alone in the flat, often for the whole day. Their father had stayed in the Basque country and did not wish to live in Madrid; he was a simple working man who would have been out of his depth in the capital and, increasingly, with his wife. The situation was becoming highly unsatisfactory for everyone: the children were growing up isolated, uneducated and, for long periods, uncared for. La Pasionaria's dilemma was how to combine the roles of salary-earner and mother without prejudice to either career or children.

In the end, the solution was an extreme one: the Party suggested she send the children to the Soviet Union. In the spring of 1935 they were dispatched there. Rubén and Amaya were not alone. A number of children of Spanish communists and other left-wingers, particularly those who had been killed or imprisoned in the bloody Asturias uprising of 1934, were also sent to the Soviet Union to continue their education and many more were to follow during the Civil War. At first, they were well looked after there, in the Soviet fashion, but it was not easy for La Pasionaria's children to adapt to life so far away from home in addition to the traumas of their parents' separation. Nor was it easy for La Pasionaria herself: for all her toughness, she was always racked by guilt about parting from her children for such a long period. 'She thought that children should not be separated from their parents and maintained that to the end of her life,' said Santiago Alvarez, a veteran communist and associate of hers through the Civil War and the long years of exile.[2] (His own son was also brought up in the Soviet Union.) Amaya remembered: 'She was very sad to say goodbye to us. She loved us very much. She had lost four children; we were the only two left. She did not want to be separated from us but the struggle obliged her to.'[3] At first the plan was for them to spend just a few months in the USSR in the hope that the political climate in Spain would improve and allow them to return. In the event La Pasionaria would not be reunited with her children for four years, when she was forced into exile in the Soviet Union after the Civil War – and Rubén would not be with her for long.

Amaya went to a home for foreign children in the city of Ivanovo. The other children came from similar backgrounds: their parents were communists who had been killed or imprisoned or who were living clandestinely: Italians, Chinese, Japanese, and many other nationalities. Rubén became an apprentice in the Stalin Car Works in Moscow. After a few months there, he went on to an aviation school.

Amaya's feelings were mixed: 'In that era the Soviet Union was regarded by us as paradise; but at the same time to part from our mother was hard. But we were very politicised children so we understood that we had to leave our mother's hands free so that she could fight.' The children found it hard, particularly being separated from each other. They were in an unknown country and at first knew nothing of the language. 'The first two years were hard, very hard,' Amaya recalled. She was homesick, suffered from culture shock and missed her mother's love. The only contact was the occasional letter. Life improved when more Spanish children arrived, as the Civil War started to go against the republic. Amaya went on to homes that were exclusively for Spanish children; she spent a total of seven-and-a-half years in such institutions and the constant chopping and changing that she went through seriously affected her education. Despite her troubles, she always retained a great affection for and gratitude to the Soviet Union for the shelter it had provided; it became her adopted country. She saw Rubén only occasionally; when he was in Moscow, she was in Ivanovo and when she was transferred to Moscow he was sent to Stalingrad. But when they met Amaya remembers him treating her with great affection.[4]

Rubén was by all accounts a warm, witty and engaging personality. When he first arrived in Moscow, he was billeted with a local family, who had asked the Comintern if they could take an exiled Spanish child. The parents were both ardent revolutionaries. According to their daughter, Olga Lepeshinskaya (later a well-known actress), they were asked if they would take two, Rubén and Amaya, but Amaya preferred to stay in the international children's home. Rubén came and stayed with the family for two years. He was then about 16. More than half a century later Olga still remembered Rubén vividly:

> He always had a broad smile. He was very funny and liked girls. He always asked us, about any girl: 'Is she beautiful?' He didn't speak Russian very well at first but he soon improved. He was a great chatterbox and loved talking on the telephone and flirting with the girls. He also liked to play the guitar and sing. He soon became like a member of the family. Everybody liked him. He adapted to life in the USSR very well.

But beneath the jolly exterior Rubén appears to have had mixed feelings about his parents. Olga remembered him being dismissive about his father's lack of education. And he once let slip a revealing remark about La Pasionaria.

Once my mother tried to punish him and told him: 'You have such a famous mother and yet you behave so badly.' Rubén retorted: 'She never educated me. I was a child of the streets.'[5]

He also had plenty of Latin pride. The Comintern treated him as a favourite son and once sent him some fresh fruit, as rare in Moscow then as now. He wanted to share it with the family but they declined, thinking his need was greater than theirs. Because they wouldn't eat it, he refused to as well – and he was famous for his enormous appetite. The family found that he became more serious as he grew older, particularly when news came of the outbreak of the Spanish Civil War.

Back in Spain, working in secret was not only causing big problems on the domestic front for La Pasionaria: it also made foreign travel extremely difficult. There were pressing engagements overseas, the first of which was an international Aid to Asturias conference in Paris in the spring of 1935. She and a man called Manuel Colinos were nominated to represent the Spanish Communist Party. Travelling to Paris presented a problem. They could not travel openly or they would have been arrested at the French frontier. The only way to get out of the country was the age-old expedient of walking across the Pyrenees. Not only was it extremely hazardous, particularly for people unused to such arduous physical exercise, there was also the constant danger of being spotted by Civil Guard patrols, who were mainly on the look-out for the many smugglers who made a living from ferrying contraband goods across the mountains. One of these acted as a guide for the communist pair and a hair-raising journey ensued. They started out by night. La Pasionaria described the journey:

> We walked like blind men, guiding ourselves largely by sound and sometimes by touch, following the unfaltering steps of our guide, who never tripped . . . How many more hours had we to walk, how many more hills to cross, valleys to pass, rivers to wade, before reaching the place where we could rest our tired feet? . . . Before us loomed the Pyrenees, like an inaccessible fortress.

Towards dawn they were forced to deviate from their original path and wade across a river to shake off an approaching police patrol with dogs. After they had succeeded in getting across the water, Manuel Colinos contrived to fall in, ruining a new suit he had not yet paid for. He was too poor even to have an old pair of trousers for the journey,

46

which gives an insight into the quality of life of a leading communist travelling to an international conference on behalf of his Party. The journey took nearly 48 hours, including a day spent hiding in a cave without food or drink. After the conference, they had to go through the whole thing again to get back home. Three months later La Pasionaria had to walk across the Pyrenees for the third time, this time in the company of the Party general secretary José Díaz, as the first stage of a journey to Moscow to attend the VIIth Congress of the Communist International, from 25 July until 17 August.[6]

It was at this Congress that Georgi Dimitrov, the Comintern's Bulgarian secretary-general, pronounced the Communist Party's historic conversion to the idea of Popular Fronts of anti-fascist forces. Henceforth, individual Communist Parties were to cease their policy of sectarian isolation and seek alliances with other left-wing parties to fight the common enemy. This tactical volte-face opened the door for the Communist Party to emerge from its semi-clandestinity and isolationism and play a full and open part in Spanish politics. José Díaz prepared the Spanish Party and public for the forthcoming U-turn in a major speech in the Monumental Cinema, Madrid (which was to become a favourite location for communist rallies), in which he called for left-wing unity in a 'Popular Block'. Díaz's reward in Moscow was to be given a place on the Comintern's executive committee. La Pasionaria was elected as an alternate member. It was a significant mark of approval from the Kremlin.

The return trip to Spain was not as arduous as the journey out, although the Spanish delegation had trouble crossing several frontiers, particularly the Austrian one. La Pasionaria was spared another tramp over the Pyrenees by a clever ruse thought up by a Spanish communist colleague. A couple of sympathisers managed to 'borrow' a yacht to take her and Díaz from St Jean de Luz, on the French side of the border, to the Spanish port of San Sebastián. It worked perfectly and the communist pair sailed into San Sebastián without hindrance from the authorities. Ironically the yacht belonged to the unsuspecting owner of the right-wing newspaper *ABC*, a lifelong adversary of La Pasionaria and all she stood for.[7]

The Spain to which she returned was in turmoil. The shadow of the brutal putting down of the Asturias rebellion lay over the country and its repercussions resounded throughout 1935. The government became enmeshed in financial scandal and collapsed in the autumn. The curbs on the left-wing parties were relaxed and political activity burgeoned again. The Communist Party had pronounced itself in favour of a Popular Front but its potential allies did not rush to the altar. The communist line was to call for an alliance with the socialists, which they hoped would gradually lead to a merger between the two Parties, and a similar merger between the two big trade union organisations, the communist CGT and the socialist UGT. Many socialists were understandably wary of the communists' ultimate intentions. But after long and tortuous negotiations the agreement to form a Popular Front was signed between the socialists, communists and the republican parties on 15 January 1936, to fight the general election called for 16 February.

At the time La Pasionaria was back in prison. Although candidates had not yet been chosen, she had been campaigning for the Party in Galicia. For many people it was the first time they had been able to attend a Communist Party event openly. In the electric political atmosphere of the time, public meetings frequently ended in scenes of violence and disorder. At a meeting in a theatre in La Coruña on New Year's Day 1936, a group whom La Pasionaria suspected of being anarchists started heckling her during her speech. The Party news-paper *Mundo Obrero*, on the other hand, reported rumours that it was local right-wingers who had planned the disruption.[8] It may have been both. The police then entered and started laying about them with vigour.

La Pasionaria was arrested in the fighting that followed, which appears to have resembled a gigantic Wild West brawl. When news of her detention spread, so did the disorder. La Pasionaria was released the following day. But in late January she was back in prison, along with Vicente Uribe, editor of *Mundo Obrero*. They were held on charges relating to events some six months previously, which may have been a deliberate attempt by the Right to put two of the communists' star electoral turns out of action during the campaign. (Both La Pasionaria and Uribe had been selected as candidates for Asturias.) The paper naturally campaigned for their release, calling La Pasionaria a 'formidable agitator' on behalf of the Popular Front.[9] They got out of jail in time to ensure their election as deputies of the Cortes in the historic poll on 16 February. The result was a clear triumph for the newly-formed Popular Front. Although it gained only a narrow majority of individual votes over the right-wing National Front (4.6 million to 4.5 million) and less than the total of the Right and the Centre parties (who gained a total of 5 million votes), the Popular Front had a comfortable majority of seats. The communists ended up with 15 deputies, including La Pasionaria and Vicente Uribe in Asturias, and José Díaz in Madrid.

The Popular Front victory set Spain alight, almost literally. Hopelessly divided into two bitterly opposed factions, the country collapsed into sectarian lawlessness – intimidation, murder, the burning of churches, coup plots. The Left was jubilant; the atmosphere bordered on the revolutionary. The Right was defiant; many in the army, including General Franco, and other influential right-wing figures such as José Antonio Primo de Rivera, son of the former dictator and leader of the neo-fascist Falange movement,[10] and wanted an immediate coup before the Popular Front could get its hands on the levers of power. But President Alcalá Zamora and caretaker Prime Minister Manuel Portela Valladares refused to countenance a putsch. On 18 February the President asked the former President Manuel Azaña, the symbol of liberal republicanism, to become Prime Minister. Right and left were now implacably entrenched. The result was effectively an unofficial civil war which took the country to the edge of chaos before real hostilities broke out six months later.

As crowds gathered immediately after the election, the most popular call was for amnesty for all those imprisoned after the Asturias uprising. In Asturias La Pasionaria, fresh from her personal electoral triumph, took matters into her own hands in a celebrated incident which was to enhance her fame and reputation.

The political prisoners in the region's two principal cities, Oviedo and Gijón, had already rebelled on hearing the election result. La Pasionaria went first to the Gijón jail and talked to the communist prisoners there, leaving with a promise to do all she could to get them released before the new parliament met. In Oviedo things looked more serious. The rumour that political prisoners would be freed had spread and by the time La Pasionaria arrived at the prison on 20 February a huge and expectant crowd had gathered outside. All day it grew until by 4.30 pm it was estimated by one source at 20,000 people, chanting their demands for all the prisoners to be released.[11] It was potentially an explosive situation. La Pasionaria spent some time trying to sort it out with other deputies and officials and finally called on the military governor, Caballero, who agreed to release only 60 men. When La Pasionaria and the other deputies returned to the prison, they discovered that Caballero had sent an infantry company to surround the building and ordered the crowd to move back. The deputies were then admitted to the prison and allowed to talk to the prisoners, who were in no mood for compromise. They were adamant that they should all be released or none would go. The deputies could only tell them that although they sympathised they had to wait for orders from Madrid (which were unlikely to be forthcoming given the paralysis in the capital).

La Pasionaria does not appear to have addressed them at this stage. Outside, things were turning ugly. The crowd was pressing forward and demanding action. The prison director pleaded with La Pasionaria to calm them down. In a typically impetuous gesture, she promised the crowd she would free the men and got them to move back for the time being. Her charisma did the trick but when she went back inside the jail she found the prisoners straining to break open the inner doors and two soldiers setting up machine-guns in case they should break through. She rushed past the machine-gun posts and shouted a warning to the prisoners, who could not see the guns, that they risked being shot. They ignored her and burst through the doors. The soldiers did not fire but the director ordered the outer gates to be closed, trapping La Pasionaria inside with the rioting prisoners.

The other deputies had meanwhile tried and failed to get a decision from Madrid. It was an impasse, with the prisoners on the loose inside, the crowd growing more impatient by the minute outside and the prison staff and soldiers close to panic in between. The director asked La Pasionaria to his office. Fearing a trick, she at first refused until he gave his word she would be allowed to return to the prisoners after they had talked. She told him the only solution was to release all the men immediately. When he, not unnaturally, still hesitated, she asserted her new authority. As deputy for Asturias, she declared that she would take full responsibility for the decision. She may have been on doubtful legal ground but the director gratefully clutched at this straw. 'Here, take them and open the doors,' he said, handing her the keys. She grabbed them and ran through the corridors, waving the keys and shouting 'Everybody out!' Her hands were shaking so much she could not get the key in the lock of the main gate. [12] The prisoners had to take it and let themselves out, to be welcomed by an exultant crowd, who took them off round the streets in an enormous demonstration. By 10 o'clock in the evening of that extraordinary day, all the inmates in the Oviedo jail, whether political prisoners or common criminals, had been freed. The news swept through Spain. La Pasionaria's image as a fearless revolu-

50

tionary heroine, a woman who scorned convention to get things done, was further enhanced.

She and her fellow communist deputy, Juan José Manso, set off for Madrid by train but at the historic walled town of Avila they found a massive and excited crowd waiting for them at the station. They would not let the two deputies go any farther until they agreed to spend the day being fêted in the town. In Madrid, *Mundo Obrero*, aware of the propaganda value of the Party's new deputy, had been preparing its readers for her triumphant return, announcing the time of her arrival at the Estación del Norte (it had to be postponed because of the unexpected interruption of her journey at Avila). When La Pasionaria and Manso finally got to Madrid, they were greeted by one of those set-piece demonstrations which the communists were so good at organising: hundreds of young women wearing red scarves and carrying red flags and banners adorned with the hammer and sickle, and the names of various communist youth organisations. Thousands more crowded on top of stationary trains, waving flags and singing the '*Internationale*'. When the train finally arrived at 9.35 pm, the crush was so great that La Pasionaria and her party could not get off for 20 minutes. She and Manso were finally manhandled into a car which made its way slowly to the offices of *Mundo Obrero*, accompanied by a huge crowd cheered on by people waving clenched fists from pavements, balconies and trams. At *Mundo Obrero's* offices, La Pasionaria and Manso, although hoarse from all their recent exertions, delivered brief speeches before the crowd would disperse. 'Long live Madrid! Long live the future Spanish soviet!' Manso shouted optimistically.[13] After all their recent tribulations, the communists really did think the revolution was nigh – or that it had already arrived.

The following weekend was one of huge communist demonstrations in Madrid. On the Saturday 100,000 people crowded into the Las Ventas bullring to hear La Pasionaria in excitable mood: 'We are living in a revolutionary period,' she said, after paying her usual tribute to the Asturian miners. 'We are happy to support the [Popular Front] pact but the government must accelerate change . . . The people are hungry for bread and hungry for justice and they must be satisfied.' She warned (prophetically) of a right-wing backlash and was dismissive of 'legality': 'We will impose legality with our strength and with our revolutionary spirit . . . We have started on the journey that leads to justice.' An Asturian orphan, whose parents had been killed by a grenade dropped from a plane, added a few moving words. The next day some 600,000 people took to the streets for a Popular Front rally. The newly-elected communist deputies were mobbed by the enthusiastic crowd. La Pasionaria was given a particularly fervent reception from the women present, many of whom surged forward and embraced her.[14]

The atmosphere of revolution was everywhere. In Madrid, huge posters of Marx and Lenin adorned buildings, Soviet style. In her speeches and writings over the next few months La Pasionaria took an increasingly extremist line, scorning the legalism of bourgeois society which she clearly thought would not withstand the waves of revolution much longer. Her criticisms were not just of the right-wing parties (although she was venomous in her hatred of them too): she was equally impatient with the many elements in the Popular Front who proposed a gradual approach to reform, within the legal norms governing Spain at the time: a sizeable part of the Socialist Party and the various republican groupings. La Pasionaria and the communists were all for revolution there and then, although they would perform a smart U-turn within a year.

She called for a general amnesty not just for political prisoners but for all common criminals, on the grounds that they were merely victims of the old system. She cited 'hundreds of letters, full of emotion, hope and feeling' which were being sent by prisoners demanding their freedom.[15] Her postbag certainly contained a good proportion of correspondence from prisons around the country. 'We have had the news that various left-wing deputies, among whom you figure, have an amnesty plan for common criminals . . .' wrote an inmate of Duero prison, adding, perhaps unnecessarily, 'We support it and would like to know what chance it has of succeeding.' A deserter from the Navy sought her help: did he qualify for amnesty along with the recently-pardoned General Sanjurjo, imprisoned for rebellion in 1932? His situation, he wrote, was complicated by the fact that he was now in prison in Madrid for a criminal offence under an assumed name. A civil servant asked to be included in any amnesty for those persecuted by the 1933-6 government for having left-wing beliefs. An agricultural worker from La Piñera wrote on behalf of his son, imprisoned for 17 years for allegedly shooting a fascist. 'He was denounced by priests but he is innocent,' he wrote. A group of guards employed at a Barcelona prison wrote that they shared La Pasionaria's reform plans and denounced the governor as being 'in the service of feudalism rather than the service of the prisons', a telling little insight into an increasingly polarised society.[16]

La Pasionaria bearded the governor of Madrid's Modelo prison in his office and accused him to his face of victimising 'jailed revolutionary workers', adding menacingly: 'We are ready to end this situation immediately.' (She walked away without giving him the chance to reply.)[17] Amnesty was a constant theme of hers at that time. Writing in *Mundo Obrero* on 19 March, she defended her stance and pledged that she would not rest until the prisons were emptied and their occupants replaced by the likes of the right-wing politicians Alejandro Lerroux, a corrupt demagogue and founder of the Radical Party, who rose to fame in a tough area of Barcelona and was Prime Minister in 1934, José María Gil Robles, founder of CEDA, a lawyer and monarchist who flirted with fascism, and José Antonio Primo de Rivera, the founder of the Falange.

She had drastic solutions for inequality: 'The dream of citizens' equality before the law is no more than a beautiful dream, a meaningless phrase, as long as the right to private property exists,' she wrote.[18] At a press conference in Barcelona in mid-March she drew a distinction between the communists' conception of parliament and that of the other parties in the coalition: 'We shall try to link Party action with the struggle in the street. We do not concede a fundamental importance to parliament but consider the mobilisation of the masses more important.'

Direct action was always her preferred style. In her first months as a deputy La Pasionaria became involved in a series of confrontations with authority on behalf of the poor and underprivileged. Ordinary people had never seen anything like it. Members of Parliament did not act like this, in their experience. When news arrived in Madrid of a strike and sit-in at the Cadavio mine in Sama de Langreo, Asturias, La Pasionaria travelled to the mine and joined them, promising to stay until their wage demands were met. Such unprecedented action became something of a cause célèbre: the public was not used to deputies, least of all woman deputies, getting involved in such a personal way. The factionalism of the Left cut short her stay down the mine: anarchist miners were not at all pleased to see a communist deputy stealing their thunder, and La Pasionaria left, to avoid a damaging split. She pursued the miners' case when she returned to Madrid and they won a total victory.

In the capital, she was just as ready to drop her parliamentary duties to help people in need. When told of a group of tenants being evicted on to the streets for non-payment of rent, La Pasionaria went to the scene, halted the proceedings, seized a hammer and began smashing the new locks the landlords had put on the doors. Fired by her example, the tenants followed suit and were soon back in their apartments. When two poor women about to give birth were thrown out of a maternity hospital 'for refusing to pray', La Pasionaria whipped up a demonstration and helped to carry one of the women, by now in labour, back into the hospital. A friendly doctor was summoned and the woman gave birth to a daughter, who was duly named Dolores in gratitude.[19] Such incidents were meat and drink to La Pasionaria. For all her narrow devotion to Stalin and all his works – 'The USSR is the country which defends peace in the most positive and efficient way,' she said in a speech in February 1936[20] – she had an enormous empathy with ordinary people, a big heart, unlimited personal courage and an impetuous nature – an explosive cocktail of qualities which when ignited tended to produce spectacular results.

As her fame spread, she came to be seen by ordinary people all over Spain as a sympathetic figure who would listen to their pleas for help. Some saw her as a quasi-mystical figure, a modern saint, whom they addressed in a deeply reverential tone. A widow from Cartagena seeking an increase in her pension wrote: 'If you can obtain it for me, I will render the most fervent devotion to La Pasionaria, to that brave woman who deserves the name she has been given because she knew how to stand for the ideal of passion for the humble and the underprivileged of society.' Indeed, people used to touch her as they would a saint.[21] The mayor of Escalona, in the province of Toledo, was more down to earth. 'With great satisfaction,' he informed her, the town council had unanimously voted to change the name of one of its main thoroughfares to 'La Pasionaria Street'.[22]

It was around this time that Santiago Carrillo, who was to succeed her as the PCE's leader in 1960, first met her. He said later:

> She moved me from the moment I saw her; she wore rope-soled sandals, a big shawl of very pretty colours and, as always, black clothes. In spite of this simplicity, she seemed like a queen to me. She radiated a dignity, a majesty which you often find among the men and women of our common people . . . What seduced me, apart from her beauty, was her extra-ordinary charm, when she laughed and spoke. In that period she was the great tribune of the party who stirred the masses because she had a voice which brought a lump to your throat and an extraordinary talent as a

public speaker. Above all, she had political intuition, a popular instinct to position herself which was always very sure. It's true that from a tactical point of view she would go somewhat further than was necessary, carried away by her passionate and truthful character. But from the moment she entered Parliament she achieved enormous respect and her first speech was a major event.[23]

For all her dismissal of the Cortes as an outdated relic, La Pasionaria played a full part in its activities and made an enormous impact as a parliamentary speaker in the six months of normal life that was left to the institution. It is difficult to avoid the suspicion that she enjoyed life as a deputy more than she let on. She was by now a popular and accomplished public speaker and one of the few deputies who could bring both friend and enemy rushing back into the chamber to listen to her when she rose to her feet. She did not so much debate as fulminate. The Cortes had never seen anyone like her. It was used to the sonorous cadences of middle-aged men addressing each other courteously. Where, for example, a British MP would refer to an opponent as 'the honourable member' for such-and-such a constituency, Spanish deputies talked of 'su señoría' – literally 'your (or his) lordship' or 'ladyship'. Into these genteel proceedings La Pasionaria burst like a black-clad fishwife. Her language was direct and so was her message. Her speeches were laden with insults to the right-wing leaders seated in the same chamber, whose imprisonment she regularly recommended. 'Neither reactionary attacks nor the more or less undercover manoeuvres of the enemies of democracy will succeed in breaking or weakening the faith the workers have in the Popular Front and in the Government that represents it . . . If there are reactionary little generals who at a given moment, egged on by elements like Calvo Sotelo [a leading right-winger], may rise against the Government, there are also heroic soldiers who can keep them under control,' was one typical phrase. The other deputies soon realised that her ferocious reputation was well deserved. She was the public face of one side of a bitterly polarised society apparently heading towards a bloody confrontation without thought of retreat or compromise. The new communist deputies soon made their presence felt. At the first session of the new Cortes after the election, the strains of the 'Internationale' were heard in the chamber for the first time in its history. The communists led the singing when the Speaker of the Assembly, Diego Martínez Barrio, tried to terminate the session against their wishes. To their surprise, a noted right-wing deputy appeared to join in. He later claimed he was singing the National Anthem.[24] After La Pasionaria's first speech, the leading Socialist Party politician Indalecio Prieto was so impressed by her forceful personality that he wrote: 'En las Cortes ha entrado una mujer' – 'A [real] woman has entered parliament.'

She prepared her speeches by rising early in the morning (a lifelong habit) and making notes on which she would extemporise when called to speak. Her instant success became something of a burden. The other communist deputies were so impressed that they kept choosing her to speak on the Party's behalf, whatever the subject, to such an extent that she eventually became very angry about it.[25] Their own reluctance to speak may perhaps have been due to the fact that many of them were simple working people who were in awe of their new surroundings and understandably afraid to expose their inadequacies before such a demanding audience. La Pasionaria had no such fears or, if she did, concealed them well. She never had any time for fainthearts and never hid her feelings about people. Her colleagues probably received the rough edge of her tongue as regularly as her enemies.

As the early months of 1936 ticked away, the political situation deteriorated steadily. The anarchists, communists and the revolutionary wing of the Socialist Party made all the running; the military hatched plots with the backing of Spain's homegrown fascists, the Falange, which, for the moment, came to nothing; the centrist republican parties, the symbol of which was Manuel Azaña, who became President in May, lost their grip. The government seemed powerless to halt the growing violence perpetuated by both sides: the church burnings by the Left, the importing of arms by the Right.

In the Cortes the widening gap between the two extremes came to a head in the historic debate of 16 June, on a motion proposed by the right-wing CEDA Party criticising the state of public order. La Pasionaria played a central role in the proceedings. Indeed, the repercussions were to haunt her for the rest of her life.

The first two speakers were the right-wing leaders José María Gil Robles, of the CEDA Party, and the charismatic José Calvo Sotelo, of the monarchists. They bitterly attacked Spain's decline into anarchy and chaos. 'We are present today at the funeral service of democracy,' concluded Gil Robles. Calvo Sotelo went further; he all but called on the Army to intervene and overthrow the government. His speech, not unnaturally, set the place alight. The atmosphere was electric as La

Pasionaria rose to her feet. The monarchist newspaper *ABC* was scathing in its report:

Sra Ibárruri, Communist, gave the long-awaited speech signalled several days ago by the marxists as one which would produce a major sensation in Parliament. Let us say it once and for all: Sra Ibárruri spoke in the chamber as if it were a public rally, with unproven primary arguments, and with all the cutting phrases . . . which at election times always win applause and cheers of passion and hate. The speaker paraded before the chamber what she usually says about the supposed repression in Asturias and several times demanded the punishment of the guilty. And she glorified the Asturian revolution, considering it the purest and most perfect of any that has ever been attempted by the proletarian masses of any country. The strange thing about all this is that a demagogic speech, glorifying the marxist revolution, which aimed at destroying the very foundations of a bourgeois society, should be applauded with great enthusiasm by the left-wing republican parties which figure in the Popular Front and which call themselves bourgeois. We have never seen a greater inclination towards suicide.[26]

It was certainly an emotional speech. La Pasionaria attacked the Right for lamenting the collapse of public order when, she said, it was they who had caused it. She accused them of smuggling arms into the country for their supporters to use against the Left. She charged Calvo Sotelo with being a collaborator of General Martínez Anido, a former civil governor of Barcelona notorious for his brutal repression of the Left during the dictatorship of Primo de Rivera. 'The republic has not yet served justice on Martínez Anido, nor on Your Worship,' she said menacingly to Calvo Sotelo. She read out a list of workers who, she claimed, had been murdered by 'hordes directed by . . . a few cretinous gentlemen who hanker after the bloody glories of Hitler and Mussolini.' When she referred to a journalist, Luis de Sirval, who had been murdered by three Foreign Legion officers in an Asturian prison in 1934 for criticising the Legion's bloody repression of the uprising, several of her parliamentary colleagues and left-wing journalists on the press benches stood up and applauded. She spoke of women being raped and children's eyes being torn out in Asturias. 'When Spain begins to know the truth, the result will not be long in coming.' She demanded that the government jail right-wing leaders, insurrectionary generals and landowners who oppressed their tenants. She concluded with a final reference to the Asturian uprising, vowing that next time they would go one better: 'The socialist masses will know how to proceed to another Ninth of October and even beyond.' As she finished, several Popular Front deputies went across and shook her hand. *Mundo Obrero*, predictably, called her speech 'brilliant and magnificent' and noted 'the spontaneity of her gestures, of her movements . . . the vibration of her rich and mellow voice . . . her proud disdain for the smallness of her detractors.'[27] Even her bitter enemy *ABC* noted that 'the remaining speeches were hardly listened to'.[28]

But this impassioned debate was to be best remembered for something that was almost certainly never said. Calvo Sotelo briefly spoke again: 'I consider that a soldier would be mad who, faced with his destiny, was not ready to rise up in favour of Spain and against anarchy . . .' As he sat down amid general uproar, someone is said to have shouted: 'That was your last speech.' The blame for this inflammatory remark was placed firmly on La Pasionaria and rapidly passed into accepted fact, at least among anti-Popular Front ranks.

On 13 July Calvo Sotelo was assassinated (he was taken from his house by a group of armed men and shot dead as he was being driven away). There was widespread belief that La Pasionaria's 'threat' had been carried out. In the feverish atmosphere of the period, many people probably believed she had ordered the murder personally. The importance of this cannot be overstressed because Calvo Sotelo's death was the outrage that made the Civil War inevitable. The link with La Pasionaria was one more element in the horrific image that her opponents so successfully created around her person: as well as allegedly killing priests with her bare hands and sucking their blood, she ordered her opponents to be murdered.

Even in the twilight of her life, the allegation lingered on. When she travelled to Bilbao in August 1977 for the funeral of her long-separated husband Julián, a middle-aged man broke through the police cordon that surrounded her (she was not long back from exile in the USSR), rushed up to her and screamed: 'Murderer, murderer, you killed Calvo Sotelo!'[30]

But La Pasionaria always denied that she had ever made the remark, describing it as an 'infamous lie'.[31] Her long-time secretary Irene Falcón supported her.[32] Hugh Thomas wrote: 'There is no record of the remark in the Diario de Sesiones [the Hansard of the Cortes], nor was it heard by two such reliable witnesses then present as Henry Buckley [an American journalist] and Miguel Maura [a former

Minister of the Interior].'[33] It would appear that this is another classic example of the Pasionaria myth exceeding reality.

The myth clearly had plenty of mileage left in it. It was disinterred again after La Pasionaria's death, and presented again as truth by the right-wing historian Ricardo de la Cierva, a former Minister under Franco,[34] and Federico Jimenez Losantos, a columnist in *ABC*.[35] 'The whole of Spain remembered it; dozens of witnesses confirmed it,' wrote de la Cierva, although he did not name these witnesses. Both writers linked the purported death threat directly to Calvo Sotelo's assassination and therefore to the start of the Civil War. Thus it could be claimed that La Pasionaria was responsible for the Civil War, ignoring the thousand and one causes that had been building up since the turn of the century. It is no wonder that her opponents hung on to it so keenly for so long.

The truth of the matter appears to have been established by Ian Gibson, the biographer of Federico García Lorca and author of several books on the Civil War period, including a biography of José Antonio Primo de Rivera. His investigations reveal that a death threat was made in the Cortes, but it came from the lips of José Díaz, the PCE's general secretary, and he made it against Gil Robles during a debate on 15 April 1936. Díaz shouted to Gil Robles: 'Your excellency will die with his boots on!' However, La Pasionaria did then become involved. When several deputies protested at Díaz's remark, she shouted: 'If that bothers you, we'll take off his shoes and put his boots on!' Gil Robles replied in robust fashion: 'It will take you a great deal of trouble, with boots or without.'[36]

La Pasionaria cannot therefore be cleared of all guilt in uttering menacing statements against her opponents during those volatile months before the Civil War broke out. It suits her defenders to portray her as a sort of secular saint, but a glance at any of her speeches of that time shows that she used language of the most basic and blood-curdling kind; so indeed did her opponents. They did nothing to lower the political temperature. Quite the reverse; they fanned the flames of discord and hatred. But a few speeches in Parliament were not the sole causes of the Civil War. They could not compare, for example, to the bitterness and divisions left by the Asturias uprising. They were all part of the process of a society slowly destroying itself.

Whatever was or was not said in the great debate of 16 June, the government won the vote but it was a hollow victory. The Civil War was little more than a month away. The sheer hatred and intolerance displayed in the Cortes left little hope that a peaceful solution to Spain's deep divisions could be found. Indeed, both sides appeared hell bent on a physical confrontation. The verbal hostilities would soon be transformed into warfare proper and democracy would be laid low for more than four decades.

Fifty years later, La Pasionaria gave a hint that she regretted the bitter speeches she and others had made in the few months of life enjoyed by the Cortes that was elected in February 1936. 'There was permanent tension in that Parliament and sometimes that tension obliged you to say things that in a normal situation perhaps you wouldn't have said, or you would have said them in a different manner,' she reflected.[37] Perhaps she was casting her mind back to the threat to Gil Robles and wondering whether it would have been better left unsaid.

CHAPTER SIX

CIVIL WAR

For millions of people, La Pasionaria was the personification of the Spanish Civil War, that dreadful fratricidal conflict and rehearsal for the Second World War which polarised world opinion between 1936 and 1939. Outsiders, unable to distinguish between a clutch of grey generals on the nationalist side and a bewildering array of warring left-wing politicians defending the republican government against the military uprising of July 1936, all knew who La Pasionaria was. A tall, dark woman, dressed in mourner's black, with a natural gift for oratory and catchy slogans, she was the republic's principal mouthpiece to the world. Tirelessly she pleaded with the world to come to the rescue of the republic. Her anguished face appeared on a thousand posters; her speeches were reproduced in a million leaflets; the world's media showed her visiting the front, digging trenches, addressing huge rallies, her message always one of defiance and hope. She seemed to represent the very essence of beleaguered Spain: a woman who had sprung from the heart of the working class to scream defiance at the old order that was seeking to re-establish its traditional stranglehold over a people enjoying their first taste of freedom and democracy. So ran the legend, which she swiftly became. In a world looking for myths and symbols to rally behind, she was an image-maker's dream.

The defence of the republic became the cause of everybody alarmed by the rise of Nazism and fascism, a cause which straddled classes and parties. She was the darling of everybody who could be grouped under the word 'progressive', an adjective that sums up the mood of a decade. New York liberals paraded down Fifth Avenue bearing placards with the words (in Spanish) 'No pasarán' (They shall not pass), the slogan she is said to have coined which became the rallying cry of the republic. It is still being wheeled out half a century later in similar causes.

La Pasionaria was Boadicea, Joan of Arc, Mother Courage rolled into one (she was even compared to Saint Teresa of Avila). The power of her image attracted many foreigners to enlist in the International Brigades of volunteers who went to Spain to fight for the republic. Bill Alexander, a British communist who was one of them, recalled International Brigade volunteers returning to Britain in the early months of the war and passing on La Pasionaria's slogans: 'One of the things which led to deep admiration and respect for her was her ability to produce a slogan which summed up our whole political thinking. One such was "Stop the bombs on Madrid and Barcelona or they will fall on London and Paris tomorrow." In that slogan she expressed a deep thought and moved many of us to go to Spain.'[1]

Much of the propaganda around La Pasionaria was skilfully orchestrated by the Communist Party for its own frequently devious purposes, and Moscow used her in the same way on the international front. But she was genuinely popular with non-communists inside republican Spain who recognised her personal courage and charisma. She was equally loathed by the nationalist side, who were just as keen to build her up as a mythical figure, in their case a blood-sucking witch hell-bent on death and destruction.

Much of the propaganda had a strong basis in truth. Many eye-witnesses testify to La Pasionaria's personal bravery, while her energy and eloquence were in no doubt. But no individual could live up to this sort of mythologising. There were other sides to her: her romance with a man almost 20 years her junior, which was common knowledge in informed circles but never publicised; and the communist politician who schemed endlessly to further the Party's interests and who, according to the testimony of her former comrades, was deeply implicated in the arrest of the Trotskyist leader Andrés Nin, who was later murdered.

She was always willing to do Moscow's bidding and the role of the Soviet Communist Party during the Civil War is murky and reprehensible. La Pasionaria's complicity in its misdeeds must be weighed against the valuable work she did elsewhere. Some communists and other republicans found the reality of her personality very different from the public image: they thought her arrogant, stupid and weak, particularly in her blind allegiance to Moscow, and never forgave her for putting, as they saw it, the Soviet cause before the Spanish one. Nobody seemed to be able to take a detached view of La Pasionaria: she was either a heroine or a villain, to enemies and colleagues alike. The Civil War was the high point of her career; at the end of it opinion about her was as divided as it had been at the beginning.

The Civil War broke out on 18 July 1936 with the military uprising in Spanish Morocco against the republican government. Rumours of an imminent uprising had been circulating for weeks as the political situation deteriorated. Calvo Sotelo's assassination brought the rumours to fever pitch. The Communist Party had been on the alert for several days, posting guards on its own premises and spies on right-wing politicians and military centres. It was a period of rumour, counter-rumour and near panic. A typical example of a misunderstanding that nearly led to bloodshed in the days immediately preceding the outbreak of war happened at a Communist Party training school in General Díaz Porlier Street at which promising young Party members from all over Spain were being indoctrinated in the principles of Marxism-Leninism under the tutelage of a Comintern agent, the Bulgarian Rubén Avramov, codenamed 'Miguel'. The young men did gymnastic exercises in the mornings before classes, then emerged in the afternoons smartly turned out. Because nobody knew who they were, they were taken for fascists preparing for an uprising. A delegation from the MAOC anti-fascist militia (composed, ironically, of young communists and socialists) arrived one day demanding to be allowed in to inspect the building or they would storm it. The young communists called Party headquarters in alarm and asked for assistance. Shortly afterwards La Pasionaria, described by one of those present as 'already the most popular and best known figure in the Party', arrived and managed to persuade the militiamen of the young communists' bona fides. Once they had gone, she talked to the trainees who said they now needed arms to defend themselves, in case the next attack came from the fascist side. A few guns soon materialised, evidence that the communists could lay their hands on arms when necessary.[2]

Immediately news that the army had at last risen started circulating, La Pasionaria was pitched into a leading role rallying the people to the defence of the republic. Hard news was scarce and rumours were rife. Had the uprising gained a foothold on the mainland? Which cities were for the government and which for the insurgents? In the capital people came out on to the streets and gathered in crowds outside public buildings, especially at the Puerta del Sol in the heart of the old city. The government in Madrid vacillated and eventually collapsed later that day. The communists and others demanded that the people be given arms. In the vacuum that was developing, it was essential to boost the morale of ordinary people, who did not know what was going on. In Madrid, it was rumoured that the troops in the Montana barracks, near the city centre, were about to join the rebellion.

José Díaz told La Pasionaria she would have to broadcast on Radio Unión from the Ministry of the Interior at the Puerta del Sol on behalf of the communists. Shaking with nervousness, and reading from a few sheets of paper she had prepared, she delivered the broadcast at ten minutes after midnight the following day. It was the most important speech of her life to date and it had an extraordinary impact. Looked at cold more than half a century on, it amounts to little more than an extended slogan but it is worth reproducing in full to give a flavour of her style:

Workers, anti-fascists, working people: everyone stands ready to defend the republic, popular liberties and the democratic conquests of the people. The seriousness of the situation is known by all through the bulletins of the government and the Popular Front. In Morocco and the Canaries the fight goes on with enthusiasm and courage, the workers united with forces loyal to the republic. To the cry of 'Fascism will not pass, the hangmen of October [ie Asturias] will not pass!' communists, socialists, anarchists and republicans, soldiers and all those forces loyal to the will of the people are destroying the insurrectionary traitors who have dragged through dirt and treason the military pride of which they have so often boasted. The whole country is shaking with indignation faced with these heartless men who, with fire and terror, want to plunge popular and democratic Spain into an inferno of terror. But they shall not pass [no pasarán]! The whole of Spain is on a war footing. In Madrid the people are on the streets, warming the government with their decisiveness and spirit of combat so that the crushing of the reactionaries and fascists who have rebelled will be achieved. Women, heroic women of the people, remember the heroism of the Asturian women! Fight alongside the men to defend the bread and security of your threatened children. Soldiers, sons of the people! Stand firm, as one man, beside the government, beside the workers, beside the Popular Front, your parents, your brothers and comrades. Fight for the Spain of the sixteenth of February; take it to triumph. Workers of all persuasions: the government has placed in your hands the necessary means of defence so that we know how to honour our obligation to prevent in Spain the shame which a triumph of the bloody hangmen of the October revolution would imply. Let nobody hesitate: let us be able to celebrate victory tomorrow. Everyone be ready for action. Every worker, every anti-fascist, should consider himself a soldier at arms. People of

Catalonia, Vasconia, Galicia, all Spaniards: defend the democratic republic; consolidate the victory won by the people on the sixteenth of February! The Communist Party calls you all to the struggle. It calls on all workers to take a place in the combat to crush once and for all the enemies of the republic and of popular liberties. Long live the Popular Front! Long live the union of anti-fascists! Long live the republic and the people![3]

The phrase 'No pasarán' was instantly picked up. It spread swiftly round Madrid and the rest of the country, and passed instantly into revolutionary folklore around the world. But was it original? It is widely assumed that La Pasionaria coined it; all the literature about her tends to repeat it and her old colleagues certainly propagate the myth. They overlook the fact that it was made famous 20 years previously by Pétain during the siege of Verdun in 1916. The phrase can be found in a variety of forms in *Mundo Obrero* at least two years before La Pasionaria's speech. On 4 October 1934, for instance, the newspaper carried a front-page drawing of a man in dungarees carrying a placard with the words 'Workers and Peasants Alliance' above the caption 'No pasarán!' Later the same month the paper carried next to the masthead what it called 'our slogan'. The paper accused a 'monarcho-clerical-fascist rabble' of 'plotting a coup to install a fascist dictatorship'. So the slogan was: 'Ni de una ni de otra forma pasarán!' (Loosely translated, 'They shall not pass in any shape or form.') The phrase had therefore been in common use in communist circles for some time before La Pasionaria made it famous. (Of course, as she was on the staff of *Mundo Obrero*, it is just possible, if unlikely, that she was the anonymous journalist responsible for it in the first place.)

The young Santiago Alvarez heard the speech at the communist training school in General Díaz Porlier Street, along with all the other students who clustered round the radio to listen. 'That was the first of the appeals of a revolutionary woman, who from then on and in the course of the conflict would succeed with her words and actions in stirring the spirits of millions of men and women who resisted fascism with all their courage,' he wrote later.[4] La Pasionaria's speech was heard outside Spain as well. William Forrest, a *Daily Express* journalist who had been keenly following the Spanish crisis throughout the year, tuned in to the Madrid radio station at his London home that night to try to find out what was happening, having got wind of dramatic events in Spain in the *Express* office the previous evening. He happened to hear La Pasionaria's voice and was electrified by her speech. (Forrest was shortly to meet her in person; he was dispatched to Spain to cover the Civil War and he reported it on and off, first for the *Express* and then the *News Chronicle*, until the bitter end.)[5]

Confusion reigned. The crucial question was: which army units would stay loyal to the republic and which would join the rebellion? The next day, 20 July, La Pasionaria went to the Guadarrama mountains, to the north-west of Madrid, to check on the Popular Front's state of preparedness in an important strategic area overlooking the capital. She was shocked by the disorganisation she found and hurried back to Madrid to report it to the Party. The communists moved to ascertain which way the military units based in Madrid would jump. The working-class militias, with the communist-socialist MAOC to the fore, took control of the city, to all intents and purposes. They besieged the Montana barracks where some 2,500 rebels were holding out; a bloody massacre ensued when the soldiers surrendered. A young communist, Enrique Castro, who was to rise swiftly up the Party hierarchy, was present and was shocked to see the number of bodies and the flies already buzzing around them. He was summoned to the Central Committee building and shown into a small office. Various Party leaders, including José Díaz and La Pasionaria, came in. Pasionaria congratulated him on his performance and presented him with a pistol. Then she asked him: 'How did you feel in the first moments [of the attack]?' 'Nothing,' replied Castro. 'You didn't have any doubts?' she asked. 'There was no reason for that, Dolores,' he replied. 'Theoretically, it was a problem solved.' She and the others laughed.[6]

More rebel strongholds were stormed or surrendered but uncertainty still prevailed at others. The First Infantry Regiment, the Wad-Ras, had a communist cell of five men who reported to the Party what was happening inside the barracks. A majority of the officers were in favour of joining the revolt but hesitated to declare themselves because they were unsure whether the ranks would go along with them. On the morning of 23 July, a communist link-man with the Party cell relayed a message to Enrique Líster, the communist militia leader who was to attain legendary status during the war: some of the First Infantry officers were trying to persuade their men to join them in rebellion. Líster went straight to the barracks. He found a group of 20 officers in one room, the colonel and other top officers in another and the ordinary soldiers wandering about the barracks obeying no one. Líster told his informant to go to the Politburo and ask for a Party leader to come to the barracks straight away. He sent another man off to the working-class area of Vallecas to bring as many workers back as he could find. A couple of hours later, La Pasionaria arrived from Party headquarters. With a group of officers loyal to the republic, Líster challenged the top brass while she addressed the other ranks, assembled on the parade square. Standing on a bench she promised land for the peasants and made an impassioned plea for them to throw in their lot with the republic. After a slight pause, the men did so. Meanwhile Líster, bolstered by his militiamen and 100 newly-arrived workers, had arrested the officers who would not support the government. He and La Pasionaria wasted no time with their haul: they took their new forces off to the Guadarrama front in a fleet of Fiat cars commandeered from a nearby showroom.[7] They got a frosty reception from the regular army unit stationed there, whose allegiance was in some doubt, but the communists' initiative had paid off. The whole incident typified La Pasionaria's approach; it was certainly proof of her persuasive tongue.

It was also typical of those first days of the war: a frantic, disorganised scramble for arms, supporters and territory, with the allegiance of many in doubt and a total absence of reliable information. In this atmosphere, the discipline and organisation of the Communist Party, in particular its militia and its youth movement, was a critical element in bolstering the shaky republic in Madrid.

La Pasionaria spent most of the those first ten critical days visiting the newly-formed fronts to bolster morale. By 24 July her voice was so hoarse from making so many speeches on the Somosierra front, that she was unable to deliver another radio broadcast, as she had planned. Instead, it was reproduced in *Mundo Obrero*: 'The spirit of the brave defenders of the republic is marvellous. They attack an enemy well supplied with weapons of war like lions,' she wrote, and urged the whole city to get behind them. She asked for supplies for the thousands of new volunteers arriving at the front daily and reminded her readers that the wives and children they left behind needed looking after too. She suggested neighbourhood committees to look after their welfare. She also appealed for blankets for the fighters at the front: the poet Luis de Tapia, who had penned the emotional tribute to her in June, turned up at the International Red Cross with 20.[8]

In Madrid, now effectively a city taken over by revolution, all the various Popular Front organisations commandeered the palaces, mansions and luxury houses vacated by their fleeing owners. The Communist Party took over the Serrano Palace, which had previously been the headquarters of the right-wing political party Acción Popular (Popular Action). A journalist found La Pasionaria there in high spirits over the Party's new home: 'It's a superb palace but the most superb thing of all is the organisational material which the Cedista Party had and which will serve us now. There are stupendous files, marvellous filing cabinets, top-quality typewriters, excellent telephones, valuable data on the homes and ideologies of thousands of citizens,' she said with relish, her last remark providing a sinister guide to what the communists would be using this treasure trove for. 'We weren't going to be so stupid as to base ourselves in a great empty house where the mounting of our organisation would have cost a fortune. We've acted sensibly, haven't we?' She showed the reporter two Rolls-Royces left behind in the rush to get out and in a cellar a dummy figure made from cloth and straw and riddled with bullet holes which had been used by the previous occupants for target practice.[9]

A few days later *Mundo Obrero* paid tribute to her:

> In this historic moment for Spain, standing magnificently on a pedestal made of her own heroism, a pedestal of rock like her own will, the figure of La Pasionaria stands out against the background of the blood and fire of the struggle. Tireless, fervent, warm in word and sure in doctrinal concept, she encourages in battle, helps in ordinary jobs like anyone else and is always alert to the little details which the brave militias may lack. We salute a comrade who knew how to pick up drop by drop the pain of the proletariat and the people and convert it into a revolutionary essence to fight for the democratic republic against fascist reaction.[10]

Hyperbolic certainly, but indicative of the image that the Party was creating around her figure. All it needed was for a latter-day Delacroix to paint her stepping off a pile of corpses and bearing a red flag.

By 29 July her voice had recovered sufficiently to make another broadcast on Radio Unión. This time her message was directed to the outside world. She appealed to the people of America and Europe to come to the aid of the republic. 'Help us prevent the disappearance of democracy in Spain. For if that should happen, it would inevitably mean the beginning of a world war which we all want to avert,' she said. It was a message she was to repeat throughout the war, with only limited results. Her warning of world war was to turn out to be all too accurate.

La Pasionaria herself provided a graphic account of a visit to the Guadarrama front in August. With José Díaz and Colonel Asensio, chief of staff in the region, she was driven from Asensio's headquarters towards the front in a so-called 'armoured car'. 'It provided about as much protection from bullets as a sheet of paper,' she commented sardonically. As they approached the front, they were sighted by the enemy, who opened fire. If the bullets had reached them, she added, 'they would have riddled us like swiss cheese.' Still under fire, they got out of the vehicle and ran for the sandbag-protected front line, the barbed wire tearing at La Pasionaria's skirt. The republican soldiers were clearly cheered to see her there. 'They took out their identity cards, personal documents, photographs of their mothers and sweethearts so we could sign them and write a kind word, an expression of affection and hope.' As night fell, it was time to leave, taking with them letters to be posted and messages for the men's families. 'We left rapidly but the enemy artillery was even more rapid. We ran an unbelievable obstacle race until we finally reached territory which was out of their firing range. Avoiding the road, we walked back to Guadarrama and then returned to Madrid.'[11]

'She didn't go to the front for political reasons. She went because of personal passion,' said Santiago Alvarez, by then a political commissar with the Fifth Militia Regiment. Her physical courage was never in question. Alvarez recalled one comical incident from the early weeks of the war. On her frequent visits to the front, the Party always sent a member along with her as a bodyguard. On her return to the Serrano Palace one afternoon with one particular young man, La Pasionaria called the official in charge of security and bawled him out. 'Look,' she said, 'when you order a comrade to accompany me, try to find out beforehand if he's afraid. The last thing I need with me is cowards. I'd rather go on my own.' And she described how her 'bodyguard', to her disgust, had hurled himself on the ground at the first sound of a bullet whistling over the Guadarrama trenches. 'She could never stand cowards or waverers around her,' according to Alvarez.[12] A militia battalion fighting at Oropesa on the Extremadura front was named after her.

La Pasionaria's extraordinary influence on the men at the front was described by a young militiaman whose job it was to teach the mostly illiterate soldiers to read and write. When they had mastered the rudiments of writing, 'they almost invariably sat down to write two letters. The first to their wives, telling them that they had learnt to write. The second to La Pasionaria, to inform her of the good news. "We are not only fighting the enemy, we are learning too, you can count on us . . ."'[13]

The pressures on La Pasionaria were taking their toll. At a mass rally in Valencia on 23 August, her voice continually faltered and eventually she had to cut short her speech through exhaustion. She was still given a rapturous ovation.[14] In the crowd was the Austrian sociologist Franz Borkenau, who related his impression of her in his classic book of reportage, *The Spanish Cockpit*:

> There were about 50,000 enthusiastic people there. When La Passionaria [sic] appeared on the platform enthusiasm reached its climax. She is the one communist leader who is known and loved by the masses, but in compensation there is no other personality in the Government camp loved and admired so much. And she deserves her fame. It is not that she is politically minded. On the contrary, what is touching about her is precisely her aloofness from the atmosphere of political intrigue: the simple, self-sacrificing faith which emanates from every word she speaks. And more touching even is her lack of conceit, and even her self-effacement. Dressed in simple black, cleanly and carefully but without the slightest attempt to make herself look pleasant, she speaks simply, directly, without rhetoric, without caring for theatrical effects, without bringing political *sous-entendus* into her speech, as did all the other speakers of the day. At the end of her speech came a pathetic moment. Her voice, tired from endless addresses to enormous meetings since the beginning of the civil war, failed her. And she sat down with a sad waving gesture of her hands, wanting to express: 'It's no use, I can't help it, I can't say any more; I am sorry.' There was not the slightest touch of ostentation in it, only regret at being unable to tell the meeting those things she had wanted to tell it. This gesture, in its profound simplicity, sincerity, and its convincing lack of any personal interest in success or failure as an orator, was more touching than her whole speech. This woman, looking fifty with her forty years, reflecting, in every word and every gesture, a profound motherliness (she has five children herself [sic] and one of her daughters accompanied her to the meeting), has something of a medieval ascetic, of a religious personality about her. The masses worship her, not for her intellect, but as a sort of saint who is to lead them in the days of trial and temptation.[15]

Borkenau was only one of many to place La Pasionaria in a quasi-religious context. And his analysis of her as 'not . . . politically minded' may sound odd in a description of a leading member of a political party, but it was essentially accurate. She was, as he repeatedly said, a simple person, a romantic, an idealist who could encapsulate in simple language the same feelings, fears and dreams of ordinary people. That is why she had such an astonishing rapport with them. Borkenau's account adds powerful weight to those who claim that La Pasionaria was the least sectarian of all the Popular Front leaders. She was always at pains to deny the allegation herself, although the same could not be said for most of her communist confrères, nor indeed of many anarchists and socialists either, as Borkenau implies in his references to other speakers at the rally.

Foreign aid and support was now a key concern. The establishment of the non-intervention committee in London was a bitter blow for the republic. But the Germans and Italians started pouring aid to Franco; the Comintern and the communist international trade union umbrella body, the Profintern, promised 1000 million francs to the republic. The fund was to be administered by a committee whose members were Maurice Thorez, leader of the French Communist Party, Palmiro Togliatti, the Italian communist who was now the Comintern's chief representative in Spain, Largo Caballero, the socialist leader shortly to become prime minister, José Díaz and La Pasionaria. She and Togliatti were also appointed to a Comintern committee on Spain. It was also decided to mount a massive propaganda campaign thoughout Europe and the USA in support of the republic. A variety of 'aid for Spain' organisations were set up, ostensibly independently-run and to raise money for humanitarian purposes; but they were really communist fronts. After a massive public meeting in Paris in July, the Comité International de l'Aide au Peuple Espagnol was set up. It soon had many branches in other countries. La Pasionaria's romantic figure was a vital element in the propaganda war overseas. Her speeches were reprinted as pamphlets and 'No pasarán' was the universal slogan.

At the end of August she formed part of a Popular Front delegation to Paris. Their aim was to persuade the French government openly to back the republic and to rally public support. The journey was notable for the hostile reception the delegation received when they stopped off en route in Barcelona, stronghold of the anarchists. It was a classic example of the internecine warfare that was to debilitate the republican cause. They emerged from an audience with Lluis Companys, self-proclaimed President of Catalonia, to find the anarchist militia who effectively ran the city claiming that their diplomatic passports needed exit visas. La Pasionaria, already shocked at the extent of anarchist power and the absence of communist influence in Barcelona, exploded with rage. The local communists to whom she turned for help were reluctant to create a fuss. Another row ensued when the passports were returned: La Pasionaria accused the anarchists of murdering communists. She claimed afterwards that the anarchists gave orders for the delegation to be prevented from leaving Spain at the border but that communist railway workers guaranteed them a safe passage.[16] It was the sort of behaviour that Orwell was to publicise the following year in *Homage to Catalonia*.

They got a warmer welcome in Paris, at least from the French Popular Front; from an extreme right-wing group called La Croix du Feu came a death threat. The Civil War had concentrated the eyes of the world on Spain and La Pasionaria was hot news. Some 200 journalists attended a press conference she held at her hotel. She made an emotional appeal for international support and condemned non-intervention as a 'legal monstrosity'. Having supper that night in a modest restaurant in a working-class district, she was applauded by her fellow-diners. 'The people of France see in her the representation of the Spanish people in their struggle,' *Mundo Obrero* faithfully reported.[17] A well-wisher sent her a bottle of perfume. 'At least someone still thinks of me as a woman,' she said – an interesting response.[18] She spoke in the packed Winter Velodrome, the cycling stadium, and unveiled another slogan which became a republican catchphrase: 'It is better to die on your feet than live on your knees.' She received a rapturous reception. She was the toast of progressive Paris; the press of all political persuasions was full of photographs and biographies of her. Three hundred thousand people marched through the city shouting 'Planes and guns for Spain!' The workers at the Hotchkiss arms factory declared a half-hour strike in protest at the government's no arms for Spain policy. Renault workers took more practical action: they built two Red Cross ambulances, filled them with medical supplies and donated them to the republican cause. Workers at an arms factory promised ten 81mm cannons and 50,000 shells.[19] But the Spanish delegation failed to persuade the French Prime Minister Leon Blum to intervene on the republic's behalf. La Pasionaria was contemptuous of his hand-wringing attitude. She claimed he even wept as he turned them down. They proceeded to Brussels and another huge rally but this time were prevented from addressing it. The delegation went on to London but without La Pasionaria: there were doubts that she would get a visa. Rather than be snubbed at Dover, she returned to Madrid on her own. There was good reason for her to do so anyway: the old socialist Largo Caballero had been invited to form a government and the communists had agreed to join it, with two ministerial portfolios. Respectability thus confirmed, the Party entered a period of increased influence and explosive growth.

As summer turned to autumn, the battle-lines between republic and rebels became clearer. The key to the republic's survival was Madrid, threatened on three sides by nationalist forces. It was during the most bitter days of the siege of Madrid during October and November 1936 that La Pasionaria attained her greatest heights as a symbol of resistance. She seemed to be everywhere, urging defiance. On 4 October she was made an honorary commander of the Fifth Militia Regiment at a rally in Madrid commemorating the second anniversary of the Asturias uprising. She did not mince words, telling the men her new status gave her the authority to talk to them in tough language. It would be a long, hard struggle, the first step in the war between democracy and fascism. 'There's a military saying,' she told them, 'that it's more dangerous to abandon trenches than to defend them. It's more difficult to save your life when you're in flight than it is to defend a parapet.' It was a message often repeated in the dark days looming. And in a variant of her classic slogan, she finished: 'Go to bed thinking "They shall not pass" and get up in the morning saying "We shall defeat them."'

Her other main theme in this period was greater military organisation and discipline. The communists were at the forefront of the campaign to create a regular army in place of the hotch-potch of militias then defending the republic's colours. This, they argued, was the only way the republic could hope to fight the professional soldiers ranged against them, reinforced as they were by well-equipped Italian and German forces on the ground and in the air. La Pasionaria put forward the Red Army as the ideal model for the republican militias and Leningrad, besieged during the Russian Civil War, as the model for Madrid. In mid-October the government created a Popular Army out of the framework of the Fifth Militia Regiment, as the communists had been pressing it to do.

More questionably, La Pasionaria introduced an unlikely figure to bolster her arguments: her long-estranged husband Julián Ruiz. On 14 October she urged the women of Madrid to get behind their men. 'You have brothers, cousins, husbands at the front,' she told a rally. 'I too have a husband at the front.'[20] This was true, in the strictly legal sense: she and Julián were still married (they were never in fact divorced) and he was certainly fighting at the front, in his native

North. But it was a gross distortion of the truth: she and Julián had been separated for the best part of five years and it smacked of the cynical to resurrect him for propaganda purposes.

In the last days of October the nationalist forces intensified their attack on Madrid. To many, the fall of the capital appeared imminent. At Getafe, 8 miles south of the city, Geoffrey Cox, war reporter for the *News Chronicle*, came across the newly-created People's Army 'in full retreat on Madrid'. He wrote: 'This morning these troops had been holding the centre of the southern front, near the village of Parla. They had been shelled and bombed and machine-gunned from the air till they had broken from their shallow trenches.' He recognised an Asturian communist who had been optimistic only a couple of days previously. Now he said: 'It's impossible. No troops in the world could stand it.' Cox went on:

Things certainly seemed hopeless for Madrid as that afternoon wore on . . . Towards dusk things got better, though the confusion remained . . . In one place a young officer was even getting a section together to march back. Green double-decker buses with fresh troops, waving their rifles and singing out of every window, rushed through to volleys of 'Salud! Salud!' And a long black Cadillac, obviously bearing someone of real importance – there were no trade union letters painted on its gleaming body – came to a stop outside the commandant's headquarters in the town hall.

From it stepped a tall woman, with greying hair, wearing a simple black dress. Immediately the men sitting round recognised her, and one cried: 'La Pasionaria!'

Still clasping their pieces of bread and chunks of herring, they crowded round her, faces alive with interest. With some of them it was just curiosity to see this famous woman communist, Dolores Ibárruri, known as 'The Passion Flower'. Famed for her oratory and her courage, particularly in the days of the Asturian revolt of 1934, she typified the old fire of Spain in a new setting. But, above all, one sensed immediately the longing for leadership amongst these men. Shattered, retreating, dispirited, they wanted leaders who would help them . . .

Amongst the crowd around La Pasionaria was a beardless militiaman, who could not have have been more than seventeen. Pressing forward, he asked me eagerly: 'What is it? Have the Russians come? Have you seen them?' And he stared down the road as if expecting battalion upon battalion of Soviet infantry in greatcoats and peaked caps to come marching up to their aid . . .

La Pasionaria walked up the road towards the line. In the glowing darkness, broken only by a fiery sunset glow on the horizon, man after man crowded after her. But there was a note of tragedy over the scene. For all her eloquence and courage, what could La Pasionaria do at this late hour to check the retreat? It seemed to me as if the dying sun were like the fading glow of the People's Government in Spain. On that autumn evening it appeared as if nothing could save Madrid and Spain from Franco.[21]

In fact during the next days and weeks, when the siege of Madrid was at its bloodiest and most intense, La Pasionaria provided much of the leadership and example whose absence Cox had noted. One militiaman recorded his admiration for her courage when she visited his unit at the front.

We passed the night and the whole morning expecting the arrival of the enemy infantry. They were preceded by enemy Junkers, throwing more bombs upon us. The planes came at the very moment that La Pasionaria, accompanied by a group of high-ranking officers and civilians, appeared on top of our trench. We were busy hiding as low as we could in the trenches, but she and her companions remained standing on top of the trenches while the bombs were falling all around us. She was calling for courage and determination to face the oncoming enemy, and she went on and on talking to us in a loud voice so as to be heard by as many soldiers as possible. She sauntered along the top of the trenches without ever a flicker of fear. Her presence and her encouragement had a good effect on our morale . . .[22]

Back in Madrid, La Pasionaria urged a practical approach to the crisis. 'Instead of building houses, why aren't hands employed in building fortifications?' she asked a mass meeting on 14 October. 'Let us kill the frivolity of Madrid, let us make it feel the war.'[23]

She did, at least once, stop retreating soldiers in their tracks by her eloquence and persuade them to return to the trenches and continue fighting. Santiago Alvarez was by now political commissar with the fourth battalion of the First Mixed regiment of the Popular Army, largely composed of Galicians like himself. They were among the troops whom Geoffrey Cox observed at Getafe towards the end of October. Two days later, they found themselves dug in in the hills above Sestena, defending the main Madrid–Andalusia highway. For four days they fought off three infantry battalions and a cavalry regiment of Moors. Cut off from any information about what was happening elsewhere, Alvarez made his way to Valdemoro to see if he could get some ammunition and supplies for his troops. Looking for the General Staff, he came across a surprising scene. In the garden of a house near the road, he found La Pasionaria, José Díaz and other communist leaders, as well as Vittorio Codovila, the Comintern delegate. He put them in the picture: the situation was critical; his men were holding out but the republican forces on their left flank were retreating and the right flank was open. He wrote:

The first to react was Dolores Ibárruri. 'What, the militiamen retreating? I'm going there with you right now.' I said: 'No, they're not my battalion, they're from other battalions but it's the same thing.' Dolores picked up her handbag and headed for the road with me. A group of retreating militiamen was approaching us. Dolores got up, on to the granite balustrade of the bridge and harangued them: 'Soldiers, comrades! Where are you going? Why are you fleeing from the front? Are you perhaps cowards? Who then will defend Madrid? What will your wives say, your girlfriends, your mothers? Don't you love the cause of the workers, of freedom, your cause? You must fight so that Madrid doesn't fall into the hands of the fascists!'

Her black figure, upright upon the parapet, her voice of steel, cutting through the air of the sunny morning, her reproaches to those who were abandoning the front, her words of encouragement, her mere presence there, at that moment, stopped the retreating men in their tracks.

Suddenly, as if moved by a spring, those in the nearest group turned right round and headed back towards the front again. Some were weeping. The others followed suit. The retreat was halted. The militiamen, soldiers now, returned to the front . . .

I confess that I always remembered the imposing figure of Pasionaria standing on the bridge at Valdemoro haranguing the militiamen, filling them with courage and prompting them to resist. For that and for other actions of hers, which I witnessed, I have always considered Dolores Ibárruri an extraordinary popular and historic Spanish figure.[24]

Alvarez insisted that the Politburo members return to Madrid as soon as possible as their safety could not be guaranteed. Even at this distance, one feels for the luckless militiamen trudging back to the front while their political masters drove off to the relative safety of Madrid. But at least the communists did not flee from the capital when all seemed lost, as the government did on 6 November, when it moved to Valencia. (William Forrest of the *Daily Express* had by now arrived in Madrid and made La Pasionaria's acquaintance. He got wind of the government's departure and, knowing he had a world-beating scoop, managed after great difficulty to dictate a report to his office in London, ostensibly about the siege of Madrid. To evade the censor, it contained a coded message: the first letter of each paragraph made up the sentence 'The government has fled.' It got through but Forrest's hurriedly-spoken explanation to the copytaker was never relayed to the night sub-editor and the scoop was lost, to his eternal disgust.)[25]

The government's departure left a vacuum that the communists filled. From then on, they led the defence of Madrid to their great subsequent benefit. La Pasionaria was at the heart of things. Her concerns were to keep up public morale and do what she could for the welfare of the men at the front. When, on one visit, she found them with no supplies or food and their base camp 10 km away, she went personally to get food, coffee and cigarettes and carried them back to the troops, dodging the bullets.[26] On 9 November she told a rally in the Monumental Cinema, organised by the communists at two hours' notice: 'Crush the enemy, make their bones serve as fertiliser for the lands of our farmworkers!'[27]

Mundo Obrero published a poem dedicated to her by one Lisa Guerrero (probably a pseudonym): 'Dolores, mother of a great people, we love you/Red eagle of a new Spain!'[28] In some outlying parts of Madrid, like the University City, the troops were dug in within shouting distance of each other. La Pasionaria's name was taken in vain by the nationalist troops in quiet moments, when both sides would exchange insults. The nationalists would shout: 'Hijos de Pasionaria!' (sons of Pasionaria!), an adaptation of 'hijos de puta' (sons of whores), one of the worst insults a Spaniard can deliver.[29] As the nationalist onslaught intensified, new hope arrived for Madrid in the unexpected shape of the first volunteers of the International Brigades, many of whom said that they had been inspired to go to Spain by the appeals from La Pasionaria, with whom they ever afterwards felt a special affinity. Against all expectations, the nationalist onslaught was checked, then repelled. Madrid was saved for the time being; La Pasionaria was the heroine of the hour.

The communists in Madrid wasted no opportunity to claim that they were largely responsible for the capital's unexpected survival. They were in triumphalist mood, but in the process they antagonised many non-communist *madrileños* who felt they too deserved credit for their city's resistance. At another rally in the Monumental cinema, held by the PCE to celebrate the anniversary of the Bolshevik revolution, La Pasionaria delivered her customary impassioned speech (which was broadcast to the rest of the world) in praise of her own Party's role in the defence of Madrid. She was so blatantly one-sided that the representative of the Republican Left Party, Régulo Martínez, felt obliged to set the record straight:

> She was praising the Communists, maintaining that they alone were defending the city. I rose to speak. It was not the Communists but the *people* who were fighting, I said. The Communists didn't take that too well, but the people stood and cheered as I spoke of the times when *madrileños* had risen to defend their liberty.[30]

Despite the euphoria of the moment, the seeds of the breakdown in trust between the communists and the other components of the Popular Front, which were to cause such damage to the republican cause, were evident already.

Thwarted by Madrid's stubborn resistance, Franco switched the focus of his attack from the ground to the air. The nationalists started bombing the city, causing heavy civilian casualties. Pasionaria condemned the bombing, claiming that the republican air forces would never stoop to such tactics. She was one of the first of many, in different wars on different continents for the rest of the century, to make the distinction between targeted and indiscriminate bombing. 'Ours [our fliers] seek vital centres like aerodromes, armed concentrations [of people] and weapons of war, while the enemy attacks defenceless cities, hospitals, schools,' she wrote. She may have had more justice on her side than many who would make similar claims after her. La Pasionaria conjured up another memorable image in the same article: 'A baby of two died with his mother. Gripped by her maternal arms in the supreme embrace of protection and agony, the paving stones of the street were his death bed.'[31] At her best, she had the sure touch of a good popular journalist.

As 1936 drew to a close, some British newspapers reported that La Pasionaria had been killed in the fighting. (During the Civil War both sides regularly reported that key enemy figures had died: the communist press certainly reported Franco's demise.) The British journalist Claud Cockburn, who reported on the war for the British Communist Party organ the *Daily Worker* under the pseudonym Frank Pitcairn, sought out La Pasionaria in Valencia to tell her of her decease. Her reaction was 'a deep chuckling laugh'. His report went on:

> 'You don't say?' she said. 'Looks like those people really are anxious about having me dead. That is the third time I have been dead in England in this war alone.'

I reminded her that when I was here in 1934 I had twice had the job of asking her the same question for the same reason, namely whether she would confirm the London newspapers' account of her death.

She started to laugh again. 'Well,' she said, 'Tell them I'm alive and kicking.' She paused. 'Mind you get that – and kicking!

'And tell them that when Franco's dead and Mola's dead and Queipo de Llano's dead, I shall start perhaps to think about dying too.

'And tell them as they don't seem to know it yet, that all those generals have arms a darned sight too short to get me – a darned sight too short.'

Still laughing, she rushed out of the room on another job in her eternally busy day as the accepted leader of the honest and decent women of Spain in their struggle against the enslavement and degradation of Fascism.[32]

Although La Pasionaria professed herself shocked and amazed at the Catholic-hating bloodsucker image of her that was by now taken as gospel in nationalist Spain, she nevertheless derived considerable pleasure and amusement when she had the opportunity to exploit it. In January 1937 she paid a visit to nationalist prisoners captured at Cerro Rojo, near Madrid. When she entered the cellars where they were being held, a 'sepulchral silence ensued,' reported a sympathetic journalist who was present. Presumably they thought they were about to be shot when they saw the black-clothed embodiment of their worst nightmares descending the stairs. La Pasionaria addressed them: 'Brothers, you lived deceived and exploited by a miserable caste which had three main pillars: the Army, the Church and the haute bourgeoisie. I know you are filled with fear because the enemy presents us as barbarians and killers. Do not fear. Your lives are as sacred as our own . . . If we had been the prisoners we would have been shot out of hand. By contrast, you who arrive full of misery, soon you will be free human beings. We shall not only respect your lives but take care that they are as pleasant as possible for you.' At this, the prisoners burst into cheers for La Pasionaria and the republic, as well they might. 'They told you the reds were killers. You see this is not the case,' she concluded.[33] Whether she was able to grant them the 'pleasant life' she promised is open to question, given the hardships Madrid was then suffering.

A similar incident happened later that year at Belchite in Aragon, a key nationalist town which was blocking any advance on Zaragoza and which La Pasionaria visited at the height of a republican offensive. A group of prisoners – soldiers, civilians and priests – was brought in to General Modesto's headquarters where La Pasionaria was. They did not recognise her and, she claimed, 'spoke of La Pasionaria with horror, of the crimes she had committed, of her cruelty with prisoners, especially with monks and nuns, of the songs about her heard on Radio Zaragoza.' She listened for a while and then asked them what they thought La Pasionaria looked like. 'They say that La Pasionaria isn't Spanish, she looks like a man,' said one. When she revealed her identity, 'they looked at me quivering with fear for their lives. I told them nothing would happen to them, but it was difficult to convince them after the "compliments" they had paid me.'[30]

On two occasions, La Pasionaria came to the rescue of groups of Catholic nuns. The first numbered about 100 who had been taken from their convents and placed in prison at the start of the war. They were clearly proving something of an embarrassment. La Pasionaria was deputed to visit them and explain that they were to be rehoused in a large empty convent, where those who wanted could do embroidery or make children's clothes. Subsequently, another group of nuns was found by militiamen hiding in a house. They too were terrified about what would happen to them at the hands of the dreaded Reds but La Pasionaria was able to tell them they could stay where they were and ensured that no harm came to them. They too were pressed into service making children's clothes after their offer to help tend to the wounded in hospital was gently turned down because 'the soldiers wouldn't accept it'. For all the social revolution going on around them, Spanish men's attitudes had not changed much.

CHAPTER SEVEN

THE COMMUNISTS IN POWER

Madrid had been saved. In the winter of 1936-7, the Spanish Communist Party enjoyed a huge and unprecedented increase in its popularity and membership. By June 1937 it had reached 400,000 members, dwarfing the socialists, who were split into two hostile factions. The communist surge was understandable. There was widespread admiration for their disciplined approach to the war; they had set an excellent example in leading the defence of Madrid; and they were inextricably linked in the public mind with the Soviet Union, which was seen as the only external ally the republic had, apart from the International Brigades, who were anyway of communist inspiration. The communists' organisation and propaganda were of a high order, which greatly aided recruitment. And there were many Spaniards who, while perhaps not greatly interested in Marxist theory, could see that it was in their own best interests to hitch their star to the communist bandwagon.

What most of them did not realise was that the Communist Party was to all intents and purposes being run from Moscow by the Comintern's representatives in Spain.

> After the intervention of Soviet Russia on the side of the Loyalists there is no question that the leadership of communist activities in Spain passed into the hands of Soviet and Comintern representatives . . . Except for public announcements and agitation, all the important functions of the Communists in Spain were carried out by the foreign commissars.[1]

The supreme practitioner of the two activities Stalin's men left to the Spaniards – public relations and agitprop – was, of course, La Pasionaria.

The Comintern's activities in Spain were headed by the future leader of the Italian Communist Party Palmiro Togliatti, whose *noms de guerre* in Spain were Ercoli Ercole and Alfredo. He was a long-time

81

friend of La Pasionaria. The most influential other foreign communists were a Bulgarian, Stepanov, and Vittorio Codovila, who had
been the Comintern's representatives in Spain before the war, a
Hungarian Erno Gero, known as 'Guere', André Marty, a paranoid,
much-hated Frenchman who was organiser of the International
Brigades, and Alexander Orlov, of the Soviet secret police, the
NKVD, who was deputed to set up a Spanish branch of the service, a
task to which he devoted himself with terrifying success. They were
an extraordinary and motley crew of hardened professional revolutionaries who had plied their trade around the Soviet Union, Central
Europe and South America, in some cases since the bolshevik
revolution, and they swiftly took control of their naïve and in-
experienced Spanish comrades, who, it must be said, were generally
only too willing to obey orders. They did not have much choice,
given the circumstances of the times. It was some time before
disillusionment set in. In La Pasionaria's case, it never did.

The republican side was deeply split over the best means to pursue
the war. The anarchists, the left-wing of the socialists and the
independent POUM (Partido Obrero de Unificación Marxista or
Workers' Party of Marxist Unification) took the radical view that
revolution came before winning the war, indeed that it was an
essential prerequisite for victory – only a completely transformed
society would have the spirit to defeat the forces of conservatism.
The social democratic wing of the Socialist Party, liberal republicans
and the communists believed, on the other hand, that the war had to
be won before they could set about the task of building a new
society. The only way this could be done was by creating a
disciplined and effective army and by all the Popular Front forces
working with a common goal. The communists now accepted that
the revolution would have to be postponed indefinitely, a complete
volte-face from their position of only a few years previously. They
thus opposed all proposals to collectivise agriculture and business,
knowing that such a move would alienate owners of small farms and
businesses. The Party gained new supporters from these sectors. The
communists put forward a programme of unity at a plenum of the
central committee in Valencia in March 1937, which was a Party
congress in all but name, and attended by representatives of other
Popular Front parties as well as foreign delegates (including Harry
Pollitt, general secretary of the Communist Party of Great Britain).
La Pasionaria delivered the opening and closing speeches. Her

concluding oration was so emotional that many delegates were moved to tears.[2]

While in public the communists made lofty appeals for national unity, the private objective was control of the army, police, secret police and the key ministries. In the army, they worked towards their goal by winning over key officers and by appointing their own nominees when positions became vacant, particularly after defeats in battle. Communists such as Enrique Líster, Juan Modesto and El Campesino took over important military commands, with some success. The creation of political commissars to all regiments was a fruitful way of extending communist influence throughout the ranks. The commissars emphasised military discipline, love of their country, Spain's independence and democracy. They never mentioned the communists' ultimate aim: the dictatorship of the proletariat. That could come when the war was won. The extent of communist predominance among the commissars was revealed by La Pasionaria in an article. She listed the commissars killed or wounded thus far: 90 per cent of them were communists.[3]

But the role of the secret police was much more sinister. It was set up in late 1936 by Orlov, on the orders of Yagoda, head of the NKVD, who was in turn acting under the direct instructions of Stalin. Orlov's real name was Nikolsky and he had operated under many other aliases, including Shwed and Lyova.[4] Under his control, the secret police devoted all its energies not to pursuing the Fifth Column of secret nationalist activists behind the republican lines but those left-wing forces whose elimination had been decreed by Moscow. Chief among them was the POUM, the party set up by the anarchist turned Communist Andrés Nin, who had in turn broken with the Communist Party in the late 1920s in protest at Stalin's treatment of Trotsky. Returning to Spain after an absence of ten years in the USSR, Nin eventually set up the POUM. It was not a Trotskyist party, as the communists dismissed it and La Pasionaria repeated in her memoirs,[5] but an anti-Stalinist Marxist party. Nin may have sympathised with Trotsky against Stalin but Trotsky later broke with the Spaniard.

Such niceties were lost on the Comintern representatives in Spain. Stalin's worldwide offensive against Trotskyism was at its height. As far as Orlov and his associates were concerned Nin and the POUM had to be eliminated. The climax to the battle between the communists and the POUM was most memorably described by George

Orwell, who fought in a POUM battalion, in *Homage to Catalonia*. It gathered pace after the socialist Juan Negrín became prime minister in May 1937 in succession to Largo Caballero. The departure of the old socialist premier, romantically but inaccurately dubbed 'the Spanish Lenin', was in large part due to the machinations of the communists. They had lost patience with him for several reasons. He was resisting their drive for a socialist-communist merger; he continued to support the notion of all-out revolution; and he refused to attack the anarchists and the POUM, as the communists wanted. Needless to say, there is no mention of these factors in La Pasionaria's own account of Largo's fall, given in her memoirs some 30 years later. She put it down to his purported responsibility for the fall of Málaga in February 1937. This was the party line at the time and ultimately it proved to be a successful ploy. But in truth the communists were using the loss of Málaga as a cover for a longer-term strategy.

For his part, Largo Caballero belatedly realised what the communists were up to. Outraged at the Soviet ambassador Rosenberg's unsubtle attempts to dictate policy to him, Largo stood on his dignity and threw the envoy out of his office. While the Soviet and Comintern men in Spain manoeuvred to get Largo out, the Communist Party general secretary José Díaz made a futile attempt to oppose them, according to the communist education minister Jesús Hernández. He recalled Díaz standing out against the Comintern representatives at a Politburo meeting in March 1937, but he received no support from his fellow Spanish communists, including La Pasionaria. They 'were waiting to hear the voice of Moscow before they risked their opinion.' By this account, Díaz's opinions counted for less and less; not that they had ever stood for very much in the eyes of Moscow. Hernández recorded a later row between Marty and Díaz which grew so heated that La Pasionaria intervened 'agitated and wild, shouting "Comrades, Comrades" like a scratched record.'[6]

The persecution of the POUM was led by the foreign communist contingent, with Orlov at its head. The Spanish Communists, ever subservient to Moscow's wishes, supported them loyally, leading the crushing of the POUM and the anarchists in Barcelona in May 1937 during the fighting which Orwell witnessed and recorded, and attacking their rivals ceaselessly in the Party newspapers. The crunch came in June. The POUM was banned and Nin arrested. Some of the Party leaders, particularly José Díaz again, were appalled.

It is here that La Pasionaria appears to have played a crucial role in supporting the Comintern's savage repression, as Jesús Hernández revealed. Hernández's evidence has to be approached with care. An able and energetic propagandist, he was a founder-member of the Spanish Communist Party who, after a colourful early career, rose to take on a succession of important jobs in the Party during the 1930s, including several cabinet posts during the Civil War. He fled to the Soviet Union after the war and considered that he, not La Pasionaria, should have become general secretary of the PCE after José Díaz died in 1942. Greatly embittered, he was expelled from the Party in 1943 and nursed a hatred for La Pasionaria that was to last the rest of his life. His memoirs, *I was a Minister of Stalin*, were published in France in 1953 and then in Spain. The fact that a book by such a well-known communist was allowed by the Franco government to go on sale in the early 1950s, when it was still internationally isolated and ferociously anti-communist, may give an idea of Hernández's approach. It is a no-holds-barred condemnation of the communists' conduct of the Civil War, a complete recantation by a man who knew the real story from the inside. It is therefore impossible to dismiss but it also has the air of a work designed to settle a lot of old scores by an excitable and embittered man. Its tone also leads to the suspicion that Hernández was seeking to ingratiate himself with the Spanish government of the time. If its aim was to allow him to return to live in Spain it failed. He died in exile in Mexico in 1971.

Despite these reservations, many of Hernández's descriptions of the innermost workings of the Spanish Communist Party during the Civil War have the ring of authenticity. His dislike of La Pasionaria emerges most clearly in his account of the climax of the plot against Andrés Nin in June 1937. Its centrepiece was a ludicrous so-called conspiracy linking Nin with General Franco, which was said to have been unmasked by the discovery of a letter (clearly forged) from Nin to Franco and a bundle of documents bearing the seal of the POUM military committee. It was a classic Stalinist set-up which would have been laughable for its crudity had its outcome not been so tragic. Indeed Hernández, no friend of the POUM, burst out laughing when Orlov told him the details of the plot.

Hernández was sufficiently concerned, however, to alert José Díaz, who was ill at home with stomach trouble. They telephoned the security chief, Colonel Ortega, who came round to Díaz's house and told them he had come from the Central Committee where Togliatti, Codovila, Pedro Checa (another leading Party light) and La Pasionaria were meeting with Orlov. They ordered Orlov to transmit a message by teleprinter to the commander of the Assault Guards in Barcelona directing him to arrest Nin and any other POUM leaders named by two Soviet diplomats in the Catalan capital. Hernández and Díaz rushed to the Central Committee where they found Codovila occupying Díaz's office.

Díaz ordered Checa and La Pasionaria to be found. La Pasionaria swept in, followed by Checa, and made a theatrical display of concern for Díaz's health. Hernández went on:

> I watched her. Her smile was forced and her question officious. Pasionaria hated Díaz. She could not forget that he had severely criticised her clandestine love affair with Francisco Antón . . . [see Chapter 8].

Díaz ignored her inquiry. 'Who ordered Ortega to order the arrest of the POUM men?' he asked.

'We did,' La Pasionaria replied (according to Hernández). They hadn't thought it worth disturbing Díaz over such an unimportant matter. 'What importance can the detention by the police of a handful of provocateurs and spies have?' she replied malevolently.

Díaz said it was a matter for the whole Politburo. Hernández weighed in himself at this point, in support of Díaz. The 'special service' knew he (Díaz) did not agree. They had promised to consult Díaz but had not done so. Why hadn't they asked the other members of the Politburo what they thought?

> Pasionaria replied cynically: 'They did inform us. But as it was urgent and we didn't have time to summon the full Politburo to deal with a simple matter, it seemed to us correct to resolve it without waiting further.' Codovila smiled. Pasionaria had behaved well.[7]

The POUM was declared illegal and 40 members of its central committee arrested. POUM battalions were disbanded. Andrés Nin was taken from Barcelona to Alcalá de Henares, where Orlov had set up his own secret prison. There he was tortured in the most horrible fashion, including, it is said, being flayed alive. Displaying the most astonishing courage, he refused to give in and sign the sort of confession that would shortly become familiar at Stalin's show trials in the USSR. This placed Orlov and the communists in a quandary. A huge public controversy had blown up over Nin's disappearance. The slogan 'Where is Nin?' was daubed on walls. The communists' response, 'in Burgos (a fascist stronghold) or Berlin' (it rhymed), was dismissed as a crude smear outside the Party. The campaign spread abroad, for Nin was a well-known figure outside as well as inside Spain. The prime minister, Negrín, summoned Hernández and demanded to know where the POUM leader was. If he did not know the precise location, he and his fellow communist leaders must have known perfectly well he was unlikely to be seen alive again. To rid themselves of Nin, Orlov and his men came up with another ludicrous plot. A group of German communists from the International Brigades was recruited, disguised as German pro-Franco commandos, to 'rescue' Nin from his cell. They 'left behind' German banknotes and train tickets in case anyone was in any doubt. Nin was in fact murdered and his body disposed of, no one has ever discovered where.

If Jesús Hernández is to be believed, La Pasionaria was deeply implicated in the Soviet-inspired plot to get rid of Nin. Her constant denials that she was ever involved in killings during the Civil War must therefore be treated with the greatest reservation: she may never have pulled the trigger but there can be little doubt about her complicity in the terrible purge of left-wingers who were as committed to the defence of the republic as she was and whose only crime was to dislike Stalin's version of communism. In her memoirs La Pasionaria made no mention of the anti-POUM purge but her hatred of POUM and the anarchists is abundantly clear in her one-sided account of the May events in Barcelona which preceded it. 'The Anarcho-Trotskyist putsch of May . . . had been in the making for months,' she wrote. 'The time for the outbreak was not chosen in Catalonia, but in the General Staff offices of Franco . . .'[8] perpetuating the solomn communist line that the POUM and the anarchists were in league with the nationalists. George Orwell was caught up in the mayhem, which he described so memorably in *Homage to Catalonia*. Orwell's detestation of communism dates in no small measure from what he witnessed in Barcelona at that time. The alleged link between POUM/anarchists and Franco was assiduously peddled by the communist press in Spain. It was faithfully reproduced by the communist press abroad and, more seriously, by gullible sympathisers with the republican cause. Orwell, however, was made of sterner and more sceptical stuff. After examining the facts, he wrote:

. . . the Communist thesis of a POUM 'rising' under Fascist orders rests on less than no evidence . . .[9]

I believe that libels and press-campaigns of this kind, and the habits of mind they indicate, are capable of doing the most deadly damage to the anti-Fascist cause.[10]

La Pasionaria's blind obedience to the party line represented all that he came to dislike most about it.

CHAPTER EIGHT

LA PASIONARIA'S ROMANCE

There was one side to La Pasionaria's life during the Civil War which the wider public never got to hear about, although it was well known in informed circles and those close to the inner workings of the Communist Party. This was her love affair with Francisco Antón Sanz, a handsome young communist who was nearly 20 years her junior. When their romance started Dolores was more than 40 years old. She had, as we have seen, effectively been separated from her husband Julián Ruiz for five years, since moving to Madrid in 1931, and their marriage had been rocky for some time before that.

But she was in the prime of life and many men, including some, like Antón, much younger than her, found her extremely attractive. A young American communist who had come to Spain to fight with the Abraham Lincoln division of the International Brigades, jotted down his impressions of her in 1938 in his diary:

> A striking woman of about 35 years of age [she was actually 41], she parts her hair on the right side, black hair mixed with thick threads of grey, and pulls it back and neatly knots it on the back of her well-shaped head. With her fine aquiline nose and smooth skin and features, she is a strong and handsome woman . . .
>
> She is about five feet seven inches tall. Today her black and steel-grey hair is pushed to the back of her head in a roll and held together by a coffee-coloured comb. Her eyes are deep-set under dark eyebrows and a smooth high forehead. Though heavy in body with high, full breasts, she looks well proportioned. Her beautifully chiselled face exposes an unconquerable personality; she radiates warmth and confidence; there is nothing artificial about her. Her voice is deep and full of resonance, almost masculine . . . What innate quality does she possess that makes a room of people suddenly halt what they're doing and stare at her with awe, admiration and affection?[1]

The writer, Philip Toynbee, then a 20-year-old communist, was visiting Madrid in December 1936 and noted in his diary: 'Though Pasionaria didn't speak to us except to say "Salud!" when we first came into the room I found her immensely impressive.'[2]

Francisco Antón's origins are obscure: he first came to be noticed as an assistant to a railway union leader. He must have been picked out as a promising young member by the Communist Party for he was sent to Moscow for training. He returned to take up the influential post of general secretary of the Party's Madrid regional committee, the position he was holding when the war started.[3] He was thus one of the Party's rising young men.

But did he embark on his affair with La Pasionaria out of love, or with the cynical (and successful) objective of furthering his own career? Feelings about Antón were decidedly mixed. Santiago Alvarez, ever the loyalist, thought their relationship was entirely normal; they lived openly together as man and wife, he said, and nobody regarded it as untoward.[4]

The onset of revolution in republican-held Spain had transformed attitudes towards sex. Young women threw off the taboos that had previously restricted them. They wore trousers, smoked in public and took part in all manner of political and social behaviour which had previously been frowned on. A more permissive attitude to sexual relations was noticeable. On occasion, marriages were solemnised by decree of a republican official or army officer. Young women visited their boyfriends at the Madrid front and made love in ruined buildings during lulls in the fighting. In such an atmosphere, the romance between La Pasionaria (never had the sobriquet seemed more appropriate) and Francisco Antón would not have seemed out of the ordinary.

Antón was an attractive man physically. Photographs of the time show him to be a short but dapper figure with dark good looks and a face that betrays just a hint of sullenness. His hair is impeccably combed back from his forehead and the parting always immaculate. Similarly, his uniform is always perfectly pressed, even in photographs taken on visits to the front line. His crisp and coiffeured figure stands out among his more crumpled, unshaven colleagues. It is easy to imagine Antón as a lady-killer. La Pasionaria is said to have been infatuated with him.

Others held a lower opinion of him. José Díaz said of him that 'he had never got his boots dirty in the mud of any trench'. Díaz disapproved strongly of the relationship, fearing that if it became public knowledge it would destroy La Pasionaria's image, which the Party had worked so hard to build up. Enrique Castro, the central committee member who was the first commander-in-chief of the Fifth Regiment, dismissed Antón as a hypocritical 'señorito', an untranslatable word laden with contempt, which roughly means a spoiled brat. He believed Antón owed his post as Madrid Party organiser entirely to the good offices of La Pasionaria. Jesús Hernández was vitriolic in his hatred:

> Pasionaria forgot she was the daughter of a miner; she forgot she had two children as old as her lover [a typical exaggeration]; she forgot that her husband Julián Ruiz was fighting on the Northern front; she forgot propriety and decency; she forgot her age and her grey hair and she settled down with Antón without heed for the indignation of those who knew of their illicit relationship.[5]

Antón then became political commissar of the Fifth Regiment under General Miaja. This promotion meant he was now the most senior political commissar in the republican army. He had a high-profile propaganda role during the first months of the war. More biting criticism came from Jesús Hernández. In a celebrated passage from his memoirs, Hernández wrote:

> A perfect example of a bureaucrat, he [Antón] directed the actions of the commissars by means of circulars and received delegates from the front swathed in magnificent silk pyjamas in a comfortable house in the Ciudad Lineal of Madrid.[6]

Antón and Pasionaria shared a house with Palmiro Togliatti, the Comintern's chief representative in Spain. Given the power and status of Togliatti and Pasionaria, this must have been an unofficial nerve centre for much communist policy-making during the war and Antón would have had access to all important information. He must be regarded as a key figure in the communist set-up. Santiago Alvarez, for one, is a stout defender of Antón. 'He didn't need Dolores Ibárruri's affection or protection to succeed,' he said. 'He was brave, capable and could make his own way in life. He played an important role in the defence of Madrid.'[7] But other contemporaries regarded him as an unprincipled rogue who used his relationship with La Pasionaria simply to further his own ends, in particular to avoid being called up to join the republican army and be sent to the front. This issue came to a head in the autumn of 1937. The defence minister, the socialist Indalecio Prieto, was becoming increasingly wary and distrustful of the communists' influence over the armed forces. He was especially concerned about the extent of the Party's control over the political commissariat. He therefore abolished many of the commissariats at the front. One consequence was that Antón was dismissed and designated for transfer as an ordinary soldier to a front-line battalion. The Communist Party vigorously opposed Prieto's actions. There is some suggestion that the Politburo had become dissatisfied with Antón's performance as commissar and was about to sack him but was now obliged to defend him. At any rate, he managed to avoid being sent to the front and it is reasonable to assume that La Pasionaria had some part in this. According to Hernández, she was already being groomed by Togliatti, Codovila and the other Soviet representatives in Spain to take over from José Díaz, who was both ill and increasingly at odds with the Comintern men. They would not have wanted to offend her over her lover. The incident terminally soured La Pasionaria's relations with Prieto, who had always disliked her. The communists had their revenge, being deeply implicated in his departure from the government the following March. La Pasionaria played a leading role, heading an enormous anti-Prieto demonstration in Madrid which helped to unseat him.

Both her lover and her husband followed La Pasionaria into exile in the Soviet Union at the end of the Civil War. Antón's journey was the more controversial. He escaped over the border into France and was for a time responsible for the Spanish Communist Party in exile in France. He was chiefly concerned with helping some of the hundreds of thousands of republican refugees to emigrate to Latin America, particularly Mexico, which took in large numbers of them. He was still in France when it was overrun by the Nazi invasion in 1940 and ended up in a concentration camp, like thousands of his compatriots. How he escaped is an extraordinary story. La Pasionaria had already got away to Moscow and Antón managed to send her a cable, pleading to get him out. She was apparently beside herself with anguish. Dimitrov, the Bulgarian president of the Comintern, and Díaz are said to have turned a deaf ear to her entreaties for her lover to be rescued: Antón was not a popular figure with many because of his unhealthy influence over La Pasionaria. Finally, she managed to get a message through to Stalin himself. He is said to have remarked: 'Well, if Juliet cannot live without her Romeo, we'll have to bring him to her.'[8] The Soviet leader ordered his ambassador in Paris to get hold of the Nazi ambassador (this was the era of the Soviet–German pact) and ask him to free Antón. It was a period when the Third Reich needed Soviet goodwill and supplies and the Germans obliged. Antón was released and, travelling on a Soviet passport, was flown across Germany to Russia in a plane placed at his disposal by the Nazis.[9] Few Spaniards in the French camps shared his good fortune. The communists in particular were in deadly danger; many indeed ended up in German concentration camps after being handed over to the Nazis by their captors. Other unfortunates were handed back over the Pyrenees to Franco's men and execution or imprisonment.

Antón set up home in Moscow with La Pasionaria and played a helpful part in defending her against an attempt to overthrow her as acting general secretary by a rival group exiled in Mexico. But the romance petered out; Antón moved to a key Party job in Paris and there fell in love with a young woman who was La Pasionaria's junior by a quarter of a century. The consequences were dramatic (see Chapter 14).

La Pasionaria's husband Julián could not have been more different from Antón. He stayed a humble working man for the whole of his life. He fought on the northern front in the Basque country until it fell to the nationalists. He made his way to Barcelona and worked for a while for the Basque government in exile. But he was not cut out for office life and found himself a job in his old trade, in the Catalonian mines. When the war ended he too fled to France, by boat, and spent three months in a concentration camp 'hungry and full of lice', as he later described it. From there he managed to get to the Soviet Union along with a limited number of other Spaniards, mainly loyal communists like him. He spent 33 years in the USSR. There were no special privileges for him, nor did he seek any. He worked in a number of factories in the Caucasus until his retirement, when he went to live in an old people's home. (He continued to work there, making wooden toys and gifts.) Unlike Francisco Antón, he at least had the satisfaction of returning in old age to Spain, to his native village of Somorrostro where he and La Pasionaria had lived together. He went back in 1972 at the age of 81 and pronounced himself 'very impressed' with modern Spain. A local journalist found him looking 'physically very good, with penetrating clear eyes and his hair a little tousled beneath his Basque beret.'[10] He was not in the least bitter about La Pasionaria. Asked about her other loves, he replied: 'I only know that I was the first. And I like to think that at the bottom of her heart she has never forgotten me.'[11] Five years later he was finding life on a small pension very difficult and went so far as to say that he would never have left the Soviet Union if conditions had been like that when he first arrived back in Spain.[12] He died on 4 August 1977, two weeks after operations on both knees. He was buried the next day in Somorrostro. La Pasionaria (she was still legally his wife, for they were never divorced) made a short farewell speech at the funeral. She had not long returned to Spain herself after her exile and she was seen to be in tears during the service.

CHAPTER NINE

MOTHER OF BATTLES

After crushing the POUM, the communists were effectively in control of the republic. It did not appear so on the surface. The new prime minister, Negrín, was a socialist, and the communists still only occupied two cabinet portfolios (out of a total of nine). But their control had spread rapidly in the army and the individual ministries, where the power really lay. The anarchists were in retreat, the socialists divided.

Another area where the Party exercised a great deal of behind-the-scenes influence was in organisations such as the Union of Anti-Fascist Women and the Anti-Fascist Writers. (Indeed, almost anything with the words 'Anti-Fascist' in the title was probably a communist-front set-up). La Pasionaria played a key role in many of these, particularly the Union of Anti-Fascist Women, which she was instrumental in founding. They played an important role in attracting sympathy and, above all, money for the republican cause both in Spain and overseas. They could be relied upon to attract good names, who would not necessarily want to appear at an event that was openly advertised as being run by the communists. Thus on 7 July 1937 La Pasionaria was one of the star speakers at the second congress of Anti-Fascist Writers at the Salamanca Cinema in Madrid (the congress also held sessions in Barcelona and Valencia). Other big names on the bill were the French writer André Malraux (a passionate supporter of the republic since the beginning of the war, when he had set up an air squadron of foreign pilots), Ernest Hemingway, Stephen Spender, Ilya Ehrenburg, José Bergamin and Miguel Koltzof. To intellectuals like these, as to so many other people, La Pasionaria appeared as a marvellous example of Spanish heroism, not a tool of Stalinist repression. They would go off and spread the word about her. Her propaganda value to the Party and the republican cause was incalculable. She was always there to greet foreign visitors who were in Spain to support the republican cause.

They included the black American singer Paul Robeson, the Indian nationalist leader Pandit Nehru, who on independence a decade later was to become his country's first prime minister, and the British Conservative MP, the Duchess of Atholl, who chaired the National Joint Committee for Spanish Relief, an umbrella organisation overseeing the work of 850 smaller outfits helping the republican cause. In 1937 the Duchess led a delegation to Spain, which included the Labour MP Ellen Wilkinson (herself something of a British Pasionaria) and wrote of her encounter with La Pasionaria:

> By far the most interesting personality I met was the woman member of the Cortes, Dolores Ibárruri, commonly known as La Pasionaria. I had been reluctant to meet her, as the nickname had suggested to me a rather over-emotional young person, but on Ellen Wilkinson's pressure I agreed to meet her.
>
> I have never ceased to be glad that I did so, for the only person with whom I felt La Pasionaria could be compared was the woman I had always regarded as the greatest actress I had seen, Eleonora Duse. [1858–1924; Italian actress famous above all for her interpretations of Ibsen's heroines.] She had Duse's wonderful grace and voice, but she was much more beautiful, with rich colouring, large dark eyes, and black wavy hair. She swept into the room like a queen, yet she was a miner's daughter married to a miner – a woman who had had the sorrow of losing six out of eight children. [The correct figure at that time was four out of six.] I could understand nothing that she said, and she talked with great rapidity, but to look and to listen was pleasure enough for me.[1]

(It is interesting that Stella Volkenstein, who interpreted for La Pasionaria on several occasions when she was an exile in the USSR in the 1950s, made a similar comment about her: 'If she hadn't been a revolutionary, she would have been a great actress.')[2]

On the first anniversary of the outbreak of the Civil War La Pasionaria spoke at the second War Plenum of the Communist Party central committee in Valencia, 18-20 July. Part of her speech was directed to 'the women of the world'. The sacrifices they were making in Spain hurt less than the lack of support the republic was getting from the rest of the world, she said. 'The flow of our tears has dried up,' she said and she appealed to German and Italian mothers to warn their sons not to go to fight in Spain. 'Tell them the Spanish workers bear no hatred or bitterness towards them. In Spain we are fighting for the liberty of all nations . . . You cannot ignore the anguished cries of our children and our women, mown down by fascist bombs . . . fight for the withdrawal of the invading army which shoots our children, rapes our youngsters and outrages our women . . .'[3]

The War Plenum's chief theme was one which the communists were pressing hard at this period: the necessity for a merger with the socialists. 'Armed with the formidable weapon of Marxist-Leninist-Stalinist theory', a combined Communist-Socialist Party would lead the Spanish revolution, La Pasionaria wrote.[4] In her speech to the Plenum, she amplified the point:

> Our claim that it is necessary for the united party to be constructed on the principles of democratic socialism is based on the experiences of the glorious Bolshevik party and on the teachings of Lenin, Stalin and the Communist International . . . We are Stalinists because the great theory of Marx-Engels-Lenin has been enriched by Stalin, who teaches us communists to be staunch even in the most difficult situations, to observe unflinchingly Stalin-like firmness in our struggle and work, to be irreconcilable towards the class enemies and renegades of the revolution . . . We are Marxist-Leninists and consequently we adjust our theories to the revolutionary possibilities of each moment without renouncing our final aspirations.[5]

Her tone at this period was one of almost unrelieved triumphalism.

The merger campaign went on for most of the year before Negrín killed off the idea. The socialists were always deeply suspicious of the communists' motives. There had already been mergers between the two parties' youth organisations and at all levels in Catalonia (to form the United Catalan Socialist Party, PSUC). In both cases the communists, although numerically inferior, had rapidly taken control through their better organisation and higher motivation. Everything indicated to the socialists that the same would happen at national level if they were unwise enough to agree to a merger.

A few days later, *Mundo Obrero* brought together two differing symbols of the world communist movement: La Pasionaria and A.G.Stakhanov, the legendary Soviet coal-miner whose enthusiasm to reach his production targets made him a symbol of Stalinist dedication and saw his name pass into the world's languages. The paper printed a message from him (doubtless penned by some anonymous propagandist in the Kremlin): 'They shall not pass because it is the people who have risen to defend their country. By increasing your output you are helping victory. More cartridges! Provide them for your able gunners, whose bullets will clean Spain of the fascist murderers!'[6]

In July 1937 La Pasionaria was brought in to play her customary propaganda role at the front, this time for the key republican offensive at Brunete, to the west of Madrid, which was inspired and led by the communists. On the eve of battle she visited the Popular Army's camp, and toured it on foot, accompanied by her lover Francisco Antón among other Communist Party notables. The Fifth Regiment's political commissar Santiago Alvarez described the scene:

> Most of the combatants hardly noticed who was with Dolores Ibárruri: the one they wanted to see was La Pasionaria. It was her whom they all wanted to greet, to talk to, to shake by the hand or embrace. Dolores Ibárruri was always a sort of idol for the masses, and even more so at those times. There was nobody else capable of arousing in the soldiers the reactions of enthusiasm and loyalty which she could. Her presence there, with us, was proof that we were about to embark on something important.[7]

Three weeks later, *Mundo Obrero* carried a long report of a return visit by La Pasionaria to the same men, who had in the meantime gone through some of the most savage fighting of the war in vain. Exhausted by 20 days of continuous fighting and eventual defeat, they had retreated to a pleasant tree-lined spot beside the Guadalix river. 'After the hell of Brunete, that place seemed almost like paradise,' wrote Alvarez.[8] The men sat on the grass and asked La Pasionaria for a speech. The reporter waxed lyrical about her effect on them.

> At first a huddle of listless stares. The memory of the fighting not yet erased. They look down, their heads droop. Little by little, as Dolores speaks, they raise their heads. Their eyes, still expressionless, fix on her. Her words hammer on the doors of reason and awareness. Now the men are looking with interest. Their expressions become more animated. Glimmers of enthusiasm come from their eyes, which previously did not see. A murmur of praise. Enthusiastic shouts. Fire has returned where before there were only ashes.[9]

The men's morale was sufficiently restored to play a prank on their distinguished visitor. The weather was hot and they spent most of their time bathing in the river. Another witness recalled:

> No one had a bathing costume, and many soldiers had never heard of one . . . Early one afternoon, two lieutenants were going along the river shouting aloud, calling: 'Please comrades, cover yourselves up, we have a woman visitor.' And not far behind, there she came, La Pasionaria! She was accompanied by a large group of officers and, as she went along the

river bank, hundreds of soldiers waited. They waited either to say something to her, or just for her to pass by before removing their clothes again and jumping back into the river. Here and there she would stop to chat with the soldiers . . . Some soldiers planned to take this opportunity to play a prank on La Pasionaria. When she was close to the edge of a deep pool they suddenly grabbed her and hurled her into the water. She soon surfaced and stood up, wiping the water from her face and throwing back her hair. She was grinning broadly and the first words she uttered were: 'My, the water is warm!' An officer helped her up the embankment. She stood there wet and laughing, and everybody laughed with her. In some ways, perhaps, the sight may not have been very glamorous, but as her clothes were wet they clung to her body, revealing a very attractive figure, especially since she must have already reached forty to forty-five years of age.[10]

The men's morale had to be restored, for they would soon be needed on the Aragon front. Thirty years later, La Pasionaria was still bitter about what she saw as the betrayal of the communist troops at Belchite by Colonel Segismundo Casado, of the regular army, who, she claimed, withdrew 'claiming an indisposition.' She made plain what she would have done with him: 'Instead of putting him before a firing squad as a traitor, the War Minister played the nursemaid.'[11] She was to cross swords with Casado personally in the dying days of the War. He remained one of her hate figures for the rest of her life.

The process of semi-deification of La Pasionaria went on apace. The name of the Beatriz Theatre in Madrid was changed to Pasionaria 'as potent proof of the love of the people of Madrid for the tireless fighter Dolores Ibárruri'.[12] If Stalin's Soviet Union was being glorified by the communist press and by La Pasionaria in her articles and speeches, the Spanish republic's struggle to survive was getting similar treatment in the USSR. The Russian Theatre of Kharkhov, for example, put on a play entitled *Salud España!* (*Greetings Spain!*) to help to raise money for Spain. It included a portrayal of La Pasionaria. Ksenia Sukroskaia, the actress who played her, sent her a message which appeared in a communist propaganda publication:

For the first time we the artists, and particularly I, had to play a real person, a woman known throughout the world – you, beloved of millions of working women . . . you cannot imagine with what deep emotion this play originated. We love our country and if the enemy attacked we would defend it to the last drop of our blood. For that, your sufferings are also ours. I am sorry I don't have a good photograph of you. I only have newspaper illustrations to go on. It would give me great pleasure to get your photograph.[13]

By the autumn of 1937, hostility to the behaviour of the communists was growing in the ranks of the other Popular Front parties, especially the socialists. There was also a growing realisation in all republican sectors except the communist that they were slowly but surely losing the war. But the communists were aware of their unpopularity and made some effort, in public at least, to offer the olive branch to their enemies. On 2 October the Cortes held a session (they had been reduced to half-yearly events to give some semblance of parliamentary democracy to political life). La Pasionaria had been elected vice-president of what was left of the parliament; naturally, it was now missing all of its right-wing members. She made overtures to the anarchists in the hope of tempting them back into the government. 'We must find means of getting the really revolutionary workers in the ranks of the CNT to take a share in the government,' she said. 'We must put aside personal differences for the common good.'[14] Rumours were circulating that some republicans favoured negotiating with Franco to bring an end to the war. Indalecio Prieto, the minister of defence, who certainly took a gloomy view of the future, was the communists' chief suspect. La Pasionaria denounced all thought of pacts: 'The only commitment would be to crush Franco,' she said. Prieto was indignant. He had become increasingly disillusioned with the communists. His response to La Pasionaria's speech was to crack down on the army's political commissars, who were mainly communists and included Francisco Antón. That confirmed her hatred of Prieto, which she nurtured until she helped to overthrow him the following year.

At the end of November 1937 La Pasionaria was back in Paris to raise more money and support for the increasingly embattled republican cause. In an interview with *Le Soir* she put a brave face on the situation despite the military reverses recently suffered, in particular the loss of Bilbao and the north of Spain: 'We are certain of victory in spite of what happened in the north. Our military situation is better than ever,' she said. 'The whole country is armed.' She made a prophetic reference to France's imminent fate: 'We need international aid to achieve a quicker victory and halt our people's suffering – and so that Hitler and Mussolini, defeated in Spain, cannot put other countries to the torch. And in saying that I am thinking especially of France.'[15]

In another interview she was more honest about the real situation facing ordinary people. 'We have had difficulties which we do not wish to hide. We are forced to mobilise considerable numbers of men who would otherwise have gone to work. In addition, the normal population of those regions under republican control has been swollen by millions of fugitives from the rebels; and finally the import of certain products is absolutely necessary. We have large quantities of oranges but we lack flour; gallons of oil but lack potatoes; wine but no milk.'[16]

The most important military event of the winter of 1937-8 was the battle of Teruel. Republican forces launched a surprise attack on the town in December and a bitter two-month battle ensued in atrocious weather. The advantage swung first to the republican attackers. La Pasionaria visited Teruel shortly after it had been captured to talk to the troops. On her return to the capital, she addressed a meeting of the Madrid Communist Party in the Monumental Cinema and described the first phase of Teruel as a glorious page in the history of our people'. She went on to renew her call for unity within the Popular Front; indeed, she was extraordinarily conciliatory: 'We communists must be flexible and give way in some cases. We have been accused of being militarists and anti-revolutionary . . . we must unite for victory.'[17] Republican hopes of a stunning victory at Teruel were soon dashed. After holding the town for six weeks, they were in turn encircled by a nationalist counter-attack (which included a notable cavalry charge) and were forced to abandon Teruel, with probably 20,000 dead, and 40,000 wounded or suffering from the ferociously cold weather conditions.

The defeat led some leading republicans, notably La Pasionaria's old adversary Indalecio Prieto, to hint at opening negotiations with Franco to bring an early end to the war. The communists vigorously opposed such talk. They also feared Prieto's determination to reduce their own influence within the army. Accordingly they launched a campaign to unseat Prieto as they had done with Largo Caballero the previous autumn. La Pasionaria featured prominently in the attacks on Prieto and his fellow 'defeatists' that became a central theme of the Party's propaganda. Prieto was angered by her words. He commented that parts of a critical speech by her on 1 March should have been cut out by the censor.[18] The campaign culminated in a big communist-organised march, with La Pasionaria at its head, to the Pedralbes Palace in Barcelona where the cabinet was meeting. The crowd broke down the gates and ended up outside the windows of the room where the cabinet was assembled. La Pasionaria delivered a speech attacking Prieto and then led a delegation to see the prime minister, Negrín. In her usual forceful way she demanded that he continue to prosecute the war. He assured her that he would and the crowd dispersed peacefully. After that, the writing was on the wall for the pessimistic Prieto and he left the cabinet shortly afterwards. The communists agreed to lose one of their two ministers as part of the deal by which he was eased out but the reality was that they continued to wield the power. In fact, Moscow had at first instructed the communists to quit the cabinet altogether in protest at Prieto's behaviour, a move bitterly opposed by Jesús Hernández. At a meeting of the Politburo he argued that the public would not understand it but see it as a withdrawal of communist support for the government altogether. During the debate, he wrote later, La Pasionaria remained silent: 'Her silence was tacit support for Moscow's proposal.'[19]

Since the bitter experiences of her life as a young wife and mother, La Pasionaria had been what we would now call a feminist, although the word was not in vogue at the time. The first year of the revolution in republican Spain, in which women had taken enormous steps towards equality and emancipation, must have given her cause for optimism. But by the beginning of 1938, Spanish men appeared to be lapsing back into their bad old ways. La Pasionaria went on the attack in a speech to the Party's provincial congress. Why weren't women joining the Party, she asked and came up with an answer: 'Don Juanismo' among male Party members. It would appear that the comrades had been engaging in rather more than discussions about dialectical materialism with the ardent young women who had been attending Party meetings. Her suggested solution was the creation of women-only cells. More women would attend meetings if they weren't held at times like 10 pm, she said, and proposed the creation of crêches and nurseries where women could leave their children while they went to work and collective kitchens where women could eat and be liberated from the drudgery of cooking for their men. The 7,000 female Party members in Madrid could be tripled with such measures. Spanish women, who had learned how to use weapons and machinery, would now be trained as engineers and technicians. She gave the example of a woman employee in an arms factory. Previously ignorant of factory life, she had set herself the task of mending broken machines which were hindering production. The result was that production went up from 80,000 to 250,000 cartridges a day.

La Pasionaria went on:

> I have known many comrades who call themselves very revolutionary and when asked why they don't bring their wives to Party meetings say: 'My wife doesn't understand. My wife doesn't know anything. My wife has many children.' Your wife shouldn't just be the woman with whom you sleep. She shouldn't be the one who darns your socks and has the supper ready on time. Your wife should be your comrade who shares with you the sorrows, the weariness, the troubles and also the joys of the struggle. Women should be economically independent. Only when a woman can look a man in the face and say 'I don't live off the pennies you give me, I'm capable of earning my own living' will women be truly emancipated.[20]

But La Pasionaria's enthusiasm to liberate her fellow women did not always have happy results. One day she called Enrique Castro, founder and first commander-in-chief of the Fifth Regiment, into her office. (He remembered it was adorned with large portraits of Lenin and Stalin and huge bouquets of flowers, while on her desk lay several detective novels, of which she was apparently fond.) She told him she wanted to create a powerful women's movement. Women had, after all, played an important role in creating the Soviet Union. She ordered Castro to set up fighting units of militia women within the Fifth Regiment. Castro suggested women would be better employed in back-up, auxiliary roles. La Pasionaria would have none of it. Within two weeks, Castro had formed three such units. La Pasionaria, accompanied by Francisco Antón and Irene Falcón, came to inspect them. 'Upright, silent, with a cold, deep gaze,' she passed up and down the women's ranks and then delivered a ringing speech to them. Within a month, 200 of the militiamen stationed at the same barracks had gone down with venereal disease – and refused to say how they had caught it. Castro ordered La Pasionaria's militia-women to be examined medically. When he received the doctor's report, it showed that 70 per cent of the women had VD; most of them were not keen communists at all but prostitutes who had been swept up off the streets. Castro drove to the Party headquarters in Serrano Street and threw the report on La Pasionaria's desk. A blazing row ensued. She accused Castro of being against the idea from the start (which was true). He replied that he knew about soldiers and plenty of them would be happy to get VD to get out of fighting. She threatened to take the matter to the Politburo, which could have serious consequences for Castro, given her status and influence. 'Why, between combatants and whores, do you prefer whores?' he asked. Castro got his way; the women's militias were dissolved, the prostitutes sent back to the streets and the remaining women reassigned to other tasks, such as hospital auxiliary work.[21]

Despite such setbacks, La Pasionaria continued her campaign. On 8 March 1938 she demanded more rights for women in a major speech to a women's rally in the Monumental Cinema. She wanted, she said, 'a free, happy Spain where women are no longer slaves to men'. Spain was 50 years behind the 'democratic countries'. Women should receive equal pay for equal work.

A fascinating, if rather excitable, portrait of La Pasionaria at this period of the Civil War appeared in the Cuban magazine *Mediodía*, of Havana, which described itself as a 'popular weekly'. It was written by Juan Marinello, a prominent Cuban communist poet, essayist and politician with a wealthy background, who was then 40 years old. He knew Spain well; he had studied at the University of Madrid in 1921. As a leader of the communist front party, the Partido Unión Revolucionaria (PUR), which was trying to reach an accommodation with the military government of Fulgencio Batista, he also knew all about Popular Front alliances promoted by the Comintern. (A survivor almost in La Pasionaria's class, he became a minister in Batista's cabinet in the 1940s, president of the Cuban Communist Party in the 1950s and rector of the University of Havana after Castro's revolution of 1959.)[22] Even after taking into account his sympathies with La Pasionaria and her cause, his article is still worth quoting at some length for its vivid observation. Marinello was bowled over by his heroine:

All those who visit loyal [ie to the Republic] Spain have one intense unconfessed desire: to see the woman who personifies the popular movement in its most intense incarnation, to touch physically the purifying and restless flame which burns in Pasionaria . . . She smiles from inside the little car which is her office and her study and disappears. She goes to the trenches, to the Party, to the Cortes, to the asylum, to the hospital, to the meeting, to the barracks, wherever her presence may matter most each time. The crowds are overjoyed and excited at the sight of her . . . You only have to talk to Dolores Ibárruri for her inner qualities to shine through the external trappings . . . Her big eyes, sweet and firm, clear and alert, are in their beauty and fire her very life . . . Her elegant yet strong hands, subtle when she chats and implacable when she is making a speech, are the flower of her best revolutionary virtue, the most faithful voice of her tragic people . . . You cannot see her, at once aristocratic and of the people, without thinking of her as the people on the march, the long-awaited redeemer from the eternal earth at the heart of Spain . . .[23]

Marinello wrote of her as the quintessential Spanish woman, the rightful descendant of Saint Teresa of Avila and Queen Isabella. He went on to describe in detail her performance at a rally organised by the joint communist-socialist youth movement in the Capitol Theatre in Valencia. Her audience was predominantly young. They stood throughout most of her speech.

The group of girls next to me wept at the sound of her stormy yet storm-taming voice. 'Yes, yes, Dolores,' they murmured at each unanswerable statement. At the end of the speech they whistled for a long time. For an hour, such was my impression, the rally saw this enlightening woman as their own mother . . .

He observed her at several rallies and gave a detailed description of her in action.

The crowds received her political message as an unanswerable dictat. Her mouth was truth itself. That was greatly influenced by her speaking style, which was masterfully adapted to Spanish reality. There were no lyrical paragraphs . . . [It was] popular language without playing to the gallery, elegance born not from literary conceit but from knowledge of language at its most basic. Her presence on the platform of war, her platform, is beautiful. Her head, proud and untiring, the tremble of her noble hands, the proud beauty of her black clothes, and above all else, her luxurious voice, a voice firm but not sour, deep but not opaque, powerful but feminine. And filling her voice and giving it unbreakable validity, the breath of sincerity of a great leader at her best.

It is wildly over the top but interesting none the less, for it is an indication of how strongly some pro-republicans felt about her and the cause and it does demonstrate the sort of effect she could have on both audiences and journalists.

Having observed her from afar while she dashed off to Madrid, then to the front at Belchite, Marinello was allowed to watch his heroine from closer quarters, which provided more fascinating insights. La Pasionaria declined to be interviewed or to provide any biographical details:

We revolutionaries, at least as long as we're alive, shouldn't have a history. At best, we belong at the end or commit mistakes which are the equivalent of treason. I believe I will be faithful to the end of my days to my Party and the Revolution.

So there was to be no interview but she allowed Marinello to sit in with her as she worked in her office. They had several such sessions. He soon discovered that 'the terrible woman, the sadistic harpie' of nationalist legend was in reality 'a woman of consummate femininity'. He noted her concern for her 'comrade' (whether this was Francisco Antón or her husband Julián he did not specify) and her children, whose portraits adorned her desk. On one occasion she talked of the latest letters she had received from her children in the USSR 'with the most tender affection'. To gauge her reaction, he accused her of having a romantic side and elicited some touching and unexpected revelations about her private life and her distress at losing touch with the little pleasures of ordinary life.

And why, she replied spiritedly, shouldn't I be a woman? I am a woman. That's why we are fighting, for men and women to be themselves . . . Look, do you know what I most hate about my popularity? Well, not being able, as I was previously, to go out at night to look in shop-windows at my ease, to take long walks through the city. Now I can't because they [the people] see me, they come up to and soon it's turned into a demonstration. Moreover I'm forbidden to do so, for other reasons which you will understand . . . And why shouldn't I like that, to see the fashions, elegant clothes?

The 'other reasons' were presumably the Communist Party's fears that she could be assassinated if she were to walk the streets alone. La Pasionaria went on to talk of the fascists' image of her as, in Marinello's words, 'a drunk and cruel virago among a band of bandits, firing a gun all the time'.

If only people knew, she said, how I used to go to the trenches from necessity. I went because I believed my presence . . . carried life and joy to the comrades, and meant an interesting contact between the rearguard and the front lines. And they saw in me a woman, a comrade, who would find out their real needs and wanted to resolve them. As things changed, my visits to the battle fronts grew fewer. This war obliges us to fight where we're most needed. Now we have a disciplined, powerful, well-equipped Army. Relations between the lines and the rearguard are good. My visits aren't needed. I'm sorry about it. It's a great thing to have

106

contact with our heroes . . . they call me from everywhere . . . but we are going through a time of maximum responsibility and one has to block one's ears to requests.

Marinello concluded with another paeon of praise:

She is greater than Saint Theresa because Pasionaria does not display Theresian symptoms, the negation of life in the final instance, but is the symbol of our own time . . . the militant Spanish mother whom her enslaved people still need. But [she is] the complete woman, utterly Spanish, who with her shadowless smile and fearless eyes brings a world without chains nearer.

It was no wonder that the legend of La Pasionaria flourished around the world when this is the sort of portrait of her that was being fed to readers in places like Cuba (a country she finally got to visit in 1963 to be lionised by Fidel Castro, whom she admired enormously and who reciprocated the feeling).

But the reality was that from now on it was downhill all the way for the republican cause until final defeat within a year. The communists kept up their vigorous propaganda barrage, pumping out the message that the war would be fought, and won, but it was increasingly an illusion. In May La Pasionaria delivered a major speech to the Plenum of the central committee in Madrid, counselling continued resistance, a united army and improved production in war-related industries – all familiar themes. She was anxious not to appear too revolutionary. She proclaimed the Party's loyalty to the government and dismissed rumours that it was intent on establishing a dictatorship of the proletariat.

In July she received a huge ovation every time she appeared on stage at the Party's fourth War Plenum in Madrid. She quoted the foreign press (including the *Daily Telegraph*) as saying the republic was far from beaten, proposed national mobilisation and demanded unity and a supreme effort to win the war.

The second anniversary of the war arrived, on 18 July 1938, with most of the optimism that had marked the first having evaporated. La Pasionaria travelled back to Paris for another rally in defence of the republic in the Winter Velodrome, this time organised by the Rassemblement Universel pour la Paix and attended by intellectuals, fellow-travellers, republican defenders like the Duchess of Atholl and progressive politicians like Pandit Nehru. But feelings about the Spanish communists had clearly changed since the first heady days of the war. Word had spread abroad about the purge of the POUM and the increasingly totalitarian stance of the Spanish Party. This was brought home to La Pasionaria when the organisers asked her not to speak for fear that the rally should be seen as too pro-communist. But the request did not go down well with many of the delegates, including Nehru, who saw her, rightly or wrongly, as a symbol of the republic over and above party politics. The French president of the meeting, Pierre Cot, a former air minister, turned down a request for the ban to be rescinded, at which the British Labour MP Ellen Wilkinson got to her feet and shouted, 'Let her speak!' La Pasionaria took advantage to make her way to the platform. Someone ordered the lights and microphone to be turned off. Amid accusations of sabotage and general uproar, the power was turned on again and La Pasionaria received a standing ovation. A Chinese delegate approached and presented her with his group's flag as a gesture of solidarity. La Pasionaria made her speech after all; it was her usual fighting performance, stressing that the Civil War was the first round in the coming battle between fascism and democracy. 'Fascism is brave to the extent that democrats are cowards,' she said. 'Don't forget that the guns with which our cities are destroyed are also aimed from the frontiers of Irun and Catalonia towards France and democracy.' It was a slight exaggeration (Spain stayed neutral in the Second World War) but not much of one, as France found out when the Germans invaded from the other direction within two years.

As she spoke, the battle of the Ebro was getting under way back in Spain: another republican advance with early successes which seemed to herald a reversal of the tide, but which was to end in nationalist victory. As autumn approached the future looked bleak for the republic. The Munich Agreement in September raised hopes that a similar deal could be arranged for Spain, including an end to a war of which all sides were now thoroughly weary. But the republic's doom was sealed when Stalin decided to wash his hands of Spain in favour of an understanding with Germany. To this end, he proposed that the International Brigades should withdraw from Spain under the super-vision of the League of Nations.

The Brigades' final parade in Barcelona on 29 October was the occasion for one of La Pasionaria's most famous, eloquent and moving speeches.

It is very difficult to pronounce words of farewell to the heroes of the International Brigades because of what they are and what they represent.

A feeling of anguish, of infinite pain, rises to our throats and grips them . . . Anguish for those who are going, soldiers of the highest ideal of human redemption, uprooted from their own countries, pursued by the tyranny of all peoples . . . Pain for those who remain here for ever, merged with our soil and living on deep in our hearts, enhanced by our feelings of eternal gratitude.

From every country and every race, you came to us as our brothers, as sons of immortal Spain, and in the hardest days of our war, when the capital of the republic was under threat, you, brave comrades of the International Brigades, helped to save it with your fighting enthusiasm, your heroism and your spirit of sacrifice.

And Jarama and Guadalajara and Brunete and Belchite and Levante and the Ebro sing with immortal verses the courage, the unselfishness, the ferocity, the discipline of the men of the International Brigades.

For the first time in the history of people's struggle, we have seen the spectacle, astonishing in its greatness, of the formation of the International Brigades to help to save the liberty and the independence of a threatened country, of our Spain.

Communists, socialists, anarchists, republicans, men of different colour, of different ideology, of opposing religions, but all of them deeply loving liberty and justice, united to offer themselves to us unconditionally.

They gave us everything: their youth and their maturity; their knowledge and their experience; their blood and their lives; their hopes and their desires . . . And they asked us for nothing. That is to say, yes, they did want a place in the struggle, they wanted the honour of dying for us. Flags of Spain! Greet our heroes, bend before so many martyrs!

Mothers! Women! When the years pass and the wounds of war are staunched; when the cloudy memory of the sorrowful, bloody days returns in a day of freedom, love and well-being; when the feelings of rancour die away and when pride in a free country is felt equally by all Spaniards – then tell your children. Tell them of the International Brigades. Tell them how, coming over sea and mountains, crossing frontiers bristling with bayonets and watched by ravening dogs wanting to tear at their flesh, these men reached our country as crusaders for freedom. They gave up everything, their loves, their country, home and fortune – fathers, mothers, brothers, sisters and children – and they came and told us: 'We are here. Your cause, Spain's cause, is ours. It is the cause of all advanced and progressive mankind.' Today, they are leaving. Many of them, thousands of them, are staying here with the Spanish earth for their shroud, and all Spaniards remember them with the deepest feeling.[24]

Then Pasionaria turned to the Brigadists themselves, parading together for the last time.

> Comrades of the International Brigades! Political reasons, reasons of state, the welfare of that same cause for which you offered your blood with boundless generosity, are sending you back, some to your own countries and others to forced exile. You can go proudly. You are history. You are legend. You are the heroic example of democracy's solidarity and universality. We shall not forget you, and when the olive tree of peace puts forth its leaves again, mingled with the laurels of the Spanish republic's victory – come back!
>
> Come back to our side, for here you will find your country, those who do not have a country, friends, those who have to live deprived of friendship, and all of you, all, the love and gratitude of the entire Spanish people, who today and tomorrow will enthusiastically cry: 'Long live the heroes of the International Brigades!'

It was an intensely moving occasion, which the departing Brigadists would remember for the rest of their lives, and it was one more reason why La Pasionaria had a special place in their hearts. The socialist trade union organisation, the UGT, held a big dinner in honour of the International Brigades at the National Palace in Barcelona on 4 November, where 'La Pasionaria's mere presence electrified the audience', according to an American veteran of the Abraham Lincoln Brigade who was present.[25] Many of the brigadists had become disillusioned with communism because of the Spanish Party's totalitarian tactics (some had tried to desert and been shot on the orders of the Soviet-controlled secret police), yet they somehow did not identify La Pasionaria with the Communist Party's darker side. They still believed in the republican cause and she had become the personification of the Spanish people's struggle against oppression and injustice. This ability of hers to appear as a living Statue of Liberty while in reality being fully aware and indeed approving of her Party's underhand side was the secret of her success.

But did La Pasionaria realise that in the ringing final phrase of her Barcelona speech she was not only pronouncing the epitaph for the International Brigades and the three years of international solidarity with the Spanish republic, but for herself as well? For she was now only a few months away from as long and unhappy a period of enforced exile from her homeland as any of the volunteers she mentioned in her speech.

CHAPTER TEN

GOODBYE TO SPAIN

The decline of the republic continued remorselessly. Final defeat on the Ebro was concluded around the time La Pasionaria was saying goodbye to the International Brigades. It was followed by the nationalists' advance through Catalonia, which was sealed off by the occupation of Barcelona at the end of January 1939. In December the communists had planned an offensive in Estremadura to divert nationalist troops from Catalonia. It was badly bungled: first the army switched the plan to make it an attack on Granada on the other side of the country, then went back to the Estremaduran offensive. It was early January before it got under way. When it failed, Palmiro Togliatti was in no doubt that the communists had to shoulder the blame because of their indecision and arguments among themselves. The offensive was launched by the Army of the Centre-South, of which Jesús Hernández was political commissar, but he left the scene just when he was most needed. La Pasionaria was dispatched to the front to see if she could sort it out, but it was far too late.[1]

Madrid and a sizeable portion of the country still remained in the republic's hands. It seemed unlikely that the capital could hold out but the communists still maintained their public posture that victory would be theirs and continued to oppose any talk of negotiating with Franco for a swift end to hostilities. However even the most dedicated Party members knew in their hearts that on the republican side the battle now was not for control of Spain but for an honourable settlement. Even La Pasionaria, the symbol of total resistance, admitted much later: 'I must admit to a great deal of ingenuousness on our part. Our faith in the people and in our victory, in the possibility of continuing the resistance, was unbreakable and at times blinded us to reality.'[2] The position of the prime minister, Negrín, was ambivalent. He protested to doubters that he was determined to continue the war, while leaving others the clear impression that he and many of his supporters were already planning their own retreat. The key lay in the army, many of whose commanders had become disillusioned with the war and, in particular, with the Communist Party, which they had embraced with enthusiasm for its discipline and fighting spirit at the beginning of the war. There were by now extensive underground contacts between the republican army and the nationalists to explore a ceasefire. The man at the centre of this was General Segismundo Casado, head of the Army of the Centre, whose loyalty to the republic had long been doubted by the communists. La Pasionaria's opinion of him, in retrospect, was: 'It is difficult to imagine a slyer, more cowardly old fox.'[3]

Returning in early January 1939 to Madrid from Catalonia, where disaster was staring the republic in the face, she went to see Casado to seek his help in finding storage for two shiploads of aid sent from abroad by anti-fascist support groups. The idea was to organise food kitchens for children and dispensaries for nursing mothers in the capital. Casado was extremely helpful. La Pasionaria admitted that she had no idea he was not wholeheartedly behind the resistance. The fact that she was so badly duped was probably behind the intense hatred she was to bear Casado for the rest of her life.[4]

Party secretary José Díaz had left for the Soviet Union the previous November for medical treatment for a persistent stomach complaint. He never saw Spain again. In his absence La Pasionaria had been charged with organising the Party's Vth Congress in Madrid. With the collapse of the republic more likely by the day, she shelved the congress, although she went ahead with a provincial congress of the Party from 8 to 11 February. In her speech, she attacked Casado and General Miaja, commander of the Army of the Centre, and other 'traitors'. Togliatti was highly critical of the speech for its sectarianism. 'It could not be understood by the people,' he wrote later.[5] After the congress, La Pasionaria set to work trying to organise food supplies to factories and to children. Although she claimed to have recruited 6,000 women volunteers in a week, sectarian disputes with the socialists impeded the success of this venture – a good guide to the state of republican morale by this time.

What was left of power in the disintegrating republic was divided: the government under Negrín was in Valencia while the communists still ruled the roost in Madrid, where Casado had his headquarters. (President Azaña had already fled to Paris and was refusing to return; he knew it was all over.) The relationship between Casado and La

Pasionaria started to break down. Casado ordered the arrest of communists in the capital who were involved in the publication of a declaration in Catalonia which attacked as cowards those who proposed to surrender. When La Pasionaria protested, he rescinded the order. A few days later, Casado invited her to his office. Her record of the conversation is that Casado thought the war had always been a mistake. His plan was that the government should retreat to the southern port of Cartagena and organise its resistance from there. In reality, this was a proposal to make an orderly retreat via the sea. La Pasionaria saw through it immediately and dismissed it as insane but, by her own admission, she still did not realise that Casado was determined to surrender.[6]

On 12 February she headed a communist delegation to meet the depressed and defeatist Negrín, who had travelled to Madrid to assess the situation. They told him they would support him, whichever course he took. If he fought on, the communists would fight on too; if he sued for peace, the Party would not be an obstacle. Negrín said he would continue to resist but left La Pasionaria and the other communists with little confidence that he meant it.[7]

On 25 February the Politburo held what was to be its last full meeting of the war. Afterwards the Party published a defiant communiqué: the fight would go on. The thinking now was that the international situation was becoming more uncertain by the day: if the republic could hold on for a few more months, it might be saved by events outside its frontiers. War in Europe would mean a drastic re-evaluation of the republic by Britain and France, which had hitherto stood aside and allowed the Axis powers to do as they liked in Spain, riding roughshod over the non-intervention pact. The Spanish communists did not yet realise that Stalin, with one eye on a deal with Hitler, had abandoned them.

The end was rapidly approaching. Negrín moved the seat of government south from Valencia to a small town called Elda, inland from Alicante. The communists, not wishing to lose touch, moved their own headquarters to El Palmar, not far away, giving it the code-name 'Position Dakar'. Enrique Castro described this, the communists' last official headquarters in Spain for the best part of 40 years, as 'a beautiful country house' with comfortable bedrooms. Pretty girls waited on the Party leaders; the food was good for the times, although most of it came from tins. The countryside around was 'quiet and enchanting'. The communist poet Rafael Alberti and his wife María

113

Teresa León were also there; Castro observed them walking sadly among the trees. It was in this idyllic place that La Pasionaria found herself when news came through that General Casado had risen in Madrid and set up a National Council of Defence, which intended to negotiate a peace treaty with Franco. Communist militants were being rounded up and arrested. Castro went in search of the Party leaders to seek permission to march on Madrid with troops loyal to the communists and put down the uprising. He found La Pasionaria playing cards with the military chiefs Juan Modesto and Enrique Líster. They told him to go to bed.[8] Although the Madrid militants were fighting on, the Party leadership (and in particular Togliatti, who to all intents and purposes had taken charge) had given up the ghost. Togliatti described them as 'demoralised and disorientated'.[9]

They agreed that La Pasionaria should leave Spain as soon as possible, fearing that Casado's rebellion would soon spread and that the Party leaders would be a welcome gift to Franco. The propaganda coup of capturing La Pasionaria would have been incalculable. Her eventual fate if that had happened was in no doubt to anybody. 'In the conditions we were in, we could not guarantee her life,' wrote Togliatti.[10] At first she refused to go but it was no use. 'The Party had decided that I should go, and go I did.' She gave away many of her possessions to the girls who had looked after them at El Palmar. She burned a copy of a Blasco Ibañez novel which contained a personal dedication to her by Julio Just, a former minister of public works, in case it fell into the wrong hands and implicated Just. She was anxious about her secretary Irene Falcón, who had gone off to Albacete, and not yet returned. But she could not wait. A small number of aeroplanes had been assembled for the Party's use at the little airfield of Monovar, a few kilometres away. It was there that she went on 6 March, the day after Casado's uprising. 'We have been defeated . . . We did our duty and the people understood us,' she said. An élite group of communist guerrillas which had been formed to fight the advancing nationalist armies behind their own lines had been assigned to guard the airstrip. They paraded to say farewell to the symbol of the Communist Party. La Pasionaria embraced them, then embarked in the waiting Dragon Rapide. Her last sight of Spain was the guerrillas saluting her, waving their guns aloft.

Her fellow passengers were Jean Cattelas, a French communist deputy later executed by the Nazis, the Bulgarian Comintern delegate Stepanov and Jesús Monzón, a young communist lawyer originally from Pamplona who had finished up as civil governor of Alicante. Most of the other communist leaders fled by plane the same day or soon afterwards. Their decision to do so while communist militants in Madrid were fighting and dying in the streets in the useless battle to counter Casado's coup was a priceless propaganda gift to their enemies. At the same time, hundreds of thousands of republicans were jamming all the roads as they headed for the ports and the French frontier in the hope of escaping from Franco's armies. Few of those who tried to get out by sea managed to do so, while those who did get across the border to France had to endure the most appalling privations both on the way and in the concentration camps the French set up for them. One who made it to France in conditions far removed from his mother's comfortable passage was La Pasionaria's son Rubén. He had returned to Spain from the USSR to enlist with the republican army at the age of only 16. He was a member of a communications unit with Líster's army in Catalonia and made his way across the Pyrenees to France with his comrades after the republican collapse.

The Communist Party's total failure to prepare for defeat was to be a source of much mutual recrimination over the next months and years. So obsessed had the Party been with victory, even long after it had become a fantasy, that hardly anyone had set their minds to building a network of members and material that could carry on the struggle under a nationalist government. This lack of foresight was to cost the Party dear.

La Pasionaria's immediate destination was Oran, in Algeria, then a French colony, where she received a heroine's welcome. Rafael Alberti reached Oran shortly afterwards. They were held in a hangar at the airport while the French authorities sought a way of getting rid of their embarrassing and uninvited guests as quickly as possible. It was a time of enormous sympathy around the world for the Spanish republic, as the realisation grew that it was doomed. Such was the excitement that La Pasionaria's arrival generated that the soldiers guarding the building pushed pieces of paper and family photographs under the door for her to autograph 'like some great actress', the poet remembered.[11] A boat was found which was leaving for Marseilles shortly. La Pasionaria, Alberti and his wife were driven to the dockside and put on the ship. Irene Falcón had meanwhile got on a flight to Oran and was frantically searching for La Pasionaria. She too was interned in a hangar. 'I made a huge fuss,' she recalled. 'I hadn't slept for ten days. I shouted to the workers outside, "Where is Dolores Ibárruri?" I discovered she was at the port. Eventually they put me in a car and took me there. I borrowed some money and ran for the Marseilles boat. On board, I opened a cabin door and a hand grabbed me. It was Dolores.'[12] The crew paraded in front of their distinguished Spanish passengers with the clenched fist salute. During the voyage, a group of sailors knocked on La Pasionaria's cabin door and warned her they suspected the captain of planning to hand her over to Franco's forces as they passed near Barcelona. But the radio operator was a Party member and would tip them off if he heard any suspicious messages. If the captain tried anything, they said, they would take over the boat. La Pasionaria did not feel safe until they were out of range of Spain. At Marseilles she received another big welcome and caught the train to Paris the same day. Most of the leading figures in the defeated Popular Front had also managed to make their way to the French capital.

The nationalists entered Madrid on 27 March. Final victory was achieved on 31 March. The same day there was a meeting of the permanent committee of the Cortes in Paris, which La Pasionaria attended in her capacity as vice-president of the Cortes. Negrín gave a detailed account of the last days of the republic since the fall of Catalonia. The discussion that followed was bitter and rancorous; insults and blame for the defeat of the republic were freely traded. La Pasionaria declared that she had 'neither blood nor gold' upon her hands, a reference to Spain's gold reserves, most of which the republican government had entrusted to the Soviet Union for safe keeping in 1939. It was worth around $500 million and it was never returned.

Where were the hundreds of thousands of republican refugees in France to go? Many, disillusioned with their rough treatment by the French, opted to return to a highly uncertain future back home. Many Latin American countries, particularly Mexico, opened their arms to them and various ad hoc bodies sprang up to cope with the massive task of supervising their transportation there. Francisco Antón was heavily involved in this work. The Chilean communist poet Pablo Neruda, a diplomat in his country's Paris embassy, was one of many foreign sympathisers to help. In Paris the communists set up a committee to vet those Party members who wanted to emigrate to the USSR. La Pasionaria was a member. Not all those who applied were successful: some 3,500 were finally approved. The Party leadership also headed for Moscow to lick its bruises and consider what, if anything, could be rescued, from the ruins. La Pasionaria travelled to Le Havre, disguised in a hat and dark glasses, to catch a Soviet ship bound for the USSR. She thought it would be a brief journey, after which she would return to France. But she would be trapped in the USSR by the outbreak of the Second World War; it would be five years before she would be in France again – and 38 years before she could return to her native Spain.

CHAPTER ELEVEN

RETREAT TO MOSCOW

During almost all of the 38 years that La Pasionaria spent in exile, she was a non-person in Spain. The Spanish newspapers, carefully controlled by the Franco government, seldom mentioned her. On the rare occasions that they did, it was in scornful and insulting terms. The same applied, of course, to the other leaders of the Spanish Communist Party. From being household names they passed instantly into myth in their own country, a myth that would in a curious way develop and grow over the years. The Spanish people regarded the communists with a mixture of fascination and horror, which was in part helped by the Franco régime's detestation of them. The fact that they were banned during the whole of the Generalissimo's long rule and that their leaders lived in exile while constantly and hopelessly plotting their return lent them a certain glamour in younger Spaniards' eyes as memories of the Civil War started to fade. But for those who had opposed them, fought them, lived under their rule or, above all, lost members of their family to 'Red' atrocities, the wounds never healed; hatred of the communists stayed alive in their hearts for decades.

In the immediate aftermath of the Civil War, the Communist Party was defeated, divided and demoralised. Its members were, literally, all over the place. Many of those who had not managed to escape from Spain had been rounded up and were now in Franco's jails. The new régime's courts worked systematically through them, sending many to the firing squad and condemning the others to long terms of imprisonment in harsh conditions which broke many spirits. Some stayed on in France, the others were slowly dispersed around the world. Many found their way to Latin America, particularly Mexico, Argentina and Chile, which had governments of a left-wing or nationalist hue and were sympathetic to the republican cause. Because there was no problem with the language or the culture they found there, many of the Spaniards prospered. For Latin America the period of the Second World War and the post-war years was one of peace and prosperity. After the turmoil they had been through many Spanish exiles took advantage of these conditions and were able to establish new and successful lives for themselves and their families.

The leading figures in the Communist Party split up in much the same fashion. The central leadership group, including La Pasionaria, went to Moscow to link up again with the Comintern leadership and find out what Stalin had in mind for them; they were followed by the 3,500 Party members selected as suitable for Soviet exile. Some key figures, including Francisco Antón, stayed in France to supervise Party members' evacuation into exile and to organise a nucleus of the Party as close as they could to Spain; while, after brief periods in the USSR, a number of activists just beneath the controlling group went on to Mexico City to look after the Party's activities in exile in Latin America. The 7,000-mile gap that separated the Party's two new power bases, Moscow and Mexico City, was to be the cause of growing friction between the two, exacerbated by slow communications and the onset of world war.

When La Pasionaria arrived in Moscow the trauma of defeat and exile was alleviated by reunion with her two children, Rubén and Amaya, now 18 and 16 respectively. She had certainly not seen Amaya since 1935 when she had sent both children off to the USSR. Rubén had returned to Spain to fight in the republican army towards the end of the Civil War but does not appear to have seen his mother at that time. After the republican defeat he was interned in the French concentration camp of Argelès-sur-mer. He escaped and made his own way across Europe to Moscow. He told the Russian family with whom he lived that he had escaped from the prison camp by hiding in a coffin in the company of a corpse.

As an alternate member of the executive committee of the Comintern, a leader of the Spanish Party, and one of the best-known figures in the world communist movement, La Pasionaria was granted considerable privileges and perks. She was given an apartment in Pereulok Street in the centre of Moscow. José Díaz and his family had a flat in the same building. La Pasionaria also had a car and chauffeur as well as access to the sort of facilities reserved for leading Soviet Party officials. She was given a 'large and comfortable' office in the Comintern building, where she devoted herself to a life of 'meetings, debates, reading and reflection'.[1] She lacked for little, in contrast to the privations suffered by many of the Spanish communists who followed her into exile in the USSR. This became a source of considerable hostility towards her in the years to come. Apart from La Pasionaria, other Party leading lights who went to Moscow included Jesús Hernández, Pedro Checa and Vicente Uribe, as well as a number of military commanders, such as Enrique Líster, Juan Modesto, Enrique Castro and the folk hero 'El Campesino ' – 'The Peasant', real name Valentín González, whose exploits early in the Civil War had made him a popular legend. José Díaz was by now a somewhat pathetic figure, ill and isolated. He had missed the dramas of the last stages of the Civil War, which he had observed helplessly from Moscow. Having been a loyal tool of the Soviet Union throughout the 1930s, he had towards the end of the decade started to display an occasional independence of mind which was not at all welcome to the Soviets. He was seriously ill, three operations having failed to cure what had been taken to be stomach ulcers but now turned out to be cancer. He had outlived his usefulness in the Kremlin's eyes and had to all intents and purposes been written off by them. This did not prevent him from pestering his newly-arrived compatriots for details of the Casado uprising and the other disastrous events of the last days of the war. Stalin himself wanted to know why it had turned out so badly. To come up with an answer, a mixed commission of inquiry was set up, with five members each from the Comintern and the PCE, among them Díaz and La Pasionaria. Its conclusions were never revealed; perhaps Stalin lost interest, in the face of impending world conflict.

But an unofficial inquest went on among the Spaniards (indeed, it continued for decades). The outcome was that the comrades all blamed each other. In the clinical atmosphere of the Soviet Union, suddenly far removed from any Spanish reality, the communists were able to give full rein to long-pent-up quarrels, both personal and sectarian.

Disputes and hatreds which had been suppressed by the hectic pace of life in Civil War Spain, and by the need to demonstrate unity, now flourished. There was ample time to nurse grudges and brood over what might have been. The exiles' culture and customs were very different from those of the USSR. Suffering from the shock of defeat, uprooted from their native land and treated with indifference by their hosts, their situation was not promising.

The military élite of the Spanish Communist Party were assigned to

МАНДАТ № 190

Тов. Долорес Мария

От компартии Испании

С РЕШАЮЩИМ ГОЛОСОМ

Секретарь ИККИ

Москва, июль–август, 1935 год.

(Top) La Pasionaria's delegate credentials to the VII Congress of the Communist International held in Moscow in 1935 (ACP)

(Above) Addressing a rally at Las Ventas bullring in Madrid in February 1936 (FDI)

(Right) Addressing troops on the Guadarrama Front; figure in background known as General Walter (FDI)

(Below) Speaking at a Communist rally in the Monumental Cinema in Madrid in 1936 (FDI)

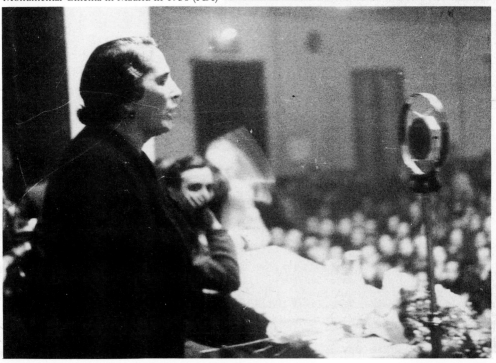

Visiting troops during the defence of Madrid in 1936 (FDI)

(Below) Addressing a battalion of the International Brigades in Spain during the Civil War with the legendary Communist military leader Valentín Gonzalez or 'El Campesino' (the Peasant) who later fell out with the Party (ACP)

Signing an autograph
during the Civil War
(FDI)

With fellow leaders of the PCE in Valencia
in 1937, La Pasionaria *middle*, José Díaz
2nd from right (FDI)

(Above) Addressing a pro-Republic meeting in Brussels in 1938 (FDI)

(Below) With her two children Rubén and Amaya in 1939–40 (FDI)

(Left) With Rubén in Red Army uniform in Moscow in 1940 (FDI)

Meeting at Spanish Centre in Moscow in 1940; portraits of José Díaz *left,* still secretary of PCE, Stalin *middle* and La Pasionaria *right.* La Pasionaria *7th from left* , Irene Falcón *4th from right* (FDI)

Addressing V Congress of PCE in Czechoslovakia in 1954 (FDI)

Meeting Mao tse-
Tung in Peking in
1956 (FDI)

With PCE delegation
in China in 1956;
Sebastián Zapiraín
2nd from right (SZ)

Visiting Cuba in December 1963 with Che Guevara *front row 2nd from left* (FDI)

Home at last: La Pasionaria, with Santiago Carrillo, general secretary of the Spanish Communist Party, waves to well-wishers on her first full day back in Spain in May 1977 after 38 years in exile abroad (Derek Ive)

staff colleges, including some of the top names from the republican army such as Enrique Líster, Juan Modesto and El Campesino. The last-named, a brave but primitive figure, did not find Soviet military discipline at all to his liking, swiftly fell out with his Russian superiors, was labelled a Trotskyist and was expelled from the military academy. Aghast, his Spanish colleagues there referred his case to the PCE Politburo for disciplinary action. The fiery Campesino hit back by accusing La Pasionaria of having got her lover Antón out of France while other Spanish communists 'were left to rot'. He also charged Líster with having raped five young Spanish girl refugees in a drunken orgy at a school in Kaluga.

El Campesino refused to accept the PCE's authority and the case was referred up to the Comintern, which appointed a special committee to look into the affair. Among its members was La Pasionaria, even though she was one of those whom El Campesino was citing. According to El Campesino, she told the committee that he was an individualist who would never admit he was wrong and was still refusing to do so. 'He fails to understand that a single member, no matter who he is, cannot be right when he is in opposition to the International.' Other Spaniards, including Irene Falcón, joined in the attack. El Campesino demanded unsuccessfully to be judged by the entire Spanish community in the USSR. After sitting for a fortnight, the committee came up with a verdict: El Campesino was to be put to work as a labourer building the Moscow Underground. Even he admitted it was a lenient judgment.[2] In Stalin's Russia, people were liquidated for a lot less.

El Campesino's life after that was worthy of a picaresque novel. He escaped from Moscow just ahead of the Nazi onslaught in 1941 and for a time ran his own robber band in Uzbekistan (another such band was composed entirely of Spanish refugee children). Returning to Moscow when the Germans had been repulsed, his path crossed La Pasionaria's once more. He was attempting to leave the USSR and, without any friends in the capital, foolishly went to the Spanish Communist Party for assistance. He rapidly became involved in a bitter and noisy row with Vicente Uribe, who was in charge of Spanish refugees in the USSR, and others.

The door opened and in rushed La Pasionaria and Líster. They joined in the row at once. Out of their own mouths I heard it was they who had prevented my release which my wife had nearly managed to obtain, and

121

they who had arranged for my deportation to Kazakhstan. They boasted that they could do what they liked with the lives of Spanish refugees, with the help of the NKVD, and threatened me with the full use of their power.

After further insults had been exchanged, La Pasionaria turned to El Campesino's wife and threatened her: 'You'll pay dear for helping this Trotskyite dog!'[3]

Having gained protection from the elderly Soviet President Mikhail Kalinin, El Campesino's adventures continued. He managed to get out of the USSR by walking across the Persian border with two other Spaniards but was captured by NKVD agents and taken back to the USSR. He spent several years enduring the most appalling conditions in labour camps, survived an earthquake in one of these which killed most of the inmates, and finally managed to escape to Persia again in 1948.[4]

To return to Moscow in 1941: most of the Spanish exiles, including La Pasionaria's husband Julián Ruiz, were put to work in factories. Disillusionment was frequent. At the top level, Jesús Hernández and Enrique Castro, as well as El Campesino, eventually parted company with Soviet communism, while many in the lower echelons suffered hardship, deprivation, loneliness and ill-treatment in their adopted country and were still bitter about it half a century later.

Some of the central disputes that sprang up among the Spaniards in the USSR in the early 1940s centred around the personality of La Pasionaria. The main one concerned the leadership of the Party as Díaz's star waned and he spent more and more time convalescing. From the start, La Pasionaria was the Soviets' only candidate for the job. First, she replaced Díaz as a full member of the Comintern executive. By late 1939 she had taken over effective running of the PCE Politburo. She needed to deploy the utmost mental agility to cope with the events of that autumn, particularly the Nazi–Soviet pact of 23 August. All of a sudden the old enemy was now the ally and La Pasionaria applied herself diligently to cope with this new development. The Comintern poured out a stream of propaganda justifying Stalin's volte-face and the PCE, mainly in the shape of La Pasionaria's writings, followed suit. In one article she described the old Poland, now carved up between the USSR and Germany, as:

a state artificially created by the Treaty of Versailles . . . a republic of concentration camps, of governments which betrayed their people, which was constituted in the image of the democracy of the Blums and Citrines! Social democracy weeps for the loss of Poland, because imperialism has lost a point of support against the Soviet Union, against the fatherland of the proletariat.[5]

This, and other such articles justifying the Nazis' occupation of France, Belgium, Denmark and Norway, constitute a shameful episode in La Pasionaria's life. They demonstrate all too clearly that for all her voracious reading she remained uneducated, credulous and pathetically subservient to Stalin's policy, whatever it might be at any given moment. She was of course not alone: the whole apparatus of the Comintern – Dimitrov and Togliatti among them – did the same. She was now publicly supporting the same Nazis whom she had spent the past decade haranguing, of whose evil power she had vainly warned the rest of Europe. Of this sad episode she made no mention in her memoirs. In Civil War Spain she could be partly forgiven for being such a monolithic communist because of the courage and vigour she also often displayed. But in the cold, clinical atmosphere of Stalin's Russia all that was left was the obedient party hack.

The Spanish communists' dutiful support for the Soviet-Nazi alliance was brought to an end by Hitler's invasion of the Soviet Union on 22 June 1941. La Pasionaria and her colleagues could safely revert to a more comfortable ideological stance. She was with her family at her dacha in Pushkino, outside Moscow, when the news was brought to her by Irene Falcón, who had heard the news on German radio. La Pasionaria's son Rubén, who was at a military academy, immediately left to volunteer for military service. 'Mother, I will act like your son,' he told her as he left.[6] For La Pasionaria and her fellow communists it was out of the frying pan of Madrid under siege into the fire of Moscow under siege. (Although even at this critical period she could not bury her old housewifely instincts. On one occasion she noticed that Palmiro Togliatti was wearing a tattered old jacket. Offended by this sight, she told him to take it off while she got out her needle and thread and performed some repair work.)[7]

Much of their energy at this time went into the creation of the institution which was to be their strongest link with Spain for the next two decades: Radio España Independiente, Estación Pirenaica (Radio Independent Spain, Pyrenean Station). Financed by the Communist International, the station pumped out communist propaganda to Spain, first from Moscow and later from the Romanian capital Bucharest where it moved in the 1950s. It was called the Pyrenean

Station in order to give to listeners the illusion that it was being beamed at them from somewhere in the mountainous north of Spain, giving the impression that the communists were operating in force inside the country. The broadcasters would occasionally try to maintain this illusion too. In February 1943, for instance, La Pasionaria said in a broadcast: 'We are in Spain, although because of the difficult conditions in which we have to carry out our work it may sometimes be impossible to deal with matters with the speed which we would wish to.' (She was referring to listeners' inquiries and requests.) In May 1943 she was talking of 'all the news we have been able to glean in this corner of the Pyrenees.'

Even in Moscow, conditions were tough enough. The station operated from underground studios because of the German bombing. As hardship in the capital grew the Spaniards often had to work by candlelight. They had no idea what listeners they were attracting. It was not until much later that they learned of the slow development of a faithful audience.

La Pasionaria was devoted to La Pirenaica, understandably, as it was virtually her only way of addressing the Spanish people. She often broadcast several times a day, either commentaries on current events or, more originally, in the form of dialogues between two 'typical' working-class women living in Madrid whom she christened Juana and Manuela. Her commentaries were predictably fiery, bloodthirsty and over-optimistic, with constant predictions, even in the early 1940s, that the Franco régime was on its last legs. On Franco's birthday in 1942, for example, she broadcast to Spain, calling the general a 'miserable traitor'. She went on: 'The curses of millions of wives and mothers whom you left without sons, whose husbands, fathers and brothers you sentenced to death, rise toward you . . . the hour of justice approaches.' On another occasion she called the diminutive Generalissimo 'the dwarf of the Pardo [Franco's palace home]'. In January 1943: 'No one believes the Falange [the only political party permitted by Franco] can remain in power much longer. The strength of the opposition to the government grows daily.' Virtually every broadcast contained an insulting reference to the Falangists, whom La Pasionaria would routinely describe as pigs or cretins. Thus on 8 February 1943: 'To expect dignity and common sense from a Falangist leader is like asking a mule not to kick.' Or the next day: 'Spain's hour approaches. And the hour of Spain's resurrection is the hour of the Falange's death.'[8]

Her Juana and Manuela dialogues, although as simplistic as the British war propaganda film scripts they resemble, are none the less of a higher quality than such harangues. Inevitably, they show a great deal of wishful thinking but La Pasionaria did have a good ear for ordinary speech and a gift for the occasional telling phrase. The scripts are an interesting guide to the communists' preoccupations of the 1940s, although they were probably based on out-of-date and unreliable information filtered back from Spain. A random sample of the concerns voiced by La Pasionaria's housewives, chatting to each other from their windows in the old quarter of central Madrid (the series was called 'From Window to Window') shows that in December 1942 Juana and Manuela bemoan food shortages: food goes either to the Falange hierarchy or is exported to feed the Germans. Why don't the Spanish rise up in protest? In April 1943 Juana is indignant that German submarines are buying fish from Spanish fishermen. If the fishermen refuse, the Germans show them a letter from the Spanish government ordering them to supply them with their catch. (The theme that Spain was becoming a German vassal was a constant one.) Manuela and Juana plan to produce a newsletter for anti-fascist women and a manifesto for the First of May to be distributed at the market and in poor areas. In January 1944 the two women complain about the lack of coal for their fires. It has all been commandeered by the steel industry in order to maintain supplies for Germany. Women who stand in queues should storm the coalyards and seize what they need.

Since the first days of exile, the communists had applied themselves to the job of rebuilding the Party within Spain. It was a dangerous and thankless task. Franco's repression was in full and efficient swing and the rest of the world, preoccupied with war, turned a blind eye to what was going on behind the Pyrenees. The Party's biggest problem was that, blinded by its own rhetoric that the Civil War would eventually be won, it had completely failed to make any provision for what might happen after the defeat which had long appeared inevitable to almost everyone else. So when Franco was victorious, the communists had no underground organisation in place to carry on the struggle. This planning failure was to be the subject of bitter debate and recriminations for many years. All the party had was a lot of members in jail, awaiting the firing squad or long prison sentences, while those who had managed to avoid capture were fragmented, and totally isolated from the leadership, which was safely abroad. Some tried to wage a guerrilla war against the régime from hideouts in remote mountainous areas. They were a brave but foolhardy group who achieved little; they never achieved their aim of winning over local people and slowly orchestrating a growing campaign of resistance, but some of them survived a surprising length of time against overwhelming odds before being hunted down by the civil guard. Others tried to rebuild the party in the cities and factories where support for the communists was strongest. Their activities amounted to little more than leaflet dropping and the occasional urban guerrilla attack; the party in exile would regularly send in courageous souls, usually from Latin America, who attempted to contact them and get some sort of organisation on its feet. Just as regularly, they were rounded up by the security police and, after routine torture, usually executed. The early years of the Second World War brought nothing but disaster for the Communist Party within Spain.

The German army's swift advance on Moscow meant that La Pasionaria and any other Spaniards left in the capital were forced to leave in a hurry. Most of them, largely children, had already been evacuated. La Pasionaria helped to organize the departure of the last group and then on 16 October 1941 set off herself on the long train journey eastwards to the city of Ufa, capital of the Bashkir soviet republic, where the Comintern had relocated its headquarters. It was a chaotic and appallingly slow journey, the train taking nine days to crawl 700 miles to Ufa, nestling at the foot of the Urals on the banks of the river Belaya. La Pasionaria took her children with her: Rubén happened to be at home, recovering from wounds sustained at the front; Amaya was at school. At the station in Moscow, which was packed with thousands of people trying to flee, La Pasionaria was caught up in the crowd and separated from both of them. When the train set off, there was no sign of them. It was only many hours later that she learnt that they were on the following train and would meet her in Ufa. She discovered Irene Falcón on the train; another passenger was Sir Walter Citrine, general secretary of the British Trades Union Congress, who had been surprised by the Nazi advance on a visit to Moscow on behalf of the newly-formed Anglo-Soviet Trades Union Congress. His lukewarm support for the Spanish republic had been the target for La Pasionaria's abuse during the Civil War: she did not record whether she subjected him to her robust critical style face to face now that she had him as a captive audience, while they proceeded

126

across the frozen landscape at a stately 20 miles per hour. Citrine found two peasant girls and their luggage in his compartment when he got on the train (they were swiftly thrown out by the guard) and found the unheated train a trifle too cold for comfort. The first morning, he recorded, 'I awakened almost frozen, and had to summon up sufficient will-power to crawl out and complete dressing. Washing was very perfunctorily performed owing to lack of water.'[9] Citrine got out at Kuibishev, where he was to meet Molotov, after a mere five and a half days travelling.

It is hard not to sympathise with La Pasionaria as she contemplated the remote city where she was to spend the next two years, along with a number of other Spanish exiles: 'How far from my Gallarta, from our Madrid!' she wrote many years later.[10]

Rubén was fortunate to have survived his first spell of duty in the front line. In June 1941 his unit had been deployed against the invading Nazis in forest between Minsk and Smolensk. They were overrun and forced to retreat in some disorder. Rubén was wounded in the arm and lost contact with his unit. He spent three weeks on the run, and was reduced to eating grass and birch bark to survive, until he found his way back to the Soviet lines. He spent two months recuperating in a hospital in Kuibishev before travelling to Ufa. His sister Amaya was found a school in which to continue her studies.[11]

The year 1942 was to be as hard a one as even La Pasionaria ever faced. She suffered personal tragedy and hardship in addition to the responsibility of taking over the official leadership of the Spanish Communist Party. Despite her privileges, life in Ufa was gruelling: the temperature reached -30°C. The Soviet Union was fighting for its life against the Nazi invaders and there were shortages of everything.

La Pasionaria took charge of the Party in March. José Díaz died in the Georgian capital, Tbilisi, where he had been dispatched to try to recuperate. He fell from the window of the fourth-floor apartment he occupied with his wife and daughter. The official cause of death was given as suicide and certainly Díaz had every excuse for ending his life: he was seriously ill with cancer; a shy and uneducated man, he had not adapted well to life in the Soviet Union, so far away from his native Spain; his grip on the Party reins had been gradually loosened by his illness and the necessity for him to live in a healthier climate than Moscow's; Stalin and the Comintern had long since decided he had no future as leader; and it looked as if the Nazi-Soviet war was going to end as badly for communism as the Spanish Civil War had.

Díaz left La Pasionaria a hand-written letter. It began: 'Dear comrade Dolores: the end of my life approaches and I don't want it to pass without you receiving a few lines from me.' There followed a series of platitudes about the need for Party unity. It was an extraordinarily banal way to say a final farewell to such an old comrade. It was, alas, all too typical of Díaz. Perhaps he may just have felt unable to say anything intimate to someone he was said to have greatly disliked. The communist renegades Jesús Hernández and Enrique Castro both recorded examples of his disapproval of her in their memoirs. The tone of La Pasionaria's wartime letters to Díaz in Tbilisi was warm and affectionate, however, and she never said a bad word about him before or after his death.

Another apostate, El Campesino, believed Díaz was murdered. He claimed that in his last months Díaz was furious at La Pasionaria for conspiring to replace him and sent her a stream of letters and telegrams protesting at the ill-treatment and even the liquidation of Spanish exiles in the USSR. El Campesino said a friend of his who happened to be in Tbilisi at the time of Díaz's death told him that two agents of the secret police, the NKVD, were in the next room to Díaz's with a doctor when he fell from the window.[12] As a right-wing historian mordantly observed, a post mortem would have been of no help in clarifying matters, since the injuries suffered by a man falling from the fourth floor would be the same whether he jumped or was pushed.[13]

La Pasionaria flew to Tbilisi in a military plane to attend the funeral, stopping off in Stalingrad en route. She paid a fulsome tribute to Díaz in a speech at the graveside and then flew back to Ufa. The succession had already been decided by the directorate of the Comintern and the PCE leadership: La Pasionaria was the unsurprising and unanimous choice. In her memoirs she claimed she told Dimitrov, the Comintern's Bulgarian chief, that she doubted she was up to the job. 'Dolores, leaders are made in office,' he replied. Her takeover was not as trouble-free as might have been expected, however. In Stalin's Russia it went as smoothly as one would expect, but Latin America was a different matter. There were more Spanish communist exiles there than in the Soviet Union and not everybody wanted to see La Pasionaria in the top job. Her principal enemy was Jesús Hernández, who, like her, had been waiting impatiently for Díaz to depart from the scene. As he made clear in his memoirs, published in the 1950s, he too disliked La Pasionaria intensely and within a year launched a bid to oust her.

But before this, personal tragedy struck La Pasionaria again: Rubén was killed in action during the siege of Stalingrad. It is a terrible thing for any parent to lose a child; for La Pasionaria the blow was doubly hard: she had lost four children in infancy; Rubén was her only son and, in every way, the ideal son for a woman of her nature and stature: he was good-looking, intelligent and courageous, and had clearly inherited his mother's headstrong nature (as well as having doubts about her). He was only 21, yet he had been through more than many men twice his age. He had returned to Moscow, where he had the best possible medical treatment at the Kremlin Clinic, as befitted the son of a distinguished communist. But he itched to return to the front. To do so, he presented himself at a barracks as far from the centre as he could find, where there would be less likelihood of getting VIP treatment. 'As you can see, Colonel, I'm ready,' he told the officer in charge and thumped the table with his good arm to emphasise the point. He re-enlisted in the 35th Division of the Guard, with the rank of lieutenant.[14]

La Pasionaria's enemies claimed that Rubén could not bear to be near her while she flaunted her relationship with her young lover Francisco Antón and lived in comfort with him at the same time as his father Julián Ruiz was working in a factory and living in reduced circumstances. But this is probably an exaggeration: the truth is probably less complex: Rubén was simply a brave young man who liked to be in the thick of the action. After all, when still in his teens, he had volunteered to return to Spain and fight for the republic in its dying months, so it was entirely in character to want to do the same in the Red Army.

La Pasionaria received what turned out to be her son's last letter to her on 13 August 1941:

> Dear mother: I have not written before because I did not know which front I would be sent to. Today I can tell you. I am in a place I know and love. It is the city where I studied to be a pilot . . . I wish to see action as soon as possible. You can be assured that I will fulfil my duty as a young communist and soldier.[15]

The place was Stalingrad, where perhaps the most savage and bitter battle of the entire war anywhere in the world was beginning. Reading between these sparse lines, was this a farewell note from a boy who wanted to die rather than face further dishonour? Or is it the sort of letter any young soldier would send home?

The evidence is that Rubén loved his parents equally, and it would be natural for him to regard Antón as an interloper. But it is stretching the imagination to believe, as did La Pasionaria's enemies, that Rubén preferred to return to the front before his wounds were properly healed than see his mother disgrace herself with Antón. It is more likely that he was propelled by the idealism of a 21-year-old steeped in communist mythology and tradition. There were many like him in the Second World War who were inspired by the same ideals and suffered the same fate.

Three weeks after this letter, La Pasionaria received the news of Rubén's death from a man whose name would be world famous 15 years later: Nikita Khrushchev, who in 1942 was a member of the Stalingrad war council and heavily involved in organising the defence of the city. His own son Leonid, a fighter pilot, was a friend of Rubén. They had met in the casualty ward at Kuibishev, where both had been recovering from war wounds. Leonid too was later killed in action. Nikita Khrushchev wrote:

> The machine-gun company headed by Rubén Ibárruri [Khrushchev got his name wrong: it was Rubén Ruiz Ibárruri] destroyed the first enemy lines . . . In this battle Lieutenant Rubén Ibárruri fell mortally wounded and was taken by his comrades to hospital . . . Despite the doctors' efforts to save the life of the young Spaniard, at dawn on 3 September 1942 Rubén died.[16]

Rubén was buried where he died, in the little village of Srednaya Ajtuva. He was posthumously awarded the title of Hero of the Soviet Union, to add to the Order of the Red Flag which he won for his earlier exploits. In November 1949 his body was removed and borne across the River Volga to the Square of the Combatants in Stalingrad itself where it was reburied with full military honours and in the presence of his mother. 'How to speak of my pain?' she wrote. 'It was the pain, the deepest of all, that of a mother who loses her son.'[17] In a way, she never got over Rubén's death. The memory of her son could reduce her to tears decades later.

CHAPTER TWELVE

COUPS AND DÉBÂCLES

The Nazi invasion of the Soviet Union may have imperilled the very existence of the opinion formers of the Spanish Communist Party but it did at least allow them to return to a more comfortable ideological position after the hideous contortions of the previous two years. Now they could again fire happily away at their old enemies, Hitler and his fascist allies. Churchill, once condemned as an imperialist warmonger, was suddenly a clear-sighted statesman and valued ally. The communists could now attempt to rebuild their bridges with their old Popular Front allies. Those few whom they had not alienated at the time of Casado's uprising in Madrid in 1939 had parted company with them when the PCE backed the Soviet-Nazi pact. For two years the PCE had effectively been isolated from the other anti-Franco parties also operating in exile.

Now the Party seized the new opening granted by Hitler to extend the hand of friendship to these parties again. First the central committee published, on 1 August 1942, an open letter to the Socialist Party, still headed by Juan Negrín, the former prime minister, who was living in exile in London. It appealed for a 'National Union', or coalition, to work against the Franco régime. It would be open to all, whether of left, centre or right, and its aim would be a government of national unity, headed by Negrín. The declaration gave every indication of having been written by La Pasionaria herself. It received a cool reception from the socialists, few of whom were inclined to forgive the communists for their previous volte-face. Bitter experience of communist duplicity had left them extremely cautious of throwing themselves into the Party's arms again. The open letter was followed on 16 September by the 'Manifesto of National Union', which was written by La Pasionaria and approved by the central committee. It was a radical break with the past in that she appealed not only to left-wing forces to unite against Franco but to anybody at all

131

who wanted to see the end of the dictator: everybody was welcome, even monarchists, provided they opposed Franco. Their task, as she saw it, was to purge Spain of the Falangists, restore freedom of the press, of assembly and of free speech (this being proposed without hint of irony from the heart of Stalin's Russia), prior to democratic elections for a constituent assembly which would draw up a new constitution. At the same time, La Pasionaria proposed guerrilla warfare against the régime throughout Spain.

Her manifesto caused astonishment in the ranks of the Spanish communist exiles in Latin America, who had to get used to yet another policy U-turn. One wonders whether the death of Rubén, which had been announced only a few days previously, influenced La Pasionaria to feel more conciliatory towards her old allies. She could not be blamed for feeling nostalgic about her country at a time of such deep grief, and for wanting to heal old wounds when she had suffered such a painful new one. But the gesture came to nothing: the Spanish socialists, republicans, anarchists, and regionalists, scattered round the world, did not take the manifesto seriously. The wounds of the Civil War had plainly not yet healed, even though communists and socialists in other countries, notably France and Italy, were reaching accommodations, faced with the common enemy of Nazism.

Although La Pasionaria was now preaching the message of brotherly love to the world, it did not appear to be having much effect within the PCE itself, which was seriously divided over the leadership question. The principal malcontent was Jesús Hernández but he was not alone. Many in the Spanish community in the Soviet Union were unhappy with the way La Pasionaria was running affairs. There was a widespread feeling that she and Francisco Antón, along with a few intimate cronies, had created a privileged inner circle with a lifestyle which was far removed from that of their fellow exiles. Life in wartime Russia was proving difficult for the Spanish. Their natural homesickness was accentuated by the shortages, deprivation and hardship that everybody in the Soviet Union was experiencing. Most of the Spaniards were working in menial manual jobs with arduous norms and targets to fulfil. There were considerable numbers of Spanish children without parents, killed, missing or imprisoned in the Civil War; at first they were provided with good conditions and education, but as the war worsened they too were set to work, often in grim circumstances. It was natural for them to feel abandoned and increasingly hostile to community leaders like La Pasionaria.

This was fertile ground for Hernández, who had never liked La Pasionaria. He had always considered himself superior to her in intellect and ability, and more deserving in every way to be general secretary of the Party. There was some justice in his claim: he had much more administrative experience, having been minister of education for two years in the Popular Front government under the premierships of both Largo Caballero and Negrín, and subsequently chief commissar of the army's Centre-South region. Hernández was an extraordinary figure by any standards, even among the many exotic people who strode the Spanish stage in the 1930s. He was an intense, hard-working man with an ascetic appearance. His gaunt, bespectacled face had something of the spoilt priest about it. Nothing could have been further from the truth. His early life was highly colourful. Born in the south-eastern province of Murcia, he was brought up in the Basque capital of Bilbao and lived a rackety life, being equally addicted, as one writer puts it, to the three 'p's': politics, pistols and prostitutes. The political atmosphere of Bilbao in the 1920s was violent: disputes were often settled with guns. At the age of only 15, Hernández became a bodyguard to Oscar Pérez Solís, then general secretary of the nascent Communist Party. He was still only 16 when he took part in an assassination attempt on the rising socialist politician Indalecio Prieto, then editor of a Bilbao newspaper. (During the Civil War, they were members of the same cabinet, where Hernández carried on plotting against Prieto, this time successfully albeit non-violently.) He quickly rose in the communist ranks until he was forced to flee the country in 1931 under suspicion of murdering two socialists in a Bilbao restaurant. He went to the Soviet Union where he stayed for two years and was groomed for the starring party role he was to play later in the decade. He was an extrovert and a womaniser who scandalised Party puritans by making off with the beautiful wife of a senior colleague. His impulsive nature helped to lead to his downfall.

It was obvious that nothing could be done in the USSR to further his ambitions. The Comintern's choice was La Pasionaria and contested elections were not the norm under Stalin. Hernández reckoned his best chance of taking over the PCE was to appeal to the exiles in Latin America. The obstacles were immense, not least merely getting out of the war-torn USSR. At the start of his exile in Moscow, Hernández had been placed on a five-man committee to supervise the PCE in Latin America. He had tried to travel there in 1940 but had been forced to turn back by the Nazi advance through Europe. Two years later the deaths of José Díaz and Pedro Checa, who was in charge of the Party organisation, left Hernández the senior member of the committee. It was high time that Moscow re-established control over the Latin American comrades, who were taking an increasingly independent line, notably over the Manifesto of National Union. It was also believed that the PCE's efforts to send its members back into Spain to link up with the underground resistance had been infiltrated by US intelligence operating through agents in the American Communist Party with which the Spanish in Latin America insisted on co-operating against Moscow's wishes. The Americans passed on the names to Madrid, and Franco's security services had no trouble in picking up the communists when they reached Spain.

Hernández set off for Mexico, ostensibly with the task of sorting out things there. But his real purpose was to start a revolt against La Pasionaria. His plot is sometimes called 'Operation Lux', after the Hotel Lux in Moscow where many Spanish and other exiles lived. It was a natural focus of discontent and the conspiracies beloved of the Left. Hernández had the support of many of the Spaniards who lived there and also of the Comintern's second-in-command, Dmitri Manuilski, with whom he had started planning his trip in 1942. It was not until the summer of 1943, however, that conditions had eased sufficiently for him to be able to set off for Latin America.

In the meantime, the Comintern had been dissolved. The organisation that had nurtured Communist Parties all over the world, and had been such a crucial promoter and protector of La Pasionaria, had been declared by Stalin to have outlived its usefulness. It was all part of his efforts to show his wartime allies they had nothing to fear from Moscow. He would no longer be pulling the strings of puppet Communist Parties, which would instead sink or swim by their own efforts. Only the gullible were deceived. Moscow's control continued in other ways.

Did La Pasionaria suspect Hernández's plot? It may well be that she did, or that someone tipped her off. For her would-be successor had company on his long and accident-prone journey to Mexico: Francisco Antón. On the face of it, this was easily explained: Antón was also on the Latin American supervisory committee and was a senior member of the PCE directorate. But as La Pasionaria's lover it is likely that he played a crucial role in foiling Hernández. The saga that ensued after this pair left Moscow contained many elements of farce. They had a tortuous journey, waiting two months in

Vladivostock, a fate to test the most ardent revolutionary, for a ship to Canada. Their passage through North America was rudely interrupted by the US immigration service, who viewed Hernández with the deepest suspicion and proposed sending him back to Russia. Only a public campaign on his behalf rescued him: he and Antón were grudgingly allowed to proceed south after a month in detention. (The US authorities also kept an eye on communications to La Pasionaria from Latin America, intercepting her mail and, if they thought it worthy of wider distribution, passing on the contents to other security services, such as Britain's. For instance, in February 1943, the British embassy in Washington was passed the contents of a letter to La Pasionaria which had been intercepted by the US censorship authorities. It was from a sympathiser in Havana passing on information he had gleaned about conditions inside Spain from four people recently there. He described a bitterly anti-Franco atmosphere among the middle-class and the clergy, the majority of the Spanish people anxious for an Allied victory, and severe shortages, with the suspicion that food and other supplies were being diverted to Germany. But the Foreign Office did not consider the letter to be 'of any special interest'.[1])

When Hernández and Antón finally got to Mexico, things did not improve. Hernández's objective was to force an election for the post of general secretary, which was in theory still vacant. La Pasionaria had been nominated by the central committee to take over but the membership, scattered as it was around the USSR and Latin America, had not yet been consulted. Hernández had a complicated manoeuvre to perform: he had to mount his anti-Pasionaria campaign and win the support of the PCE's leaders in Latin America, Vicente Uribe and Antonio Mije; but he was also highly critical of their political effectiveness and planned a putsch against them in turn. He failed in both objectives. Uribe, a former Cortes deputy and editor of *Mundo Obrero*, and Mije were old comrades of Hernández from the Civil War but were jealous of interference in the empire they had built up in Latin America.

Hernández conducted his campaign in the clumsiest possible manner. In a report to Moscow, he claimed that Uribe believed that Antón had fallen for his (Uribe's) wife. This nonsense was presumably concocted to arouse La Pasionaria's rage. Hernández attacked Uribe's and Mije's leadership, particularly their opposition to the National Union Manifesto. His proposal was that he should become general secretary while La Pasionaria was given the figurehead post of Party president. But he only succeeded in alienating everybody and his suave shadow, Francisco Antón, made sure that all his erratic attempts at taking over the Party were blocked. In January 1944 the Party struck back: Hernández was forced to write two 'self-criticisms' before being expelled from the Party in April, accused of being a Trotskyist.

His ally, Enrique Castro, was not so lucky. He had stayed behind in Moscow and as Hernández's closest associate suffered the consequences: he was arraigned by the central committee of the PCE for 'anti-party' activities. In May he had to submit to a virtual trial before the committee, headed by La Pasionaria, plus the Bulgarian Comintern apparatchik Stepanov (real name Mineff), another veteran of the Spanish Civil War, who proposed Castro's expulsion. La Pasionaria supported this while at the same time suggesting Castro be given 'a chance to save himself', a curious echo, as the historian Gregorio Morán points out, of her Catholic upbringing. The hearing was notable for La Pasionaria's only recorded admission of her liaison with Francisco Antón: 'If I have had relations with Antón, I have had them in a normal manner, as communists do' – whatever that might mean.[2] The principal inquisitor was La Pasionaria's protégé Ignacio Gallego, a former leader of the joint socialist-communist youth movement. The inevitable outcome was Castro's expulsion.

La Pasionaria emerges with little credit from the sequel. Castro applied to leave the Soviet Union with his family but La Pasionaria bitterly opposed it, even writing to the Comintern's former head Dimitrov to explain that she believed Castro would 'continue fighting against the Party and our common cause'. The Soviet government chose to take a charitable line with Castro and ignored her request. He was allowed to rejoin Hernández in Mexico, where they set up their own revolutionary party. It never prospered and Castro, who had not surprisingly become disillusioned with communism, soon fell out with his old friend. Hernández never lost faith with revolutionary politics and moved his base of operations to Yugoslavia, where he set up an Independent Spanish Communist Party, hoping that something of Tito's success in forging a separate path from Moscow might rub off on him. It did not. Both he and Castro vented their spleen on the PCE, the Soviet Union and La Pasionaria by writing vitriolic memoirs, which provide valuable insights into the workings of the Spanish Communist Party in the 1930s and 1940s. Castro had the consolation of being allowed to return to Spain in 1963. He died there in 1965. Hernández ended his days running a coffee shop in Mexico City, where he died in 1971. He had never succeeded in dislodging his old rival, La Pasionaria.

CHAPTER THIRTEEN

THE GUERRILLA DREAM

The Spanish communists had a fourth base of operations, besides the USSR, Latin America and clandestine activity in Spain itself. This was France, where a considerable number of members had remained after fleeing over the border at the end of the Civil War. Most lived in the south, as close as possible to their own country. Their headquarters was Toulouse. Many of the Spanish exiles became involved in the French Resistance, and played a courageous and valuable role in fighting the Germans, whom they had extra reason to hate for their key role in Franco's victory which would probably not have been achieved without the active support of the German air force and the massive flow of German arms and supplies to the nationalist side from the start of the Civil War. There were links with the communist resistance inside Spain, but they were generally tenuous because of communications difficulties. Throughout the early 1940s, the PCE in Spain was beset by every difficulty imaginable: many of its members were still in prison or concentration camp, where they none the less maintained a tight organisation and planned for the future; the Franco government kept up its guard and was merciless when it uncovered any underground communist activity; and the country itself was sick of war and offered little encouragement to revolutionaries: most people were too busy struggling to exist, in a country where food and most other commodities were in short supply.

The unofficial leader of the PCE in France (there was no official one) from 1940 was Jesús Monzón, who had flown out of Spain in the same plane as La Pasionaria in February 1939. He had the reputation of sending many people to the firing squad during the Civil War, first as a prosecutor in Bilbao when it was held by the republic, and later as governor of Alicante. He was a larger than life character, flamboyant, extrovert and a notorious womaniser, with a penchant for cloaks, wide-brimmed hats and cigars: after he returned to Spain in 1943, to organise the Communist Party there, a colleague described him as always looking as if he were just off to a bullfight. He was also responsible for the biggest of the many débâcles suffered by the PCE during the 1940s: the Aran valley invasion.

The German retreat throughout Europe in 1944 raised the hopes of Spanish exiles, whatever their party persuasion, that the Franco régime's days might be numbered too. Their optimism was understandable amid the general euphoria over the now-inevitable defeat of Nazism. Surely Franco's fascists would soon go the same way as Hitler's and Mussolini's? The morale of the Spanish communist element of the French Resistance was further bolstered when they took part in a number of successful actions against the German army. La Pasionaria herself wrote in her memoirs: 'We thought that the defeat of Hitler must cause the fall of Franco.' But, she added, it would not happen automatically. International help would be needed.[1] But Monzón and the Spaniards in France were blind to reality. They failed to understand that the political situation in Spain could not be compared to that of France and other countries being liberated from the Nazis. On his secret return to Spain in 1943 Monzón set up a Supreme Junta for National Union, an alliance with which he hoped to attract all anti-Franco forces, on the lines of La Pasionaria's Moscow manifesto. An indication of the fantasy world in which the PCE in exile lived was the announcement by Antonio Mije in Mexico that 70,000 people had demonstrated in Madrid in November on the anniversary of the defence of the city in 1936: it was of course a figment of someone's imagination.

In February 1944 the resistance in Madrid launched a call for 'national insurrection' in which they appealed for a Spanish De Gaulle or Tito to unite the military against Franco. A series of similar proclamations were made during the year as the Germans fell back throughout Europe and the Allied victory became more and more inevitable. Monzón appears to have believed that the Spanish people would rise up and join in the liberation of Europe. In August 1944 he ordered the PCE HQ in Toulouse to start preparing a full-scale attack on Spain. The Party had several thousand members under arms fighting the Germans; now they would switch their attentions to their own country. The location Monzón chose for the assault which he clearly believed would spark the fall of the Franco régime was the Valle de Arán (the Arán valley), which cuts through the Pyrenees in Galicia, north-western Spain. The attack was launched over the frontier on 17 October with a force of more than 5,000 men, infiltrating Spain in a number of different units. The operation was a complete disaster. The communists were trained to fight a guerrilla war and expected the local people to greet them as conquering heroes: instead, they came up against well-organised formations of the Spanish regular army, who had been expecting the attack for some time. They were under the command of General Juan de Yague, who with Franco had ruthlessly suppressed the Asturias rising of 1934 and soldiered through the Civil War. After five years of relative peace he took great pleasure in exterminating some more communists. The remote Arán valley was in any case an odd place to choose for an attack. The guerrillas took over a few small villages but could make no impression on Viella, the valley's principal town. They were badly-equipped, lacked communications or even good maps, and were picked off without mercy by Yague's army. After 11 days they were ordered to retire in disarray back over the Pyrenees. They lost 129 dead and 218 taken prisoner, plus 241 wounded; more in a week and a half than had been suffered in the entire war against the Nazis. The order to retreat came from a young communist leader who had just been instructed to go to France by La Pasionaria to sort out the mess. His name was Santiago Carrillo and he had soon established himself as the new leader of the PCE in France. Eventually he would take over the Party from her.

Santiago Carrillo became the most significant and best-known Spanish communist after La Pasionaria. He also rivalled her in the violent hatred he excited among his countrymen. He was widely regarded as a consummate political operator but also as devious and ruthless in the extreme. He showed these qualities from the very start of a political career which spanned more than half a century, nearly all of it at or near the top of the Spanish communist movement. He came from a political family; his father Wenceslao Carrillo was a socialist deputy and a leading light in the UGT, the socialist trade union organisation. A moderate and close ally of the socialist prime minister Largo Caballero, Wenceslao was director-general of security and under-secretary of the interior during the Civil War, staying in Madrid even when the rest of the government fled to Valencia. Santiago was a political prodigy: nicknamed 'the chrysalis in spectacles' by his opponents, he started out as a socialist like his father and at the age of only 19 became secretary of the Socialist Party's youth wing. At the same age he was jailed for his part in the Asturias uprising. After his release he moved closer to the communists and was one of the principal architects of the union of the socialist and communist youth movements to form the United Socialist Youth (JSU) of which he became the first general secretary when barely 21 years old. At the outbreak of the Civil War he joined the communist Party and the JSU rapidly fell under Communist domination. In November 1936, with Madrid under siege, he was placed in charge of public order in the capital, an immensely powerful position. His performance in this job for the two months that he held it was the source of intense controversy and was at the heart of the hatred he aroused in the nationalist camp. He was held by them to be responsible for a particularly gruesome massacre at the villages of Paracuellos de Jarama and Torrejón de Ardoz, just outside Madrid, when more than 2,000 political prisoners were removed from the city's jails and shot by the republicans, who feared that the capital might be overrun at any moment. Carrillo always denied responsibility for, complicity in or even knowledge of the massacre. Whether or not he personally ordered it, he must have known all about them, as the historian Ian Gibson made clear after a rigorous investigation of the affair.[2] Gibson's conclusion was that Carrillo turned a blind eye to the many murders of nationalists that took place in Madrid during his period in charge.

At the end of the war he was the last communist leader to leave Madrid. He popped up everywhere in the first years of exile – the US, Argentina and North Africa, from where he sent La Pasionaria in Moscow a brief message in late 1944: for two months he had had 60 communists in training and was preparing to land them near Málaga to pursue guerrilla warfare against Franco. Carrillo's plan was to establish a base in the south of Spain and gradually establish links with the other guerrilla groups scattered around the country. It was as ill-conceived a plan as Monzón's and met with a firm rejection from La Pasionaria. She said later that conditions in Spain were not conducive to such a venture.[3] It would have been a mass suicide mission. Carrillo was at first reluctant to obey. La Pasionaria sent him a further order: 'Go to France to work with the Party leadership.' Carrillo did so, with a bad grace but, Pasionaria claimed, he later recognised that she was right. Carrillo's immediate task was to close down the Arán valley operation and salvage what he could.

As 1945 dawned, the PCE leaders in Moscow and Latin America

141

prepared to move to France. The need to do so was becoming urgent. After the disaster of the Arán valley, which was in part due to the Moscow-based leaders' inability to control events on the ground in France, it was imperative to regain command there. Party organisation and morale had to be restored and La Pasionaria and her comrades could now move around freely in newly-liberated France where the domestic Communist Party was highly influential.

In the Europe of 1945 there was a deep feeling that with the collapse of the Nazi empire there was all to play for. Despite the setback in the Arán valley, the Spanish communists were still optimistic that the redrawing of the European map would be to their advantage. Surely the Franco régime, isolated and friendless, could not survive much longer? France was the place to be, as close as possible to home. What the opposition in exile failed to realise was that Franco's very isolation would work to his advantage. With everything else there was to do in Europe, the Allies just did not care what happened on the other side of the Pyrenees provided Franco behaved himself. Restoring democracy in Spain came very low on the post-war agenda; it faded even further in importance compared to Spain's strategic importance as the US and Britain moved from world war against Germany to cold war against the USSR.

But that development was still well in the future as La Pasionaria planned her departure from Russia and her move to France. She had reckoned without a powerful enemy, which had no wish to see her return to the West: the British Government. In November 1944 she applied to the French embassy in Moscow for visas for herself, Amaya and Amaya's boyfriend Ignacio Gallego, a rising figure in the PCE, who was described on the visa application as La Pasionaria's secretary. The French granted the visas and she then applied to the British embassy for transit visas to enable them to travel via Iraq and possibly Palestine, both then under British control, to France. The British ambassador, Sir Archibald Clark Kerr, referred the request to London, mentioning that 'Madame Ibárruri's' stated reason for the journey was that she found the Russian climate unsuitable and wished to live in France until she could return to Spain.

The Foreign Office did not welcome this hot potato. The first official to see Clark Kerr's telegram minuted:

If the French embassy have granted a travel warrant, presumably the French Government have no objection to the return of 'La Pasionaria' to

France. Our policy up to now is *not* to encourage Spanish émigré politicians to travel to France. La Pasionaria would undoubtedly start stirring up trouble there.

His superior commented:

I agree. While we would welcome the replacement of General Franco's Govmt by a moderate régime, we do not want revolution and La Pasionaria is a revolutionary. Besides, her arrival in France would, by playing on the Spaniards' fear of revolution, be likely to have the immediate effect of bolstering up General Franco's position, as did the disturbances on the Franco-Spanish frontier [presumably a reference to the Arán valley débâcle].

He finished on a typically Foreign Office note:

I recommend that Sir A. Clark Kerr should be instructed to refuse the applications and that Mr Duff Cooper [British ambassador in Paris] should be instructed to inform the French Government that we are taking this line. To the French Government we can explain that we do not wish to further the cause of revolution or to bolster up General Franco. If the Soviet Government intervenes, we can make the second point only.

Mr Frank Roberts, acting head of the FO's Central Department, added:

The Spanish ambassador has recently made it clear to Sir A. Cadogan [Permanent Secretary of State at the FO] that the Spanish Government object to facilities being given to their political opponents . . . Sir A. Cadogan approved that principle . . . I therefore agree that we should refuse transit or other facilities (although what we have to do with Iraqi visas is a mystery to me) but without giving any reasons unless specifically asked for them.

Mr O. C. Harvey, Under-secretary in the Central Department, minuted:

I see advantage in refusing these visas unless we are strongly pressed by the Quai d'Orsay themselves . . . We do not want France to become a stamping ground for all Spanish Republican leaders at a time when their presence can only disturb security in France and strengthen Franco in Spain . . .

Clark Kerr was instructed to reject La Pasionaria's party's applications. The FO telegram added:

For your own information, HMG are opposed to facilitating the journey

143

of exiled Spanish politicians and agitators to France where their presence can only disturb security, while strengthening the position of General Franco in Spain by the fear they are likely to inspire of a further revolutionary outbreak.

Someone had noted in the margin of the file: 'Need Sir A. Clark Kerr give any reason?' Harvey replied: 'No. But there are plenty of other routes by which this party can get from USSR to France.'

Clark Kerr was still slightly anxious. He cabled back:

> Strictly speaking, we cannot I suppose refuse Iraqi visas without consulting the Iraqi Government. I propose therefore we say that the Government of Palestine have refused visas.

The FO contacted the Colonial Office whose response was that they 'would at least like to inform the Palestine Government that their name has been taken in vain'.

Such were the lengths to which the British Government was willing to go to keep La Pasionaria out of France. But it was not only the Foreign Office who were interested in her movements: on 22 December Roger Hollis wrote to the FO from 'Box 500, Parliament Street' (ie MI5) to mention that the *Daily Herald* had recently carried a little story to the effect that La Pasionaria would shortly be leaving Moscow for France. 'So far I have not been able to obtain confirmation of this statement,' wrote Hollis (who rose to become head of MI5 and after his death was the subject of speculation, never substantiated, that he might have been a Soviet agent). He was brought up to date with the FO's latest machinations towards La Pasionaria.[4]

The FO managed to keep her in the Soviet Union against her will for two months but they could not do so indefinitely. In February 1945 they had to relent because France granted her a visa on condition that she did not indulge in political activities. Mr Harvey cabled Clark Kerr in Moscow:

> In the circumstances I do not feel justified in continuing to refuse transit facilities across British and British-controlled territories. You may therefore grant the necessary visas.[5]

Before leaving the Soviet Union, La Pasionaria had a meeting with Stalin in the Kremlin on 23 February at which she thanked him for his support during her years of exile and asked him to help arm the Spanish resistance in France and Spain. Stalin agreed. She was delighted. It was now all the more important to get to France as quickly as possible. She contacted Negrín in Paris, for he was still the head of the Spanish republican government in exile and La Pasionaria was still pursuing her dream of National Union.

The journey eventually took two months. With Amaya, now 21, and Ignacio Gallego she flew to Tehran in a Soviet military aircraft, via Stalingrad and Baku. After a week in the Persian capital, she found a plane to take them to Baghdad and on to Cairo, the centre of Allied military operations in the Middle East. She hoped to be able to book a sea passage to France but there turned out to be none available: the war was still on and German submarines were still active in the Mediterranean. La Pasionaria's daily visits to the offices of Thomas Cook were fruitless. Weeks passed. She busied herself sightseeing but grew more and more impatient. Finally Thomas Cook came up with a French cargo ship carrying cotton, they hoped, to Marseilles. The British Government was now prepared to help her to get to France. The British ambassador in Cairo, Lord Killearn, cabled London on 17 March:

> French Legation have requested assistance of this embassy in securing sea passages to North Africa or France for Madame Dolores Gómez, Mme Amaya Ruiz Ibárruri and M. Ignacio Gallego Bezales, Spanish nationals from Moscow who are authorised to enter France.
>
> With the agreement of the British military security authorities passages have been applied for to competent authorities and it is probable that party will leave for Algiers by the end of March. You will probably wish to have prior warning of it as S.I.M.E. [Secret Intelligence Middle East] state that Madame Gómez is in fact 'La Pasionaria'.[6]

British Intelligence may have thought that La Pasionaria was travelling under a pseudonym to avoid recognition. They probably misunderstood (as many non-Spaniards do) the Spanish custom of using both paternal and maternal surnames.[7]

It was only several days into the journey that La Pasionaria discovered that the ship's destination was in fact Boulogne, not Marseilles. (British Intelligence notified London of her departure on 26 March, not for Algiers, but directly for 'Northern France'.[8]

They negotiated the Mediterranean safely, despite the frequent presence of mines, and passing through the Straits of Gibraltar she had the emotional experience of seeing her native country for the first time for six years but being unable to enter it. So near and yet so far.

Their long journey nearly came to a nasty end off the Isle of Wight, of all places, when their ship collided with a Polish ship in heavy fog. The passengers and crew were about to embark in the lifeboats when the captain appeared to announce that the ship had been holed above the waterline; it was not in danger of sinking. Thus passed La Pasionaria's closest opportunity to set foot in Britain. (She never did: post-war British governments proved as reluctant as pre-war ones to allow her into the United Kingdom.) For eight days she stayed on board ship in the English Channel while it was repaired. When it finally approached Boulogne it was discovered that the port had been completely destroyed during the war and the ship could not dock. La Pasionaria and her party had to travel the last mile in a motor boat before being helped ashore by British sailors.[9]

It was late April and the war in Europe was about to end. When La Pasionaria reached Paris, she found that Negrín had gone – to Mexico. Her hopes of a united front against Franco were dashed. But she was still able to celebrate the end of the war in Paris amid the delirious French, along with Santiago Carrillo and various other old Spanish colleagues. There was no better place to mark the end of what had been for La Pasionaria a hard and tragic conflict – no better place, that is, apart from her beloved Spain.

In the immediate aftermath of the war the Spanish communists' euphoria rose even further. After a decade of siege, retreat and defeat, the future suddenly looked decidedly rosy. Fascism had been crushed, the Soviet Union was triumphant, the exploits of the Red Army were already legendary and all over Europe, both eastern and western, communists and socialists were poised to reap the political harvest. In France and Italy communists formed part of new coalition governments; in eastern Europe, communists were setting up Soviet puppet governments under the protection of the Red Army; in Britain Attlee's Labour Party swept even Winston Churchill out of office on a tide of hope of a new classless society being rebuilt from the ashes of war. In such an atmosphere, how could the Franco régime in Spain survive for much longer? So reasoned the Spanish communists, converging on France to assist the dictator towards the exit.

Santiago Carrillo was effective head of the Party in France and he knew that the key to his further progress up the Party ladder lay in maintaining good relations with La Pasionaria. He found her a house in Paris, with servants and bodyguards[10] but she soon moved down to Toulouse, where the PCE had its headquarters, appropriately in the Rue d'Espagne. The southern city had become the centre for exiled republicans of all parties and for the guerrillas who crossed into Spain to fight. Spanish could be heard as frequently as French in the streets. La Pasionaria's daughter Amaya remembered this as an exhilarating period in their lives. For all those Spaniards who had been in the maquis or in German concentration camps (where many had suffered and died) it was a time of liberation, when they could once more live in freedom and a Spanish atmosphere, and look forward to returning home before too long. 'It was a marvellous period. There was great enthusiasm. We thought Spain was about to change,' Amaya recalled. 'There were lots of meetings and a very active political life.'[11] She was then 22 and threw herself into working with the Party's youth movement.

Meanwhile her mother was reliving the great days of the mid-1930s when she had first electrified the progressive world with her impassioned speeches. It was back to the Winter Velodrome in Paris, scene of some of her greatest oratorical triumphs, to harangue the World Syndical Congress with a typical call to international solidarity, with much fond reminiscing about the foreigners who had fought for the republic with the International Brigades. It was as if La Pasionaria was stuck in a time warp, almost as if the Second World War had never happened. The line-up of delegates and observers recalled too the progressive parades of the 1930s: H.G. Wells, Aldous Huxley, Jacob Epstein and Professor J.B.S. Haldane were among them.

The Spanish communists' optimism lasted longer than political reality warranted, a characteristic failing from their earliest days. At the Potsdam conference in July Stalin submitted a memorandum on Spain which proposed that the allies broke off all relations with Franco and aided 'Spanish democratic forces' to bring about a political régime according to the people's wishes. Churchill and Truman both emphasised that they had no love for Franco but opposed breaking off relations with him. Churchill thought such action would rally support to Franco, who was in his opinion 'fast weakening'. Truman said it was for Spain to sort out her own affairs. The Allied leaders were much more preoccupied with what was happening behind what was soon to be called the Iron Curtain than what was going on beyond the Pyrenees. All they agreed on in the final communiqué was that Franco's Spain should not be admitted to the United Nations. Already the first breezes of the cold war were being felt and they would bring no comfort to the Spanish Communist Party.

On 9 December 1945 La Pasionaria celebrated her 50th birthday and the PCE paid homage to her in lavish fashion, combining the occasion with a Party Plenum. She addressed 3,000 people in the Gaumont Cinema, Toulouse. One of those present was Pablo Picasso; it was the first time La Pasionaria had met him. Flanked by Carrillo and Antón on the podium, she compared the Party in her speech to an army coming together after years of dispersal after an 'unjust defeat' to regroup and prepare for 'new and decisive battles'. They were ready to start again, as in 1936; and they were ready once more for the armed struggle.

The cult of the personality was in full swing in the world communist movement. If Stalin was the Soviet Union's object of adoration, the PCE's was undoubtedly La Pasionaria. Every year between 1945 and 1956 the central committee met to mark her birthday with an orgy of adulation in language which scarcely varied: 'our guide and leader', 'forger of our Party' and so on. This phenomenon was noted by the young communist writer and intellectual Jorge Semprún, who had just emerged from two years in Ravensbruck concentration camp, and was to become one of the PCE's most important and controversial figures (he was finally expelled in 1964 along with another intellectual, Fernando Claudín, for their free-thinking ways). 'In that era,' Semprún wrote, 'La Pasionaria's birthdays were the occasion of collective ceremonies of the said cult. And cantos, odes, elegies, couplets and other poetic monstrosities formed an obligatory part of the anthology of religious fervour which was offered to Dolores on those occasions.' Semprún himself embarked on a long poem in her honour, which he remembered with some embarrassment in later life (he tore it up unfinished). He recalled an edition of a communist cultural magazine in the early 1950s containing the ringing declaration, 'Today it is the Communist Party which lives, grows and has a tomorrow. And Dolores Ibárruri is the symbol, and the incarnation of that better tomorrow, the farsighted guide who is leading the Party towards the victorious goal.' Almost all the poems in the magazine, *Cuadernos de Cultura*, were dedicated to La Pasionaria.[12]

The quasi-religious devotion towards La Pasionaria by a Party which was by its very nature atheistic remained a strong theme throughout her life. Semprún remarked on the latest manifestation of this phenomenon. Many Spanish communists, he wrote, called their sons Rubén, after La Pasionaria's dead son, Rubén Ruiz.

His death came to form part of the obligatory reference points of communist rhetoric. The religious, Christlike resonances of the use of the event are obvious. The son of God was made man to redeem us . . . through his death. And the son of Pasionaria made himself a fighter of a regiment of the Red Guard to save us from Fascism. His death is an exemplary sacrifice. The Christlike theme of Rubén Ruiz's death features in all the odes, cantos and elegies of that epoch. It figured in my verses.[13]

The constant repetition of religious imagery to describe La Pasionaria is the product of the deep influence the Catholic Church retained on Spanish people, even those who claimed to have rejected the faith in favour of communism, socialism, anarchism or whatever. More than one old friend said of her: 'Dolores was always a believer.'

She moved back to Paris, it being thought vital for the leadership to stay close to the other republican parties, which were based in the capital. The communists, with the active encouragement of Moscow, were determined to keep alive the idea of an anti-Franco coalition embracing all ideologies, from Left to Right. The French Communist Party found a house for La Pasionaria and Amaya in Champigny and the PCE took offices in the Avenue Kléber, an address which, Semprún wrote later, acquired mystical overtones to devotees like himself. He remembered his first sight of La Pasionaria there, in 1947, sweeping in and giving everyone present a cheerful greeting. He was so inspired that he went off to start writing his poem to her.[14]

The communists developed a two-pronged strategy. They supported the notion of an anti-Franco coalition; in March 1946 Santiago Carrillo joined the cabinet of José Giral's republican government-in-exile. But at the same time the communists kept up their guerrilla operations within Spain, despite their notable lack of results. They maintained their optimistic line about Franco's imminent collapse. At a meeting of the central committees of the Party and the communist-controlled PSUC, the United Socialist Party of Catalonia, La Pasionaria delivered a memorable example of overblown rhetoric: 'The German defeat at Stalingrad engraved [the wall of] the Palace of El Pardo, Madrid, with the powerful victors' hand, the tragic end, the biblical MENE, MENE, TEKEL, UPHARSIN which announced to the caudillo the collapse of his terrorist power.'[15] But the reality in 1947 was otherwise: as the cold war intensified and Soviet control over Eastern Europe deepened, Churchill and Truman were beginning to look on Franco as a comforting bulwark against communism in his part of the world. They certainly did not regard La Pasionaria as a preferable alternative.

By 1947 communism's short-lived resurgence in Western Europe was coming to an end. In that year they were driven out of coalition governments in Belgium, France and Italy. The Spanish communists departed the government-in-exile after a bitter row with their old enemies, the socialists. In March 1947, La Pasionaria opened another Party Plenum in Montreuil, in the Paris suburbs, with the usual declaration that they were in the 'dying moments' of the Franco régime.

> Francoism, mortally wounded, is crumbling and democratic Spain rises from its prostration. The workers' organisations, which Franco brutally dissolved, are being rebuilt in secret; [there are] strikes and protest demonstrations against hunger; hundreds of illegal newspapers are being published; the peasants resist Francoism.[16]

(Writing in 1976-7, Jorge Semprún wryly noted feeling a 'strange sensation' on re-reading her words: 'Isn't it just what was being said 30 years later, just before Franco's death?')[17]

The apotheosis of La Pasionaria as cult object of worship came on 20 July 1947 at a huge rally organised by the PCE in the Parc des Sports, Toulouse. It was attended by 40,000 Spanish exiles and the atmosphere was one of enjoyment and hope. It was not merely a succession of speeches (although there were plenty of those) but a day out in the sunshine and a celebration of Spanish culture, with dancing, singing and parades. The speakers' platform was dominated by huge portraits of La Pasionaria, staring beatifically into the distance, and José Díaz, dead these five years past but looking very much alive. Above them was the slogan 'Viva La República', while the park was ringed with more huge portraits, of Stalin and the other members of the PCE's central committee, gazing down on the festive Spaniards, swigging their red wine, chewing their sausages and dreaming of a prompt return home. A succession of delegations – the old and the young, party cadres and Civil War veterans – ascended to the platform bearing flowers and presents to pay homage to the beaming figure of La Pasionaria, goddess of all she surveyed, bestowing embraces and blessings on her devoted tribespeople.

But it was an Indian summer, not a Spanish spring and La Pasionaria recognised it in her speech. The Americans were the target of her hatred, as the British and French had been during the Civil War. She reminded her audience that 'the first imperialist war was organised by the yankees against Spain to wrest Cuba and the Philippines from them.' She fulminated against 'certain exile groups' who thought Spain should apply for Marshall Plan aid even though Franco was still in power. Her theme now was 'Spain for the Spanish', free of foreign (ie US, not Soviet) interference. There was more than a touch of desperation about her peroration:

> It is true that exile weighs heavily and breaks one's spirits. But we shall return to Spain, comrades, and we shall return to a liberated Spain!

In fact, she was soon moving in the opposite direction. In the autumn she was in Stockholm for a congress of anti-fascist women in solidarity with republican Spain. By 1948, with the cold war well under way, she was back, not in Spain, but in Moscow.

In October 1948 La Pasionaria, Francisco Antón and Santiago Carrillo were summoned to the Soviet capital to an audience with Stalin himself. This was unprecedented; the great helmsman had rarely bothered himself with the Spanish communists since the end of the Civil War. He had visited the sick José Díaz in hospital towards the end of his life and had called La Pasionaria in to wish her well before her return to France in 1945. But to invite three of the top four of the PCE (Vicente Uribe was the only absentee) was a novelty and meant that something serious was afoot. That something was the independent line from the Kremlin that Tito was taking in Yugoslavia and which came to a head in 1948. Stalin was afraid that the virus of Titoism might affect other European Communist Parties and he had good reason to be specially concerned about the Spaniards, who were normally so loyal to the Kremlin's line. For in February 1948 an extraordinary episode had occurred: Santiago Carrillo, accompanied by Enrique Líster, had visited Yugoslavia to ask Tito for help in the fight against Franco.

Carrillo was not merely seeking moral or financial support; he wanted arms and more besides: he wanted Yugoslavia to send troops to fight alongside the Spanish communist guerrillas. Guerrilla operations inside Spain had not been going well. There were occasional bombings and killings, but nothing on a scale to dent the régime's growing confidence. But Carrillo, far removed from the reality of Spain, still thought a military attack could spark off a general uprising against Franco. He suggested to the Yugoslavs that they should drop paratroopers in the Levante region, on the east coast, who would link up with communist guerrillas on the ground and create a nucleus of resistance to the régime which would lead to its eventual downfall. Carrillo also cited 'good communications with France', particularly by sea, as a reason for launching an attack in the Levante.

It was all the purest fantasy, and the Yugoslavs did not take long to realise it. Besides, they had enough on their plate as it was, their rupture with Moscow being imminent. The first question they asked the Spaniards was: 'Have you discussed this with the Russians?' When they replied that they had not, the Yugoslavs exchanged amused glances, which were not lost on Líster and Carrillo. The Spaniards were invited to go off and inspect various tourist sites for a fortnight while their request was 'studied'. When they returned to Belgrade, they were told they had been turned down for 'technical reasons', which did not convince Líster, for one. They were packed off with a gift of $30,000 while their hosts turned their attention to more practical matters.[18] Stalin would presumably soon have heard about the trip from his intelligence agencies and the unexpected news would not have pleased him, given his state of paranoia about Tito's rebellion. Thus the 'invitation' of La Pasionaria and her associates to the Kremlin.

At the meeting Stalin was accompanied by his foreign minister Molotov, the party's chief ideologue Mikhail Suslov and the military expert Marshall Kliment Voroshilov. The reason for the summons soon became clear. Stalin had had enough of the PCE's pointless guerrilla war and wanted a change of tactic. He did not put it quite as brutally as that but his drift was clear: could the Spanish comrades explain, he asked, why they were not working within mass organisations inside Spain, particularly the trade unions? Until now, the PCE had refused to have anything to do with the unions because they were controlled by the government. Stalin was therefore proposing an abrupt change of direction; but at first the Spaniards were either unwilling or unable to grasp the point. They expressed their hostility to having anything to do with the Francoist unions and praised the heroic efforts of their guerrillas. Doodling on a pad in front of him and never raising his voice, Stalin gave them a history lesson in revolutionary tactics. The bolsheviks had worked patiently inside tsarist organisations for years before making their decisive moves, he said. The clear message was that if it was good enough for the bolsheviks, it was good enough for the Spanish communists. The guerrillas should be a supporting arm for the political struggle, not its chief expression.

La Pasionaria, Antón and Carrillo (particularly the latter, as he was in charge of guerrilla operations) were not convinced. Blinded as they were by their hatred of Franco, they still thought the Generalíssimo was not much longer for this world. A brutal old dictator like Stalin could perhaps see otherwise. 'Patience,' he repeated, 'patience.' Seeing that the Spaniards were not getting the message, he changed the subject to less important matters. Tea, cakes and sweets were served. The penny dropped when the Spanish trio met afterwards to discuss what Stalin had said. After lengthy analysis, they came to the conclusion that Stalin was right. Given their previous history of toeing the line, this was not a surprising outcome.

The Spanish delegation returned to Paris (with a further handsome cash gift to add to that of the Yugoslavs) and reported to the Politburo, who were not at first convinced that Stalin's analysis was correct. Whether it was or not, there was not much point in disobeying it if the PCE wanted to survive as a viable political force, for without Soviet backing it would soon have disintegrated. The guerrilla war was slowly wound down, not without protest and some vicious score- settling. According to Líster, Carrillo had many guerrillas murdered for 'treason' against the Party: indeed, he accused Carrillo and Antón of a reign of terror against anyone thought to be disloyal to them.

After he split from the PCE in 1970 to set up his own hard-line Communist splinter party, Enrique Líster went public with his allegations against Carrillo, Antón – and La Pasionaria. He bluntly accused Carrillo and La Pasionaria of ordering the murder in 1945 of a veteran communist activist, Gabriel León Trilla, who had stayed on in Spain after the civil war to pursue guerrilla warfare against Franco's regime. Trilla's body was found in a Madrid cemetery; he had been stabbed to death. Carrillo denounced Trilla as an 'agent provocateur' and said he had been 'liquidated' by another communist guerrilla, Cristino García, who was arrested in Spain the same year. He was sentenced to death and executed in February 1946. Líster claimed Trilla was an honest communist whose memory had been traduced by Carrillo. Líster said that another ex-guerrilla, Antonio Núñez Balsera, described to him in 1971 in Sofia how Carrillo and La Pasionaria had ordered him, in Toulouse in 1945, to go to Madrid and pass on their order to Cristino García to execute Trilla personally. When Núñez contacted him, García had refused to carry out the order, saying he was a revolutionary not a murderer, and told two

153

members of his gang to kill Trilla, which they did. (They were later executed too).

Líster also accused Carrillo of organising the death of other guerrillas: Luis Montero, who was active in Asturias from 1945-48, and José San José, who was sent back into Spain in 1944. Líster's charge sheet does not end there: he claimed Carrillo and Antón also ordered a party loyalist, whom Líster referred to only as 'G', to 'liquidate' Jesús Hernández in Mexico in 1946 (the operation was a failure) and of wanting to eliminate Líster himself and Juán Modesto, another civil war military leader in exile. Líster said that Carrillo only pulled back from the brink when Stalin praised Líster and Modesto at a meeting. In his support, Líster called up the memory of his fellow PCE leader Vicente Uribe, whose fall from grace was engineered by Carrillo in the early 1950s. Líster said Uribe revealed details of Carrillo's murderous intrigues in Prague in 1961. Líster was also enraged by the way Carrillo blackened the names of PCE guerrilla leaders such as Jesús Monzón (architect of the Arán Valley disaster, who eventually fell into the hands of Franco's police and was imprisoned for many years), Heriberto Quiñones (executed by firing squad in Madrid in October 1942) and Joan Comorera, leader of the clandestine Communist Party in Catalonia, whom Carrillo accused of being a traitor and expelled from the Party in 1951. Comorera stayed on in Barcelona until he was arrested in 1954. Condemned to 30 years' imprisonment, he died in Burgos prison in 1958. Carrillo saw conspiracies against him everywhere and accused all three of being enemy agents: Monzón of being in the pay of the USA (as well as being a 'Titoist'), Quiñones of Britain and Comorera of France. There was little or no evidence against them, and much testimony from fellow guerrillas and prisoners that all were brave men who were tortured by Franco's secret police and two of whom gave their lives for the Communist cause.[19]

As a lifelong Stalinist, Líster's credentials as a friend of freedom and an opponent of purges are questionable; but support for his claims came from Jorge Semprún, the writer and intellectual, who belonged to a more liberal wing of the Party. 'Both "Monzonism" and "Titoism" were inventions of Stalin's Special Services,' he wrote later. He too accused Carrillo directly of having Trilla murdered. The truth would never be known, he wrote, because the victims were dead 'and from the other side, the side of the autonomous and inventive executors of Stalin's policy in the Spanish Communist Party, can it reasonably be expected that anyone will speak?'

Semprún added (he was writing in 1977, the year of La Pasionaria's return to Spain):

La Pasionaria will doubtless die without saying a word. She has not come back to Spain to speak, to tell bloody and miserable truths about the past. She has come back to Spain to die. And she will die without saying a word.[20]

He was absolutely right.

By 1948, La Pasionaria's health had begun to deteriorate. She was soon on her way back to Moscow, where in December she had an operation on her gall bladder. It was successful but complications set in: she contracted a severe lung infection which she could not shake off. Only constant applications of oxygen kept her alive. Antibiotics, were then in their infancy and most were extremely hard to obtain, but thanks to a friendly ambassador, a supply of streptomycin was brought from the United States (the irony of it) but without success: only penicillin appeared to have any effect. The Soviets were clearly anxious not to lose La Pasionaria: doctors were summoned from all over the USSR to treat her. Even Stalin himself paid her the singular honour of a visit; he ordered the nurses to make sure she recovered. She did, but it was a long business; she was in hospital for six months, and it is probably true to say that her illness marked the beginning of the end of her career as a leader of the very first rank. The initiative passed to the younger generation, based in Paris, and although she remained general secretary of the PCE until 1960 she was never quite the same formidable force again.

Health was certainly a factor but there may have been an equally important one: the psychological blow of losing her lover, Francisco Antón. In December 1948, the month of her operation, La Pasionaria was 53 years old, Antón in his mid-30s. Antón had stayed on in Paris where he had been taking a keen interest in a young colleague named Carmen Rodriguez, a Party member, fellow exile and by all accounts an attractive and vivacious young woman, whom he had known since 1947. The romance blossomed and in 1949 they were married. (They were to have two children, the second of them handicapped.) There is no official record of La Pasionaria's reaction to Antón's desertion – she made no mention of her relationship with him in any of her books or in any interview – but her actions in the following years suggested that she was deeply embittered by his rejection of her. There was only one way she could exact revenge on him and that was to attack him politically via the Party apparatus. That is what she did, in the early 1950s.

La Pasionaria's situation then, as the 1940s ended, was not an enviable one. She had only just recovered from a life-threatening illness; she was back in the USSR (a country which despite her devotion to communism she never really liked living in); her hopes of returning to her native country in triumph, which had been so high in 1945, had been dashed; as the cold war intensified, Franco looked more secure than at any time since 1939; she was isolated from her colleagues in Paris; and in her mid-50s she had been abandoned by her lover. She cut an increasingly lonely, isolated and anachronistic figure.

CHAPTER FOURTEEN

ANTÓN'S DOWNFALL

On 7 September 1950, the Spanish Communist Party in exile was declared illegal by the French government. The cold war was at its height; the Korean War had started that summer; and suspicion of communists in the West was intense. Where would their loyalties lie in the event of hostilities with the Soviet Union? It was by no means an idle fear; the general secretary of the French Communist Party, La Pasionaria's old friend Maurice Thorez, had hinted earlier in the year that French communists might well place loyalty to the movement ahead of country. The Spanish communists, organised, active and devoted to Stalin, formed a potential fifth column which the French government considered it could do without. A mass round-up ensued, and many Spaniards were deported to camps in French North Africa and Corsica. The leadership in France, headed by Carrillo and Antón, was forced into semi-clandestinity. They themselves avoided arrest because they were tipped off by their colleagues in the French Communist Party, who heard about the forthcoming purge. Líster, for example, had been living away from home for a month when the blow fell. The main effect was that the Party's operations were severely disrupted, and communications with Moscow, which were never speedy, were hampered further still. This meant that La Pasionaria, who was still convalescing in the Soviet capital, was in danger of becoming even more isolated from what was going on in France. Alarm grew in the PCE's various Eastern European redoubts (it had a strong presence in Prague, where some of its leading figures, including Vicente Uribe and Antonio Mije, fled after the crackdown in France, as well as Moscow) about the virtual collapse of the Party in France, which left it even more remote from Spain than it already was. There was intense anger towards Carrillo and Antón, particularly for failing to foresee the coming purge and make adequate preparation for a life of illegality. Carrillo made swift and adroit moves to accept some blame while looking to the future. The man who was made the scapegoat for the setback was Antón, on whom La Pasionaria was now to take ample revenge for his unfaithfulness to her.

It is an extraordinary episode, which can have few, if any, parallels in modern political history. Antón, who was in charge of Party organisation in France, received the first inkling of his fate when he was called to Moscow towards the end of 1951 to be accused of behaving in a dictatorial fashion by La Pasionaria herself, his former lover, and the rest of the ruling Politburo. He had such a torrid time that he came out in a rash and returned to Paris a broken man.

But his ordeal was only just beginning: in August 1952 he was, effectively, put on trial for his political 'errors' by those members of the Politburo still in Paris. True to form, the proceedings opened with an abject self-criticism from the accused, in which he praised 'comrade Dolores's . . . exceptional leadership qualities . . . [she is] indisput-able chief of the Party'. Antón confessed to serious misconduct because he had been 'blinded by pride'. He went through his life story, analysing his defects and repeatedly praising comrade Dolores's 'clear-sightedness' and the wisdom of her remedy, which was (inevitably) to 'study political problems and our Marxist-Leninist-Stalinist theory'. There was no limit to Antón's self-abasement, a fact that is perhaps surprising when one considers that he was under no obligation to incriminate himself; as a Spaniard living, albeit illegally now, in France he was in no danger of being tortured or otherwise physically abused to extract a confession, as happened behind the Iron Curtain. And yet he 'confessed' all in the most abject manner. The only plausible reason, apart from dogged devotion to the Party, is that Antón somehow feared being sent back to Spain, where a far grimmer fate would have awaited him.

Worse was to come. He was summoned back to a second hearing, on 8 August 1952, at which Carrillo turned on him, accusing him of 'vanity, egotism . . . and . . . a battle against the comrades in the Party leadership who lived outside [France]' – a clear reference to La Pasionaria. Antón meekly agreed, accusing himself of 'totally divisive conduct, without any mitigating circumstances'. The outcome of the session was that Antón was ordered to produce a written self-criticism, which would be forwarded to Moscow to be judged by none other than La Pasionaria herself. A month later Antón produced this document, which makes pathetic reading. He admitted what he termed his duplicity, ambition and divisive behaviour against the

Party. He said he had only wanted La Pasionaria to leave Paris for Moscow because of the 'grave danger which threatened her' (ie a supposed plot to assassinate her). He admitted to expelling some 2,000 members from the Party since 1946 (even providing a year-by-year breakdown of the numbers). He concluded by blaming his petty-bourgeois upbringing for his faults and put himself at the Party's disposal for whatever penalty it might impose. But his ordeal was a long way from being over. La Pasionaria's verdict, relayed to Paris several months later, was that more investigation was needed. It was a classic Stalinist tactic: to demand that the victim humiliate himself still further, to squeeze out more 'confessions'. La Pasionaria even raised the stakes still further by floating the idea that her former lover might be some sort of enemy agent. The sole 'evidence' for this was that he had purportedly concealed the fact that his father had been a public order official for a right-wing government in Spain several decades previously. Perhaps therefore his son had always been working for the opposition, La Pasionaria suggested. The comrades in Paris were losing patience with the Antón affair by now, for they knew full well what lay behind La Pasionaria's hatred. What most of them didn't know was that in March 1953 she abruptly ordered Antón to leave Paris and move to Warsaw, there to await news of his fate. Antón meekly did so. His wife Carmen was not even told where he had been sent: the Party suggested she might care to return to North Africa, her birthplace. She was spirited enough to take no notice and joined Antón in Warsaw in July with their two small daughters.

In November La Pasionaria delivered her final verdict: Francisco Antón had been an enemy agent since he first joined the Spanish Communist Party back in the 1930s. She even threw in as the conclusive evidence of his treachery the famous plane trip he took from France to the Soviet Union courtesy of the Nazis after the end of the Spanish Civil War. This was breathtaking: for it was La Pasionaria who had pleaded with the Soviets to get her lover out of the French concentration camp in which he was interned. Now she used it to condemn him. Tactfully, nobody in Paris pointed out the obvious conclusion: that if the accusation against Antón were true, it meant that La Pasionaria had shared bed and board with an enemy agent for the best part of 15 years. But of course everybody knew the rules of the game: everybody, including Antón, who allowed his life to be ruined for the cause.

He was expelled from the PCE's Politburo and central committee, though not from the Party itself. Incredibly, the investigation was to continue: his conduct was to be examined further to ascertain what terrible things he might have done to the Spanish Party in exile. Equally incredibly, nobody told Antón of these decisions. He lived in limbo in Warsaw, uncertain of what was happening and apparently fatalistic about the future. He would seem to have been very loyal or very stupid or very frightened; perhaps a mixture of the three. Finally, the Polish Communist Party, evidently perplexed about this Spaniard who had suddenly been dumped in its lap and forgotten, started to make enquiries. It was not until the middle of 1954 that Antón finally found out that he been cast out into the darkness. He was told of his fate by Enrique Líster, the brusque and brutish Civil War military hero who had become a Red Army general and thereafter floated around Eastern Europe in a state of simmering bitterness against his fellow PCE leaders (particularly Carrillo) which exploded into rebellion in 1970 when he quit to set up his own breakaway Communist Party, without notable success. Líster hated and despised Antón too, so perhaps he derived some pleasure from this task, although so byzantine had the whole affair become that nobody in the PCE had thought to inform Líster that Antón had been living in the same city as himself for several months. The Poles, taking pity on Antón, offered him a job in journalism but he preferred a proper martyrdom: he volunteered to work in a motor-cycle factory, where he laboured in exhausting conditions on the assembly line. His health suffered and he and his wife, who had a lowly, ill-paid job, earned barely enough to live on. Their life was in stark contrast to La Pasionaria's comfortable and cosseted existence in Moscow. Francisco Antón's life had come full circle: he had been plucked from humble surroundings by the Communist Party and had soared to unimaginable heights of power and influence because of his relationship with La Pasionaria. But once he spurned her, she and the Party combined to toss him out, back into the same sort of world from which he had come.

Antón stuck it out in Warsaw for a decade but was partially rehabilitated by the PCE within three years. In 1957 Carrillo, who was in the process of taking over effective control of the Party from La Pasionaria, invited him to attend a Plenum of the central committee. It was the least Carrillo could do for a man with whom he had once worked so closely and then betrayed. The gesture of reconciliation was not lost on the rest of the Party. Even La Pasionaria shook her former lover's hand, although she bestowed embraces on the other comrades. In 1964 Antón was readmitted to the central committee and moved to a propaganda job in Prague. He ended up back in Paris, where he died in 1976, in the back of a taxi which was taking him to hospital after he had collapsed at a Party meeting. Within a year he would certainly have been allowed to return to Spain. Unlike his former mistress he never made it back home.

The writer Gregorio Morán, whose brilliant book *The Sadness and Greatness of the Spanish Communist Party 1939-1985* provides a wealth of insights into the Party's fortunes after the Civil War, draws an interesting comparison between the Antón 'trial' and that of Rudolf Slansky and his fellow leaders of the Czechoslovakian Communist Party at around the same time. Slansky's arraignment was a classic show trial of the Stalinist era, in which Slansky, himself a dedicated Stalinist, was sacrificed for obscure internal Party reasons. No one, neither the accused nor his accusers, had the slightest belief in the truth of the proceedings. Exactly the same could be said about the Antón case, with the crucial difference that Slansky paid for his 'errors' with his life. He was executed in 1952. But the comparison between the cases goes further, as Morán points out: there were close links between the Czechoslovak and Spanish Parties, under Slansky and La Pasionaria respectively. She hoped to establish a base for the PCE in Prague, with Slansky's co-operation, that would rival Paris in importance.[1]

There was an even more intimate and tragic link: Irene Falcón, La Pasionaria's faithful, self-effacing but powerful secretary and her closest friend and aide, was the lover of Beadrich Geminder, Slansky's number two, who went on trial with him and received the same sentence. In the climate of the times she was perhaps fortunate not to have suffered the same terrible fate as her lover. It is said that La Pasionaria interceded personally with Stalin to save Irene. At any rate, after Geminder's execution, Irene was, as it were, re-exiled. She was packed off to China and did not return to Moscow to resume her work for La Pasionaria until after Stalin's death. Yet despite losing her lover in such a fashion her faith in communism, like La Pasionaria's, was never dented for a moment. They both remained faithful to the cause to the end, with the same devotion that Francisco Antón showed in accepting whatever course the Party chose for him.

*

The news of Stalin's death in March 1953 came as a thunderbolt to La Pasionaria: 'I don't know why but we didn't expect it; in some way – irrational, of course – we imagined that Stalin would never disappear.'[2] She delivered eulogies to the departed great helmsman at various memorial meetings but, like many of his devotees, the bottom had been knocked out of her world. The process of de-Stalinisation that slowly got under way and took off with Khrushchev's famous speech to the XXth Congress of the Communist Party of the Soviet Union in 1956 was the biggest factor in this: the Spanish Communist Party underwent the same cycle of re-examination and change, and as the symbol of the Stalinist old guard, La Pasionaria was an inevitable target. But there were several other elements: her age (she was 57 when Stalin died); her growing interest in her developing family life as a grandmother; her isolation in Moscow from the young turks of the Party, who were mainly to be found in Paris; and to some extent her isolation in Moscow itself from her fellow Spanish exiles.

Her domestic contentment centred on her daughter Amaya who had, in 1951, married Artiom Sergueiev, an officer with the Red Army. Both were children of the communist élite: he was the son of a famous bolshevik, who took part in the 1917 revolution and performed various acts of derring-do in the turbulent years afterwards, before dying in a mysterious train accident in 1921. Artiom was brought up as a favoured son of the Kremlin. His mother was also a formidable figure, being both a doctor and director of a factory. Artiom rose to the rank of general in the Red Army, but according to their daughter Dolores, his marriage to Amaya was not a particularly happy one. They did, however, have three children, two boys – Rubén and Fiodor – and Dolores, better known as Lola, Loly or Lolita. Named after her grandmother, Lola was always the apple of La Pasionaria's eye and was indeed largely brought up by her when Amaya and Artiom's marriage broke up in the late 1960s. But in the mid-1950s, La Pasionaria found her daughter's marriage and the arrival of grandchildren a considerable consolation for the many family tragedies she had gone through.

She still lived in comfortable circumstances. Since her return to the USSR in 1949 she had had a pleasant apartment in Stazokoniushenny Street of the type provided by the Soviet government to top Party officials, plus a car and a driver. But by its nature it was an existence cocooned from the realities of Soviet life, especially those being endured by the thousands of Spanish exiles still in the USSR whose dreams of a swift return home had long since faded away. Although La Pasionaria did a lot of work for the Spanish community, there were many Spaniards who felt she ignored them and their problems. Indeed it was widely felt that she would have no truck with anyone who criticised the Soviet Union, as many of them did. In 1956 General Franco shrewdly announced that those who wanted to return to Spain could do so and many took up his offer with alacrity. But La Pasionaria was not at all pleased. She is said to have opposed the idea energetically. For one, she could not understand anyone preferring Franco's Spain to the USSR, although plenty of the exiles evidently did. For another, she still harboured dreams of returning to Spain in triumph and she envisaged the Soviet Spaniards as a potential hardcore of revolutionary zealots who should be kept on standby for the call to arms. There were indeed many enthusiastic Party members in their number, particularly among those who had fled Spain after fighting in the Civil War. But the children who had been evacuated from beleaguered republican areas such as the Basque Country and Asturias just before they fell to Franco were often much less enthusiastic about the Soviet Union and communism. Many of these children had suffered dreadful hardship in the USSR during the Second World War. Many had been taken out of school and been forced to work in factories. They had harrowing stories of privation and discrimination to tell – all of that in addition to the continuing trauma of separation from their families and their homeland. Many had no idea what had happened to their parents and relatives; and they were scattered all over the Soviet Union so that it was difficult for the community and Party leaders in Moscow to keep track of them.

Typical of them was Anastasio Monge Barredo, a Basque boy who was evacuated from Bilbao in June 1937, three days before it fell to the nationalists. He spent his first three years in a children's home reserved for Spanish children, and thus did not lose his native language. They were indoctrinated with pro-communist and anti-Franco propaganda; the food was poor, but conditions worsened considerably when the Second World War began. He was put to work in an aircraft factory. He believes many Spanish children died in that period, but no one knows how or when. When the Civil War ended a second wave of refugees had arrived, this time military veterans and their families, who formed the core of the PCE in exile. After the Second World War, Anastasio qualified as an engineer and worked for 20 years in Siberia. It took him eight years to get permission to return to Moscow but he finally made it in 1969. Back in Spain his father had been imprisoned for 13 years; he had no word from him until the mid-1950s. Anastasio's parents had no idea what had happened to their son; there was no communication between the USSR and Franco's Spain in the 1940s and 1950s. It was 33 years before they were finally reunited. Stuck in Siberia, Anastasio had no idea that Franco was allowing refugees back. 'Nobody told me,' he said. He married a Russian girl and raised a family. In the early 1960s, he was sent to Cuba for three years to train young engineers. In the more relaxed climate of the 1970s and 1980s he was able to visit Spain, where he felt totally at home. But as his family was in the USSR he felt obliged to return there. After he retired his only ambition was to return to Spain permanently. 'I want to die in Spain,' he said. But he could see no way of doing so. His Soviet pension was worthless outside the USSR, he was allowed to take only $200 out of the country (which would have paid for two nights in a Madrid hotel) and he was not entitled to a Spanish pension. He was marooned in a country he hated, and which incidentally was collapsing around him, yet it was not of his own doing. He had had no say in the matter when they packed him off to the USSR all those years ago. What was even more galling was that many of the refugees in the second wave had been able to return to Spain to live.[3]

Few of these innocent victims of two wars, like Anastasio, had much time for La Pasionaria. They felt she knew nothing and cared less about their problems. Many were still saying that in the 1990s, when as elderly folk living on meagre Soviet pensions, they were trying desperately to go 'home' to Spain, a country they had lived in for perhaps a sixth of their lives but which they still found a more attractive prospect than the USSR. In 1991, they estimated there were 800 of them still living in the USSR, 400 of them in Moscow.

While the exiles were playing their part in building the Soviet Union in the mid-1950s and the Soviet Communist Party under its new leader Nikita Khrushchev was beginning to disengage from Stalinism, the Spanish Communist Party leadership was engaged in a parallel process: groping for a new role in a rapidly changing Europe. In September 1954, the Party finally got round to its first Congress for 22 years. This Congress, the PCE's fifth, could be said to have been postponed for 18 years, having originally been scheduled for August 1936, only for the Civil War to intervene. It was held by the side of a Czechoslovakian lake and was an unsatisfactory and inconclusive affair, distinguished only by the low standard of debate. La Pasionaria set the tone with an undistinguished opening speech which harped on about old disputes of the 1940s and gave little sign of recognising that the world was changing around her. Although nothing was said publicly, Santiago Carrillo and his coterie in Paris were looking ahead to a future in which La Pasionaria would play a largely symbolic role. It was not so much a question of political differences as a generation gap. The old guard of the PCE still held power officially in both Moscow and Paris but the young men in the French capital, led by Carrillo, were eager to take over. Carrillo himself was particularly ambitious to lead the Party into a new era and used all his devious skills to plot his path to power.

When the Spanish Party's most promising ideologue, Fernando Claudín, moved to Paris in 1955 from Moscow where he had spent most of the previous decade, Carrillo lost no time in quizzing him about La Pasionaria and her life in the Soviet capital. Claudín's reply must have been encouraging for Carrillo:

> She lived a very isolated life, as much from Spanish exiles as from Soviet society, in a little circle composed of her daughter Amaya, her secretary Irene Falcón and her first grandson, in almost permanent cold war with the mother of the young Russian General (Artiom), Amaya's husband. I used to consult her from time to time – sometimes through Irene – on questions of emigration [of Spanish exiles] but political conversations were rare. I held La Pasionaria in high esteem but in Moscow I reached the conclusion that she was not the ideal person to carry out the role of Party general secretary. In my conversations with Santiago Carrillo in 1955 I got the impression that his judgement in this respect was at least as negative as mine although he only let it be known by hints or eloquent silences. We fully agreed on the necessity to end the 'personality cult', concretely that of Pasionaria, which was the equivalent in the PCE of that of Stalin in the USSR and the communist movement.[4]

To be fair to her, La Pasionaria knew in her heart that change was inevitable – but not just yet. She continued to rule the Party from afar. She was still untouchable – officially.

The key to change was the Soviet Union's fresh attitude towards Franco. Rapprochement was in the air. The new brooms in the Kremlin gave a clear sign that they were not going to let the diehard, Franco-hating old Stalinists of the PCE get in the way of their own better relations with the new Spain. The PCE's radio station, Radio España Independiente, which was still beaming its anti-Franco propaganda across Europe to Spain, was quietly told to move its operation from Moscow to the Romanian capital, Bucharest. The station was very close to La Pasionaria's heart; it was effectively the only means by which she could communicate directly with the Spanish people, or at least those who tuned into La Pirenaica, as it was more popularly known. The Soviet order was a serious snub. La Pasionaria moved to Bucharest for a period to help get the new venture under way and put a brave face on it, expressing her delight at the climate and atmosphere of Bucharest, which she found similar to Spain's and more agreeable than Moscow's. But the move was the clearest possible sign that La Pirenaica had had its day. The Soviet Union knew its anachronistic voice, piping away from the Carpathians, was never going to bring about a revolution in Spain, even if La Pasionaria didn't. She continued to broadcast the old Juana and Manuela dialogues to the faithful.

The next big landmark was La Pasionaria's 60th birthday in December 1955 and the Party faithful, scattered throughout the world, fell over themselves to display their devotion. So many presents poured in to the PCE's Paris headquarters and so many people wanted to go to Moscow to venerate her that a special train from Paris had to be laid on to get them there. There were acts of homage in the Spanish exile communities throughout Latin America and the South of France and the poet Rafael Alberti, a fellow communist and exile, who had been with La Pasionaria in the last days of the Civil War in 1939, wrote a suitably passionate poem dedicated to her.

At the same time, a far more important historical act was being sealed: Spain was admitted to the United Nations, a move which the PCE had always fiercely opposed because it conferred international credibility on the Franco régime. For the Soviet Union, it was simply a matter of realpolitik: they allowed Spain and several other countries then in the Western sphere of influence to join while the USA gave the nod to several of the USSR's Eastern European satellites. This left the Spanish communists divided. The old-guard Stalinists who still occupied the leadership in France and Eastern Europe, like Vicente Uribe and Enrique Líster, were aghast. They broadcast a statement from Bucharest registering their disapproval of giving any comfort to Franco. But younger PCE leaders like Santiago Carrillo and Fernando Claudín, took a different attitude: they could see the advantages to the PCE of ending Spain's isolation from the rest of the world. Carrillo wrote a long article setting out their support for Spanish entry in the magazine *Nuestra Bandera* (*Our Flag*), which reflected the younger generation's point of view. There was pressure to withdraw it. Carrillo refused. Instead, publication of the magazine was delayed. The great imponderable was what La Pasionaria thought. 'Dolores must be involved,' pronounced Uribe. The young writer and rising Party thinker Jorge Semprún was deputed to tackle her personally.

In a memorable passage from his brilliant memoir *The Autobiography of Federico Sánchez* (his *nom de guerre* during exile), Semprún drew a marvellous portrait of La Pasionaria during that epoch, a severe, forbidding, yet beneath the surface lonely and unhappy woman, living in a kind of limbo in the soulless ambience of Eastern Europe. Semprún caught up with her in Prague, on her way back to Bucharest from an East German Communist Party Congress in East Berlin. She was on the train reserved for the Romanian delegation. Such was her symbolic importance that she merited a carriage to herself. Semprún hitched a ride on the train and discovered a world that, he wrote, only a novelist could do justice to (and, being one, he had a go). The train was the embodiment of the privileges which the communist élite of Eastern Europe awarded themselves in the name of equality and social justice. A 'fabulous banquet' was served for the Romanians in the dining car. There was Caspian Sea caviar, Baltic herrings, a rich variety of hors d'oeuvres, spicy salads and steaming soups, fish and meat stews topped off with desserts and ice cream. The dishes were accompanied by 'innumerable' glasses of vodka, red and white wine, pink champagne from the Caucasus and Armenian brandy. For much of this feast, La Pasionaria was engaged in conversation with Chivu Stoica, recently named President of the Romanian Council of Ministers. To her credit, she did not appear to approve of 'such long and protocolary nutritional ceremonies, hardly touched her food and drank only mineral water, fiddling all the while with a strand of white hair and only becoming animated when evoking some memory of Spain.'

Back in her private compartment, Semprún reported on the furore in Paris over the UN and gave her a copy of Carrillo's article. She listened in silence 'with a look of marble'. When he had finished, she said she would read the article on the train, consider it and tell him later what she thought. The journey lasted an 'interminable forty-eight hours more', wrote Semprún, and La Pasionaria made no further reference to the subject. Instead, she talked incessantly about Spain.

Semprún had only recently left Spain, having lived there clandestinely for some time, and La Pasionaria was eager to hear all about it. She wanted to know in detail what Madrid looked like now, how daily life was for ordinary people, what changes there had been since she had last seen the city 17 years previously. 'She compared her memories with my stories and told me tales of her life in Madrid when the Party brought her there from Vizcaya in the 1930s,' Semprún recalled. 'It all interested her passionately.' When they finally reached Bucharest, La Pasionaria invited him to dinner with the Radio España Independiente staff. There she told him that she would retract the Bucharest declaration of the Stalinists and discuss the matter of the United Nations at a Party Plenum to be announced shortly.[5]

CHAPTER FIFTEEN

LA PENSIONARIA

On 24 February 1956 Nikita Khrushchev delivered his secret speech to the XXth Congress of the Communist Party of the Soviet Union in which he denounced Stalin's terror, the 'cult of personality' and began the process of rehabilitating Stalin's victims. La Pasionaria was a delegate to the Congress, along with three other veteran Spanish Stalinists – Antonio Mije, Vicente Uribe and Enrique Líster – plus the rising young ideologue Fernando Claudín. They attended the open sessions but the real business got under way once they and the other foreign delegations had been asked to leave.

Although they knew a fresh wind was blowing through the Kremlin, they were stunned when they eventually read Khrushchev's speech. Intense secrecy surrounded its dissemination. The delegates who heard it delivered were forbidden to take notes and the foreigners received their copies in conditions of tight security. La Pasionaria was given a copy on the evening of 25 February, 24 hours after it was delivered. The text was also sent round to Uribe. He was staying in a Party guest apartment with Líster, who later described the events of that tumultuous night.

Having gone to bed around midnight, he was awoken at 2 am by an excited Uribe, who needed the Russian-speaking Líster to translate the speech for him. Líster, who worshipped Stalin and continued to do so long after almost everybody else had abandoned him, was astonished at what he read. He even suspected a coup d'état. He read and re-read it until 5 am, and then went along to Uribe's room to explain it all. Uribe was as stunned as he was. They called La Pasionaria and an hour later met her at her apartment to discuss the historic document[1] – 'the earthquake', as she later described it. It must have been a bitter moment for La Pasionaria to glimpse the truth about her great hero, if she had not already done so. Her public reaction was to support the new line, although it contradicted everything she had

169

always stood for. She announced that the decisions of the XXth Congress 'will help us to finish with narrow and sectarian concepts that have held our activities back'.[2]

In her generally uninformative memoirs, she revealed something of her bewilderment at the time:

> On analysing the personality of Stalin in his last years, the Soviet leaders showed us a sad and bitter reality, which differed from what we knew. But aside from the anguish which such a reality produced, it was preferable to know it than to live in error.
>
> If we Communists fought for justice, how were we not going to put things right when we understood that we had been wrong, even though the correction of the mistake was of such a dimension as the revision of our judgments on Stalin's personality?[3]

Much had been written about Stalin, she wrote, most of it nonsense. His true personality would emerge in due course, after proper historical research. She was quite right, though perhaps not in the way she intended. As for the ordinary communist foot-soldier, confronted with Khrushchev's revelations of 1956, the only solution, she advised, was to study the problems and correct their errors with the help of the teachings of Marx, Engels and Lenin. La Pasionaria's big problem was that if the cult of the personality was now deplored, she stood to be as big a loser in her own sphere as Stalin was becoming, albeit posthumously. The whole edifice that had been built up around her depended on the myth of her as goddess, saint and mother of the Spanish communist movement. If that sort of cult was going out of fashion, then so was she.

Santiago Carrillo was already working diligently to establish himself as the real power in the PCE. The XXth Congress gave him an unexpected boost. As Enrique Líster and others pointed out (and he himself later admitted), Carrillo had been as dedicated a Stalinist as anyone. But he was young and ambitious and tuned in to the new thinking quicker than most. In the confused post-Congress atmosphere, when communists everywhere were re-evaluating their position, Carrillo went for the kill. His two targets were, first, the Party number two, Vicente Uribe and, second, its leader La Pasionaria. Uribe turned out to be easy meat. A crude, hard-drinking bully with a fierce tongue and violent temper, he had few real friends. Carrillo launched a full-blooded offensive against him, with the conveniently topical accusation that he had built a personality cult around himself. Uribe was toppled without difficulty but La Pasionaria proved a much tougher obstacle. She was wily enough to realise exactly what Carrillo was up to and hit back with some of her old fire, starting with a meeting of the PCE Politburo in Moscow in March 1956, convened to discuss tactics in the wake of the XXth Congress. She implicitly accused the Paris Young Turks, Carrillo and his ally Fernando Claudín, of trying to isolate her in Moscow, even to the extent of delaying sending the Party newspaper *Mundo Obrero* so that it was months out of date when she received it. Instead, she said, they sent her luxury editions of Catholic writers such as Saint Teresa of Avila 'for which I thank you because in addition to adorning my library they help me not to forget my Spanish. But politically they give me nothing.'[4] It was a witty and telling thrust, followed by an attempt to turn the XXth Congress's resolutions to her advantage. The Congress wanted more teamwork, not personality cults. Well, then, Carrillo and Claudín had been going their own way for too long, over there in Paris. It was time for the Politburo to reassert its authority.

But La Pasionaria did not get her way. She in turn was out-manoeuvred – indeed, out-talked – by her former protégé Fernando Claudín, the PCE's brightest intellectual. He had impeccable references. Born in Zaragoza in 1913, he trained as an architect. He had joined the Party's youth wing in 1933 and was soon elected on to its central committee. He was instrumental, with Carrillo, in effecting the merger of the socialist and communist youth movements just before the Civil War. He also edited the Valencia newspaper *La Hora*, and fled to Moscow at the end of the Civil War. He continued to work closely with Carrillo, in Mexico and then France, before returning to the USSR in 1947 to become general secretary of the PCE within the Soviet Union. He had become renowned for his mastery of the minutiae of Soviet communist doctrine, and was much admired for being one of the few people who read *Pravda* for pleasure. He had recently undertaken a secret journey to Spain to gauge the political climate there. His report on his findings was one of the items La Pasionaria complained had been kept from her. This gave him the opportunity to hit back in public. It was the first time a high-ranking Party member had dared to criticise her openly since Jesús Hernández back in the early 1940s.

Claudín made the telling link between the XXth Congress's criticism of the personality cult and the figure of La Pasionaria. 'In the

171

light of the XXth Congress, I understand that comrade Dolores's authority cannot be elevated to leave her beyond the bounds of criticism . . . The cult of the personality has two faces: the maximum complacency and liberalism towards those in high places and the maximum toughness for those below.' Claudín plunged on. If 'comrade Dolores' had complaints about not receiving the report on Spain, why had she not asked him for one? He had been in Moscow for a month and could have supplied any facts she wanted. But she hadn't asked him for anything.[5] In fact, they had only spoken for two hours in all that time. Claudín had dared to say what everyone knew and whispered but had not the courage to say out loud: that La Pasionaria had made herself a remote and isolated figure and must now suffer the consequences.

Vicente Uribe came in for much harsher criticism from Claudín and many other speakers: he was formally deposed shortly afterwards. This happened at a Plenum of the Politburo, held in Bucharest (the Spanish communists certainly got around the high spots of Eastern Europe while tearing each other to pieces), in April. The Plenum, which lasted a marathon 40 days, was the next step in the response to the crisis caused by Khrushchev's speech. It marked a further consolidation of power for Carrillo, the end of Uribe's career and a demonstration by La Pasionaria that she had not lost all her political touch. In effect, she recognised the force of Claudín's criticisms in March, and after a long meeting with Carrillo swung behind the Young Turks, sacrificing her old comrade Uribe and gaining herself a further four years as general secretary. But it was only a superficial victory. As Claudín wrote later: 'We knew we were seeing Santiago Carrillo taking over the Party – not formally perhaps but in effect.'[6]

The central issue concerned how the Franco régime should be opposed: should the Party's posture be one of confrontation, of insisting that Franco could only be overthrown by violent means, by revolution? Or should the Party change its tactics and work as part of a broad national anti-government movement which would help to bring about a change in the political climate, leading to the eventual collapse of the Franco régime and its replacement by a democratic one? The Young Turks, or their representatives, had visited Spain secretly. They knew that the country was changing. Compared to the rest of Western Europe, it was still backward and its government harsh and undemocratic. But Franco had invested huge

172

amounts in public works; the country's infrastructure was improving and foreign investment was beginning to flow in behind the West's relaxation of its attitude towards Franco. The tourist revolution had yet to happen but the emergence of a prosperous and relatively apolitical middle class was there for any clandestine visitor with eyes to see it. For many Europeans, the symbol of the new Spain was the brilliant Real Madrid football team, winner of five successive European Cups, not the civil guard and the firing squad. The economic boom which was being generated was also producing a more prosperous working class, which would inevitably not accept Franco's restrictions on independent unions and left-wing political parties indefinitely. A new generation of students who were too young to remember the Civil War was arriving at Spain's universities and it was from among their number that the first open opposition to the régime was voiced. The communists realised this and worked actively (but of course secretly) on the campuses to recruit support. Their efforts were extremely successful.

But for all this potential future opposition, Franco still possessed one powerful weapon, in addition to the apparatus of the police state: his countrymen's terror of another civil war as a means of effecting the political change that everyone in their heart of hearts knew must come some day, after Franco. The Generalissimo was revered by a large cross-section of the population but even those who could not abide him wanted change to be carried out in a peaceful manner.

The younger communists were beginning to understand these new realities. The old guard were incapable of changing their mentality – with one notable exception: La Pasionaria. Whether she believed it deep down is a moot point: she was a creature of contradictions. She was capable on the one hand of the most ferocious hatred for Franco and all his works, expressed in the most violent possible language. Yet on the other hand she did repeatedly express a desire for national reconciliation. It may be that there were two diametrically opposed forces working within her. Her devotion to the communist cause and her bitter memory of Civil War defeat encouraged her violent side. Opposed to that was her deep and abiding love for Spain which, according to the testimony of everyone who met her in exile, never diminished in the slightest. Indeed, the opposite happened: the longer she was away, the more she longed to return and the more painful her absence became. But Franco was determined that would never happen in his lifetime.

173

Whatever the reason, she now threw in her lot with the new wave. Opening the Plenum she announced: 'Francoism today is not what it was ten years ago.' She proposed co-operation with other parties in the search for an alternative to Franco, brought about by non-violent means. And she gracefully admitted she and the other old guard had been wrong about Spain's admission to the UN. It was a total capitulation to Carrillo, and the price she was prepared to pay to keep her job for a little while longer. Carrillo criticised La Pasionaria implicitly, saying that decisions must not be taken by a few at the top but by the leadership as a whole. But this apart, he and his supporters were magnanimous in victory, heaping plenty of praise on 'comrade Dolores' as well. She had never wanted the trappings of the personality cult; it had always embarrassed her, said Carrillo. By the end of this marathon Plenum, Carrillo was clearly leader of the Party in all but name. For all his attacks on La Pasionaria's dictatorial style, it was soon clear, wrote Claudín, that the new leader would not tolerate anybody else's point of view either.[7] Throughout his career, Carrillo was a ruthless, secretive autocrat who clung tenaciously to power. He was also a great survivor.

The PCE rounded off its Grand Tour of Eastern Europe for this dramatic year by another lakeside, this time, of all places, in Goering's old hunting lodge in northern East Germany. In July it held a Plenum of the central committee there in which La Pasionaria confirmed her volte-face, pledged the Party to a new policy of 'national reconciliation' (ie peaceful change) and even appealed for a truce and a pact with the socialists, their uneasy ally of old. It was a historic change of direction by the PCE, which henceforth tried to portray itself as a modern, progressive party which none need fear, free of its old totalitarian image. In her speech, however, La Pasionaria showed herself still perplexed by the events of the year, particularly in relation to the communist movement's reassessment of Stalin. 'It hurts us like a deep burn to discover the negative attitude of Stalin which we were unaware of previously,' she mourned, then added: 'Stalin was a great Marxist and his deeds should always preside over our activities.' At least she was being honest about where her loyalties lay, unlike those former Stalinists who were falling over themselves to distance themselves from his shade.

The events of 1956 dealt a mortal blow to La Pasionaria's self-confidence. The old certainties had evaporated: her hero Stalin was now reviled; her enemy Franco was slowly being accepted not only by the West but by the Soviet Union too; a new generation was taking over the Spanish Communist Party; and she was canny enough to know that it was only the personal affection, even reverence, which she inspired among the faithful that saved her from the fate her old ally Uribe suffered. It was little wonder that 1956 left her depressed and, according to Enrique Líster, even suicidal. 'Dolores's nerviness increased day by day,' he recorded later. 'She frequently talked about throwing herself out of the window.'[8] It is a strange echo of the fate of her predecessor, José Díaz, who fell out of a window in Tbilisi when, like La Pasionaria 14 years later, he found himself isolated from his party, his country and from the sense of being at the centre of events. Then, La Pasionaria had been the beneficiary. Now she in turn was being defenestrated.

In 1956 La Pasionaria had a brief respite from the traumas of a difficult year when she was invited to head a PCE delegation to the VIIIth Congress of the Chinese Communist Party. It was her first visit to China. It took nine days to make the journey by train from Moscow to Peking, and La Pasionaria not unnaturally was enchanted to be in China: not only was it one of her revolutionary Utopias but she also retained a childlike wonderment at travelling to far-flung corners of the world and finding that they matched up to her childhood dreams. At the end of the Congress, she and her fellow delegates were received by Mao tse-Tung, Chou en-Lai and Chu-te, another veteran of the Long March. Chou talked to them in his fluent French; Chu swapped war stories; and Mao listened patiently while they explained their new policy of 'national reconciliation' before exclaiming: 'Ten thousand years to the policy of national reconciliation!' The expression baffled the Spaniards until it was explained to them that this was the Chinese way of saying 'Long live . . .'[9]

As 1956 drew towards a close, the dramatic pace of international events gave veteran communists like La Pasionaria reason to believe that the changes in the Soviet Union were no more than cosmetic. The crushing of the Hungarian uprising by Soviet troops in November was faithfully supported by her and the PCE Politburo. She linked Hungary with the Suez crisis: both were designed by 'fascist and imperialist forces' to further the objective of 'a third world war'. The Politburo praised the Soviet forces for intervening in Hungary 'to re-establish democratic order'.[10] La Pasionaria's Stalinist soul had swiftly reasserted itself and was still well in evidence 10 months later when she addressed the third Plenum of the PCE's central committee in Czechoslovakia on the subject of Hungary: even the 'most myopic', she declared, could see that the uprising had been 'a counter-revolutionary movement, organised by Hungarian fascist forces and international reaction . . . thanks to the heroic and selfless action of the Soviet fighters, the counter-revolutionary aggression failed . . .' A member of the central committee who happened to be in Hungary at the time of the invasion and who questioned whether the Soviet Union's action had been justified was thrown off the committee for his pains.

He was not the only one to have doubts. The events of 1956 fatally undermined many foot-soldiers' hitherto unquestioning belief in the inexorable advance of world communism. Fernando Claudín, for example, wrote later:

> The year 1956 marked for me, as for so many other communists, the beginning of a break with a comfortable and optimistic view of our movement's situation and propects . . . The revelations of Khrushchev's secret report, and then the revolts of the workers and intellectuals of Hungary and Poland against the Stalinist system, destroyed at a stroke this whole view of things.[11]

It was precisely these doubts, shared by many idealistic young people and left-wing sympathisers, that were to prove a fatal stumbling block to communism's hopes of feeding off the fresh thinking making itself felt in Europe. No such doubts disturbed La Pasionaria, or indeed Santiago Carrillo. All that remained for him was to gain official leadership of the Party he effectively now controlled.

Carrillo's strategy was two-fold: to try to build links with all the other opposition parties and movements, of whatever political hue, and to promote a series of demonstrations within Spain which would show that opposition to Franco was alive and well. He was encouraged by news of student disturbances and by a two-day public transport boycott against higher fares in February 1957 which was well supported by the public. It raised wild hopes in communist breasts that more overtly political demonstrations might be just as successful. At the same time Spain was opening up; it was easier to get in and out, so that communist exiles could infiltrate the country and rebellious souls from within Spain could travel abroad, sometimes with drastic consequences: a delegation of young Spaniards who travelled to Moscow in the summer of 1957 for an International Youth

Festival were arrested and jailed, along with friends and political colleagues (the total came to 100), on their return to Spain. The galling thing for the Franco régime was that they were the children of the middle class: an exultant Carrillo in Paris wrote to La Pasionaria in Moscow that the General Security Directorate building in Madrid was 'surrounded by magnificent Cadillacs belonging to the detainees' families and friends'.[12]

Carrillo and the PCE put all their energy into two demonstrations of strength which they hoped would shake the régime. The first was a so-called Day of National Reconciliation, called for 5 May 1958. It was meant to be an all-party affair marked by anti-régime strikes, meetings, demonstrations and the like. It was a complete flop, which did not stop the communists hailing it as a triumph and inventing all sorts of magnificent events which had never in fact taken place. Even La Pasionaria, who had little or nothing to do with it, gave it a cautious welcome from Moscow: 'The Day has proved that it is possible by mass action to put an end to the dictatorship in a peaceful manner.'[13]

Carrillo pressed on with the second prong of his strategy: his aim was nothing less than to bring Spain to a complete halt for a day. So was born the Huelga Nacional Pacífica: the Peaceful General Strike, known by its Spanish initials as the HNP. The communists worked hard to involve as many other opposition forces as they could. Although the socialists declined, the PCE had a good response from other organisations, particularly among students and intellectuals. The one person who was not contacted to give her approval was La Pasionaria, the clearest indication yet that the Party had ceased to regard her as its effective leader, although it may also have had something to do with Carrillo's fear that she might try to block it. When she heard about it, she was opposed to it, out of the caution that had become ingrained in her by her long years of living in the Soviet Union. She believed that it was little more than a stunt whose failure would rebound on the Party. Eventually she gave grudging approval, provided the event was 'well-organised'.[14] After months of negotiations with other parties, the HNP was fixed for 18 June 1959. But despite widespread publicity via Radio España Independiente, leaflets, wall posters and even hostile articles in the official press, the HNP was another resounding flop, as La Pasionaria had feared. French observers in Madrid reported back that they could not discern the slightest difference from an ordinary working day. Not only that, but several leading Party members who had returned to Spain clandestinely were arrested. They included Simón Sánchez Montero, a member of the Politburo/central committee and the most important Party official inside the country. Carrillo, however, pronounced it a huge success, claiming widespread strikes among agricultural workers in Andalusia and Estremadura. These claims, it turned out, were based on wildly over-optimistic reports by Party members in those regions who sent back to Paris the news they knew their exiled leaders wanted to hear, rather than what had actually happened.

If there was one person who could have made political capital out of the HNP débâcle (apart from General Franco) it was La Pasionaria. The fact that she had deliberately been kept out of it by Carrillo meant her hands were clean. But she showed no interest in taking advantage of this setback for her ambitious underling, and shortly afterwards Carrillo moved in for the kill.

In July he and the leading members of the PCE Politburo, including Claudín, Semprún, Tomás García and Santiago Alvarez, travelled to the Soviet Union to meet La Pasionaria. There are conflicting reports about the purpose of the journey. According to Claudín, it was to hold a post mortem on the HNP and prepare for the VIth Congress of the PCE. But according to another member of the delegation, Santiago Alvarez, their chief purpose, which they all agreed on beforehand, was to persuade La Pasionaria to step down as general secretary. It being high summer, they met at her dacha at Uspenskoye, 42 km from Moscow. Claudín's version is that after they had made some introductory remarks about the tasks ahead, La Pasionaria stunned them by pulling out a piece of paper from which she read out her resignation. So taken aback were they that Carrillo requested an adjournment on the excuse that he needed to go to the toilet, where he nervously enquired of García: 'What manoeuvre is she preparing for us?'[15] (Echoing, presumably unwittingly, Talleyrand's famous remark on hearing of a rival's death: 'I wonder what he can have meant by that?')

Santiago Alvarez, however, who was also there, has a slightly different version: La Pasionaria was well aware that they had come to persuade her to quit and tried to forestall them by proposing that she stay on but that a new post of deputy general secretary (presumably Carrillo) be created to assist her. The delegation turned this down, and instead proposed another new post for her, President of the Party, a purely titular position. They would not be diverted from choosing a new general secretary. Her resistance collapsed and she agreed to be

178

kicked upstairs.[16] La Pasionaria's version was that she herself raised the question, because of her age and her belief that a younger person should take over. Various options were discussed before the title of President was suggested.[17] Whichever version is correct, the result was the same: La Pasionaria's 17-year rule as head of the Spanish Communist Party, which she had held on to only tenuously since 1956, was over. In the garden of the dacha various other members of the central committee and their guests were preparing a meal of paella, to be consumed when the proceedings were over. Perhaps appropriately, while the comrades dispatched La Pasionaria inside, one of the guests outside was Trotsky's assassin, Ramón Mercader, only recently released from a Mexican jail.

The VIth Party Congress was duly held in Prague over Christmas 1959 and Santiago Carrillo was acclaimed as the new general secretary. La Pasionaria made a rambling, sentimental farewell speech, but it was Carrillo's Congress, the public confirmation of what he had been working towards for a decade or more: control of the Party. He delivered a triumphalist speech, whose main burden was that conditions for the Party had never been better since the end of the Civil War. He was right; as opposition to Franco started to grow, painfully slowly but grow none the less, the Communist Party was the chief beneficiary. From inside Spain, the Party was seen as the chief standard-bearer of opposition, and as the eventful decade of the 1960s opened it was beginning to attract a new generation of students and intellectuals. As during the Civil War, its appeal was as much to the middle class as it was to the workers.

La Pasionaria's decision to take a back seat was largely provoked by the Party's expanding horizons: she was 64 years old and knew that she was not up to the tasks ahead. To retake control of the Party she would have to move to France, where the Spanish communists were still officially banned (although unofficially tolerated) and could expect no immediate improvement of their status under the new government of General de Gaulle. In her memoirs she wrote that she would have had the utmost difficulty living and working in Paris because of her enormous personal fame: when she had last lived there, she claimed, it had been impossible to go out without being recognised.[18] It would have been equally difficult in 1959-60. She was clearly conscious that the Party was at a crossroads, and that the next generation ought to be given its head to deal with the challenges of the 1960s. So she retired gracefully; but her story was still far from over.

★

Although she had relinquished the leadership of the PCE, La Pasionaria was still kept busy by the communist movement, which tended to venerate those veterans who had escaped being devoured by purge or firing squad. She continued to be a regular on the usual round of international conferences of a progressive nature and Party congresses, where she would be given a ritual welcome by the assembled delegates, like some old boxer being led into the ring to be cheered by the crowd before the real business of the night got under way. By now, she was known by her fellow Spanish exiles in Moscow as 'La Pensionaria'.

But in Spain itself she was still regarded as the next thing to the Devil incarnate. The Spanish press (all pro-Franco; no opposition papers were permitted) occasionally reported on her activities in scornful and insulting tones. In August 1960 she made an appeal for Spain and Portugal to become neutral, non-aligned countries, a familiar communist theme. She also praised the activities of students throughout the world and their enthusiasm for political struggle (this was the beginning of the era of student unrest of the 1960s) and repeated that she was now opposed to guerrilla warfare and terrorism in Spain. The newspaper *ABC*, which usually prefixed any reference to her with the term 'the sadly celebrated La Pasionaria', commented: 'The document reveals the constant work against the peace of the Spanish and Portuguese which is carried out from the centres of international communism. The picturesque prose of the famous Pasionaria throws new light on the intrigues prepared from beyond our frontiers.'[19]

She was still as willing as ever to go into battle on behalf of the Soviet Union. In 1960 Khrushchev summoned a congress of world Communist Parties in Moscow, at which the Sino-Soviet split became public knowledge. The Chinese and Albanians declared their opposition to the Soviet leader's policy of 'peaceful co-existence' with the West and his repudiation of Stalin. La Pasionaria leapt to the defence of the USSR. After the Albanian Communist Party leader Enver Hoxha had spoken, she went to the podium to deliver a vigorous counter-attack on him which left Hoxha fuming with rage. She did the same at the 1962 Congress of the Italian Communist Party in Rome, where the Sino-Soviet split was the dominant theme. The correspondent of the Spanish newspaper *Ya* dug deep into his supply of adjectives to describe her intervention:

Tall, old and running to fat, delivering several shrieks which shook the loudspeakers and pierced the listener's ears, Dolores Ibárruri spoke to the Congress of the PCI. The hysteria of this decrepit old amazon of international communism was displayed in impressive manner in the seven or eight ovations which punctuated her harangue . . . Her blind obedience to Moscow communism was underlined by her attacks on the Chinese communists for backing the Albanians.[20]

She did the rounds of the Eastern European communist satellites, where she was as well known to the public as the grey men who made up the local Politburos. She ventured farther afield, making her first visit to Cuba in December 1963, where she received an enthusiastic reception from a country which had always had strong links with the Spanish republican cause, long before Fidel Castro's guerrillas came down from the Sierra Maestra to take power in 1959. Cuba had been home to thousands of republican refugees and a strong base for the PCE in exile during the 1940s and 1950s. La Pasionaria felt a huge emotional identification with Castro; he was, in many ways, a latter-day version of herself, with the crucial difference that he won his Civil War. They shared too a slavish devotion to Moscow.

She picked up the usual baubles dispensed to the ultra-loyal: an honorary degree from Moscow University in November 1961, the Lenin Peace Prize in 1964, the Order of Lenin in December 1965. As the cold war eased in the 1960s and new perspectives opened up for Communist Parties outside the Eastern bloc, La Pasionaria managed to visit Western Europe for the first time in more than a decade. But in the early 1960s she was still unable to travel openly to France, where the Spanish communists were still officially unwelcome. She therefore travelled in disguise, and on a number of false passports supplied by the Soviet Union. She always hated having to do so, unsurprisingly for a woman of her fierce pride, but the alternative would have been equally humiliating. Sometimes she wore a wig, sometimes spectacles, sometimes both. When she attended the VIIth Congress of the PCE in France in 1965 she passed as a French citizen, Hélène Madeleine Georgette Charre, married name Brunet, born on 31 December 1900, and resident in Champigny.[21] Wearing wig, hat and spectacles, La Pasionaria, alias Mme Brunet, flew in from Romania accompanied by Leonor Bornao, a young Spanish woman who was on the central committee of the PCE. She went successfully through passport control and was driven to the school in a Paris suburb where the Congress was being held. So terrified were the Spanish

181

communists of being found out by the French authorities that applause was forbidden, so La Pasionaria's entry had to be greeted with silent, but enthusiastic, gestures of welcome.

In later years she travelled as a Spaniard, María Pardo, a widowed schoolmistress from Avila, born in June 1896; and as Carmen Costa, another teacher, this time from Madrid, born on 15 December 1895 (only a few days after La Pasionaria's real date of birth). There could be few frontier guards who would have suspected potential mischief from the dignified old lady presenting such documents. La Pasionaria herself maintained that the best disguise was brightly coloured clothes, because she was always associated with black.

Back in the Soviet Union, she was also deeply involved in heading the team producing the PCE's three-volume official history of the Spanish Civil War, which eventually came out in between 1967 and 1971 and about which the most polite observation would be that it is not an objective work of scholarship.

La Pasionaria combined all these commitments with a solid domestic life and routine. Her apartment in central Moscow was a little corner of Spain in Moscow, decorated with Spanish paintings and trinkets, which were continually topped up by gifts brought by the steady flow of Spanish visitors. Although she had learned to read Russian fairly fluently and speak it a little less so, she spoke it as little as possible at home, always preferring Spanish. Indeed, she had no Soviet documents at all; when she travelled abroad, it was either on forged passports or stateless documents from the Red Cross.

She was a light sleeper and an early riser, at 4 or 5 am. She would spend several hours reading, or writing speeches, articles or memoranda. After that she would wake any of her grandchildren who might be staying.[22] She then did her daily physical exercises, a routine she kept up until a week before her death. They included exercises to help her lungs, similar to those of an opera singer, for she had suffered from emphysema since her operation in 1949. She was an immensely practical woman, who had lost none of the talents she had been forced to acquire as a young housewife in Somorrostro. She was a good cook, and liked to sew and knit, sometimes making her own clothes, she was good with her hands, delighting her grandsons by making catapults for them. She was still physically strong; one of her little hobbies was to move the furniture around periodically, and she liked to do it herself. She loved animals; the apartment was usually home to dogs, cats, canaries (at least two at any one time), a parrot which had pride of place for a while, and even a hedgehog rescued from the woods near Moscow. She was always well dressed and groomed and liked everyone else around her to follow suit.

For all her revolutionary impulses, she was at heart a deeply conservative person. At one time she forbade the women around her to wear trousers, although she softened on this later as these garments became more fashionable. She hated people around her smoking, and particularly women. She tried to stop her eldest grandson, Fiodor, from taking up the habit by forcing him to smoke a whole packet one after the other. She was moderate in her personal ways: she liked a little wine or beer and the odd glass of brandy after supper, but never vodka, saying it was fit only for getting drunk on, a habit she disapproved of. She would give the children a little wine at meals, mixed with water in the continental fashion. When they had colds, she would give them a mixture of brandy, milk and honey. She was, indeed, a keen amateur student of medicine. Of all her family, she was closest to her granddaughter Dolores (Lola), a lively and intelligent girl in whom she probably saw many of the characteristics of her beloved son Rubén. Lola was in turn devoted to her grandmother. She recalled:

> She had enormous personality and energy. Everyone living with her had to submit to her daily régime. She was dominating and tolerant at the same time. She made my friends welcome, cooked meals for them and me and would then retire to her room.
> She wanted me to have a career so that I wouldn't depend on anyone else. When I said I wanted to be a journalist, she said 'Fine' but it was a hard life for a woman. She wanted me to study but would then say: 'Why aren't you engaged yet? I don't care if you get married three times but it's time you got started!'[23]

It was in many ways an isolated life – isolated both from ordinary Soviet concerns and from those affecting other Spanish exiles. As well as the apartment, La Pasionaria had a car and a chauffeur, and a dacha in the country. Until 1965 it was at Uspenskoye (where the famous resignation meeting took place). But her grandchildren complained that it was too far away and they got car-sick on the way there. She asked for one nearer the city, and was provided with one at Zazechiye. The dacha had a good-size garden with four or five apple trees. La Pasionaria liked to potter about, planting strawberries and flowers. She enjoyed looking for wild mushrooms in the neighbourhood, but above all she liked to lie in a hammock, reading. But she never really enjoyed being in the country; she once told Santiago Alvarez: 'There are pines and flowers, but no people. I like human beings, not countryside.' She said much the same to Lola. Many old Communist Party figures and distinguished foreigners like herself had dachas in the area, which provoked her to describe it to her granddaughter as 'the cemetery'. She had lived in cities since the 1930s and longed for their noise and bustle. Perhaps she hated to be reminded of the loneliness and poverty of her days in the Basque Country.

La Pasionaria's longing to return to Spain grew more and more intense with every passing year of exile. Although she was in relatively good health, she must have been increasingly anxious that she would die in exile. Franco was ageing too but as the 1960s wore on he showed no sign of giving up power, and as long as he remained in the Pardo Palace there was no prospect of La Pasionaria returning home. Her granddaughter commented:

> She talked constantly of returning to Spain. She rarely spoke about the Civil War. She talked only of her adventures, never the bad times. She liked to talk about her childhood, and her family. Despite her Basque background, she always spoke of Madrid as 'home'. She would have liked to live in Italy. She tried to get us out of the USSR, but I think she couldn't persuade Amaya to leave. It was crazy to live in the USSR: so isolated, so cold, such a restricted life, but she didn't let on. At Christmas and on her birthday she drank a toast to 'next year in Madrid'.[24]

The toast had echoes of Jews down the ages saying 'Next year in Jerusalem!' at the annual Passover Seder night.

La Pasionaria kept in touch with events in Spain as best she could. Her main sources of information were the pro-Franco newspapers like *ABC*, which she read every day, and visitors from Spain, who tended to paint an over-optimistic picture of the Left's chances of over-throwing the Generalíssimo. Despite her bouts of depression, she tried to put on a good front for her guests. Marcelino Camacho, leader of the then illegal communist trade union movement Comisiones Obreros, recalled an evening spent with her and various other comrades at her apartment when she joined vigorously in a session of Spanish songs.

In the summer of 1964 her old Civil War friend and ally Palmiro

Togliatti, general secretary of the Italian Communist Party, died. La Pasionaria travelled to Rome to attend his funeral and delivered a moving speech at the graveside. This gathering of communist notables was the first occasion on which La Pasionaria met Leonid Brezhnev, who was heading the Soviet delegation. She was struck by the 'intense blue of his eyes, contrasting with his dark complexion'. She thought him an 'affable and simple character with whom one could argue about any political or human topic'. A few months later, this affable and simple character helped to overthrow Khrushchev and succeeded him as general secretary of the Soviet Communist Party. The news took the world, and not least the Spanish Communist Party, totally by surprise (Khrushchev too, by all accounts). Santiago Carrillo, in Paris, wrote to La Pasionaria to try to fathom out what had happened, in his usual cautious fashion. She arranged for a representative of the Soviet Communist Party to go to Paris and explain personally to Carrillo why the Party had carried out its latest internal putsch.

The Spanish communists were engaged in their own internal bloodletting at this time: a long-simmering revolt by the two men who could justly be regarded as the PCE's brightest intellectuals, Federico Claudín and Jorge Semprún, was coming to a head. Although Carrillo had broken with Stalinism and was trying to persuade the world that he was both modernising and liberalising the Spanish Party, Claudín and Semprún did not see it that way. With the benefit of hindsight, they can be seen as extraordinarily prophetic about political developments in Spain more than a decade later. The official PCE line, having renounced force as a means of overthrowing Franco, was that the régime would eventually weaken and crumble, forcing the bourgeoisie to make concessions which would open the way for the masses to take more power, culminating in total control (ie capitalism would disintegrate from its own internal contradictions, in the classic Marxist analysis). At the beginning of 1964 Claudín proposed an alternative scenario: when Franco finally did die, Spain's political and, above all, economic development meant the ruling oligarchy would remain in power and would control the country's post-dictatorship political development. While most communists happily imagined that a revolutionary atmosphere would be created by Franco's departure, Claudín was positing a much more gradual evolution which might lead to some sort of democratic outcome. Such a hard-headed analysis did not go down well with

185

Claudín's comrades, whose grip on political reality was tenuous at the best of times. And in the mid-1960s they were in no mood to listen to a thesis that promised the PCE only more years of patient slogging even after Franco's demise.

Claudín, supported by Jorge Semprún, put forward his analysis at a plenary meeting of the Party's executive committee, as the Politburo had been renamed in 1960, held in Prague from 27 March to 2 April 1964, and presided over by La Pasionaria. When Claudín and Semprún had spoken, she rose and launched a ferocious attack on them which reminded her audience of her great old days. 'Listening to Claudín, I could not believe it was a leader of the Spanish Communist Party speaking. I seemed to be . . . listening to the whining social democratic tones of half a century ago.'[25] In a memorable phrase, she dismissed Claudín and Semprún as 'hare-brained intellectuals'. But Semprún was not cowed: he hit back with a brave speech in which he referred obliquely to La Pasionaria's own chequered history by reminding his audience of the personality cult which had reigned during the 1950s. Everybody knew to whom he was referring. When he brought up the Czechoslovakian show trials of the early 1950s, during which a Czech communist friend of his, who had been in Buchenwald with him, was accused among his other 'crimes' of working for the Gestapo (he was executed), La Pasionaria could not restrain herself. She interrupted with the accusation that he, Semprún, had not done anything to defend him, a breathtaking comment from one who had certainly done nothing of the kind herself. The outcome was that Claudín and Semprún were suspended from the executive committee pending a decision on their future by the central committee. When putting the motion to the executive committee, La Pasionaria did not call for those against to vote. Claudín and Semprún had to remind her that they at least opposed it.

The affair of Claudín and Semprún dragged on for the rest of 1964 before they were finally expelled from the Communist Party in 1965. In later years Santiago Carrillo liked to paint himself as a reformer, the earliest exponent of Eurocommunism, as it became known in the late 1960s and early 1970s, when it became the most fashionable thing to be in Western European left-wing circles. It meant a brand of communism that was more democratic than the Soviet version, which allowed for pluralism and the gaining of power by the ballot box, permitted free speech within and without the Communist Party, and modified the old, hackneyed idea of the dictatorship of the proletariat brought about by violent revolution. In short, Euro-communism recognised that no Communist Party could hope to make progress without recognising Western Europe's devotion to the democratic process and what the communists were pleased to call the 'ruling oligarchy's' tenacity in holding on to political power. But in reality Carrillo, like his predecessor La Pasionaria, was a Stalinist by conviction and method, and his purging of Claudín and Semprún for espousing ideas which were to become common currency within the Western communist movement within a few years demonstrated the fact. The departure from the PCE of two such fine minds had little effect on the Party's immediate fortunes. It continued to gain surreptitious support within the Spanish working class as the 1960s progressed, while both Claudín and Semprún flourished once freed from the Party's stultifying intellectual atmosphere. Claudín went on to write distinguished books of political theory, Semprún to write a series of prize-winning novels, memoirs and screenplays including the film *La Guerre est Finie*, starring Yves Montand, which brilliantly captured the impotence and despair of Spanish republican exiles as the years passed and they seemed no nearer to returning home or achieving their political aims. Indeed, Claudín and Semprún admitted that this sense of disillusionment had played a big part in their rebellion against the PCE's autocratic ways. As Claudín said in a revealing aside to Carrillo: 'Listen, I'm 52 years old and I still haven't achieved anything of what I would have liked to have done.'[26] That remark summed up the feelings of a whole generation of Spanish exiles. (Claudín and Semprún both returned to Spain after Franco's death. Claudín died in 1989. Semprún joined the Socialist Party and became a cabinet minister in the government of Felipe González, serving as a distinguished and effective minister of culture.) But in the long run the expulsion of this talented pair was probably harmful to the Spanish communists. They might have brought about a more open-minded Party in the 1970s, or at least have persuaded the public that there was less to fear from the communists than they thought. As it was, the most potent symbol of the party in the public mind continued to be La Pasionaria, and that was not helpful in the long term.

While Carrillo consolidated his hold on the PCE, La Pasionaria in Moscow continued to play her role of elder stateswoman. But Carrillo still found her useful, as for example in her assistance in interpreting Khrushchev's fall. Indeed, although they had never been close personally, Carrillo was always careful to cultivate La Pasionaria and not let her feel too isolated from the PCE's activities. She might be in virtual retirement but she could be a dangerous enemy.

While the PCE was making steady progress, the Soviet Communist Party under Brezhnev was becoming increasingly conservative. La Pasionaria found nothing to quarrel about in this; quite the reverse. Her way of thinking was returning to fashion in the USSR, but it could not have been more out of place in the West, where the revolutionary Left was making all the intellectual running. As young people in France, West Germany, the United States and Britain increasingly questioned the political values of the capitalist world, a similar rebellion against the communist status quo was taking place in Eastern Europe, most notably in Czechoslovakia, and it was over developments there that La Pasionaria finally stood up and criticised the Kremlin.

The Prague Spring of 1968 and the Soviet invasion of August the same year were watersheds for Western communists, who on the whole behaved in a braver and more dignified fashion than they had over similar events in Hungary in 1956. On that occasion, La Pasionaria had led the Spanish communists' vocal support for the Soviet Union's actions, but times had now changed. While the Czech people confronted the Soviet tanks and thousands fled in despair over the borders to the West, the Western Communist Parties engaged in a heated debate over the issue, and all the important ones – the Italians, the French, even the usually docile British – condemned the Soviet action. It could not have come at a more embarrassing time for them: all the Western Communist Parties were attempting to convince their respective electorates that they had sloughed off the skin of Soviet-style communism: the French and Italian Parties were both engaged in building electoral pacts with other left-wing forces.

For the Spanish Communist Party the invasion was equally inconvenient, but it had to be addressed none the less. The Spanish communists (with a few notable exceptions) had supported Dubček's reforms from the start, but on the other hand they had also always been the Soviet Union's most loyal subjects, and a considerable number of its members, and some of its leaders, still lived there. But some also lived in Czechoslovakia – and the PCE's chief representative in Prague was none other than Francisco Antón, now rehabilitated after his fall from grace. In early August, with talk of an imminent Soviet invasion in the air, he had travelled to Paris to brief the PCE executive committee on the situation in Czechoslovakia and to support Dubček (an entirely understandable position for a man who had suffered as badly from Stalinism as Antón had). Carrillo backed this stance, with an independence that was surprising in such a strong ally of the USSR, and then went to the Soviet Union for his summer holidays, meeting La Pasionaria in Moscow to discuss the crisis and assure each other that the Soviets would leave the Czechs alone.

It was wishful thinking. The Soviet army went in on 21 August; Carrillo cut short his holiday on the Black Sea and with two other members of the PCE executive flew back to Moscow to meet La Pasionaria. Conscious above all of his need to show his democratic credentials within Spain, Carrillo was all for denouncing the Soviet action outright but La Pasionaria, indefatigably pro-Soviet, managed to restrain him slightly. The PCE sent a letter to the Soviet Communist Party saying it could not approve the Soviet invasion, 'regretting' that for the first time in the Spanish Party's long history (47 years) it had to differ with its patron, and proposing a conference of Communist Parties of East and West to seek a solution.

A couple of days later, La Pasionaria, Carrillo and three other members of the PCE executive were summoned to meet Mikhail Suslov and Boris Ponomarev of the Soviet Politburo to hear the official explanation for the Czech invasion. The Spanish delegation repeated its disquiet and opposition to the Soviet action. In the second volume of her memoirs La Pasionaria could hardly bear to recall what must have been an excruciating meeting for her. Her account of the entire episode is as follows:

> In August 1968 there occurred the most bitter moment in our relations with the Soviet leaders. The motive was the entry of Warsaw Pact forces into Czechoslovakia. The facts are well known. And so is the public reaction of the leadership of our party.
>
> Santiago Carrillo, Simón Sánchez Montero, Ignacio Gallego, Francisco Romero Marín and I argued on that occasion with comrades Suslov and Ponomarev, expressing our deep anxiety and disagreement.
>
> I had collaborated for many years with comrade Suslov, for whom I felt great respect, as I did for Boris Ponomarev. The fraternal friendship between our two Parties was proverbial, indeed historic.
>
> We considered, in spite of everything, that the most loyal, the most authentic thing, was to tell the truth, to express sincerely what we felt.
>
> Although it was painful.[27]

But the Spanish Party was by no means united on the issue: there were plenty of supporters of the Soviet action within its ranks and the argument raged on between them and Carrillo's backers. On 18 September Carrillo called a meeting of the central committee near Paris to discuss the matter further. La Pasionaria made a rare journey from Moscow to be present. She made a decisive speech in which she condemned the Soviet invasion in the clearest possible language – 'for the first time in its history the PCE has to say No to the Communist Party of the Soviet Union' – while making clear that the PCE's future lay in supporting the USSR. The Czech invasion was to be treated as a one-off. It was a clever tactic and it helped to ease Carrillo's path, for he was by then in some difficulties with the hardliners within his Party, who were outraged by his outspoken attacks on the USSR.

Nowhere was the split more evident than within the ranks of the Spanish exiles in Moscow. When La Pasionaria returned there, she went to a meeting in the Spanish Centre, the exiles' social centre, and the one place in the whole Soviet Union where they could be Spanish, speak their own language, sip Spanish coffee, play cards and temporarily forget the rigours of Soviet life. The meeting was settled in Spanish style too. So great was the antagonism between the two sides – for and against the invasion of Czechoslovakia – that a fight broke out, with punches and chairs being freely thrown. The result was a formalised split between hardliners and moderates; they even had two separate versions of the PCE newspaper *Mundo Obrero*, one with a red masthead, one with a black one.[28] La Pasionaria sided with the moderates. Carrillo returned the favour by entrusting La Pasionaria with a new task: that of coming up with a coherent policy for the Party with respect to the Spanish regions, an area of conflict that Franco's iron fist had managed to control for 30 years but which was now re-emerging into the political arena.

CHAPTER SIXTEEN

THE END OF EXILE

On 22 July 1969 General Franco proclaimed his future successor: Prince Juan Carlos, grandson of Spain's last king, Alfonso XIII, who had abdicated in exile in 1941. Franco had decided that the best way for the country to proceed after his death was under a constitutional monarchy and to this end Juan Carlos was installed as the future king before the Cortes. He would have to serve six years as heir apparent but at least the ageing Franco had laid down the structure he wished to replace him. From exile, the communists naturally denounced the restoration of the monarchy, although within a decade they were to be supporting it vociferously. And what a decade the 1970s were to be for Spain, the decade which saw the end of Franco's long reign, the slow and delicate dismantling of his government apparatus, the legalisation of long-banned political parties, including the communists, the restoration of democracy, and the return from exile of the last Civil War republican veterans, the most notable of whom were Santiago Carrillo and La Pasionaria.

Although the communists passionately opposed Franco's move, they knew it was the beginning of the end in a long game of political chess in which all they had managed to achieve was to stay in play – just. But as the 1970s opened, their hopes were higher than at any time since the end of the Civil War. Their patient strategy looked as if it might be paying off at last. There was a widespread feeling outside Spain that Franco could not last much longer and that it was time Spain rejoined the Western democratic club, although many doubted whether this could be achieved peacefully. The communists would obviously be among the beneficiaries and strove to project themselves as a Party that had shaken off its old totalitarian ways. In this task, however, they were generally unsuccessful. Inside Spain, the PCE was still widely remembered as the perpetrator of some of the worst atrocities of the Civil War (for example the Paracuellos massacre, and

191

the killing of priests and nuns) and as being dominated by the Soviet Union. The official press lost no opportunity to remind readers of these connections. That the Party was still firmly controlled by the old guard from the Civil War era did little to support its claims of being reconstituted as a vibrant new democratic force. The fact that its president, La Pasionaria, still lived in the Soviet Union and sang its praises at every opportunity, despite the Czechoslovakian débâcle of 1968, was no help either. And the emerging middle class, which had known only Franco's rule and had greatly profited from it, had a horror of returning to the instability of the 1930s which most of them had only heard and read about, but which was a powerful force for stability, moderation and distrust of the Left.

But there were positive developments too for the Communist Party inside Spain. The most obvious, apart from a generalised pressure for greater freedom of thought and expression, was the rise of the Workers' Commissions (Comisiones Obreras, abbreviated to CCOO). This was an unofficial trades union organisation, which had started in La Pasionaria's old territory, the coalmines of Asturias, in 1956, had been stamped on by the authorities but had survived to expand and prosper in the 1960s as workers in the fast-expanding industrial sector sought to improve their conditions. The Communist Party had worked assiduously to dominate the CCOO and through it had achieved a respectable platform within the working class. Its most prominent figure, who was to become its official head when it was legalised in the late 1970s, was another communist Civil War veteran, Marcelino Camacho.

The echoes of the Soviet invasion of Czechoslovakia were still affecting the PCE in exile. The Soviet leadership had not forgiven the PCE's apostasy in opposing the invasion and there was a significant pro-Soviet element within the PCE Politburo which attempted to reverse Party policy and bring it back within the Soviet fold, with the active support of the Soviets and their security machine. The two chief plotters were Eduardo García, who had been a Civil War brigade chief at 19, and Agustín Gómez, who had been evacuated to the USSR from the Basque country as a teenager and who was otherwise of interest as a brilliant footballer who rose to captain the famous Moscow Torpedo team and even to play for the Soviet Union national side. He returned illegally to Spain in 1956 and worked to restore the fortunes of the PCE in his native Basque Country before being arrested and, on release, fleeing back to the USSR. This picturesque career did not prevent him and García being expelled from the Spanish Party in 1969 for their factional activities. They were followed a year later by the grizzled old figure of Enrique Líster, who had always hated Carrillo and who subsequently set up his own Communist Party in opposition to the PCE. It never prospered, however, despite Soviet backing and a relentless intellectual shelling mounted by the old Civil War hero against Carrillo, who at one stage approached La Pasionaria to act as a mediator between the two warring camps. Torn between her loyalty to the USSR and to the PCE, of which she had after all been a founder-member, she declined to enter the fray, which effectively left Carrillo free to purge the Stalinists.

Líster was expelled at a plenary meeting of the PCE central committee, held in a Paris suburb in August 1970. The meeting was a lively one, for Líster refused to go quietly and there was uproar after he and four other hardline pro-Soviets were thrown out of the Party. But in a sense it also marked the end of the effective political road for La Pasionaria. When the fuss had died down, she presented her report on the Spanish regions, which Carrillo had commissioned from her. It was a disaster, a rambling, largely historical monologue which contained no hint of understanding what was going on in the regions and no clue as to how the Party might address itself to the growing problems there. In La Pasionaria's native Basque country, for instance, the new underground nationalist organisation ETA had emerged, assassinating members of the security forces and putting the nationalist issue back on the agenda after Franco's long repression of it. But La Pasionaria gave no sign of realising how important such a development was. Unfortunately for her, the audience contained many members of the younger generation of communists, whose first big assembly this was. They were horrified and embarrassed by what they heard from this near-mythical old figure, by now a stooped and white-haired old lady whose intellectual faculties were clearly on the wane. She would be 75 in December and the meeting concluded with the usual birthday tributes, brought forward by a few months.

But although she was increasingly being written off by the younger generation, she still had her uses. The PCE had to rebuild its bridges with the Soviet Communist Party. It might have asserted its independence but it still needed the moral and, above all, economic support which only the USSR could provide. La Pasionaria, living in Moscow and still retaining the Kremlin's respect despite her stance on Czechoslovakia, was the key link with the Soviet leadership and the channel through which they re-established a modus vivendi with the PCE. She continued her life of communist dignitary-in-exile, travelling round the Eastern bloc countries to attend conferences on this and congresses on that. Jorge Semprún, whose expulsion from the PCE she had approved in 1964, recalled meeting her by chance at Belgrade airport. She appeared to bear no animus against him. 'Federico,' she called across the transit lounge (she still thought of him by his communist *nom-de-guerre* Federico Sánchez) and engaged him in animated conversation. He went on:

> The plane to Moscow was called and off she went (would La Pasionaria remember she had expelled me to the outer darkness?), waving goodbye, followed by Irene Falcón and a little retinue of Yugoslav followers . . . [1]

She was still wheeled out occasionally to address mass meetings in France and elsewhere, for she was even now the PCE's biggest public draw; there was simply no one else in the party with her public image who could get a crowd going as she could, even if her speeches were full of ancient history and crude slogans. In June 1971, she and Carrillo spoke to a mass meeting in the park at Montreuil, near Paris, organised by the French Communist Party as part of a week of solidarity with the PCE, which used it to restore morale among the exile community after the Líster split. La Pasionaria's speech was a compilation of all her classic themes: she harked back to the great days of 1936, when she had taken Paris by storm with her fiery speeches in defence of the embattled Spanish republic; she recalled how the French intellectuals and workers had rallied to the aid of Spain; she remembered the French and Spanish who had died fighting Hitler; but she claimed not to be obsessed with the past (and clearly did not wish her exile to last as long as that of the Jews from Israel):

> We meet, not to weep like the daughters of Jerusalem over our long exile, nor to stir the ashes of fratricidal hatreds, nor to raise like a flag of battle the shroud of our dead. We meet, as communists always do, to talk of life and the struggle; of our hopes and dreams, of our confidence in the bright future of our homeland.[2]

The French authorities were displeased enough with Carrillo for speaking out so publicly to expel him from the country, although he was soon allowed to return. In an odd sort of way, the older La Pasionaria got, the greater her legend became. She was still capable of the odd shrewd and striking phrase. In July 1972, the Party held its

VIIIth Congress in another Paris suburb. It confirmed its continuing modernisation (approving, for example, the European Economic Community) and influx of young blood. But La Pasionaria warned that the old guard would not give up control of the Party just yet. As she told the closing session, 'We were, are and will be.'[3] She seemed unaware that it was precisely because the PCE was thus composed that it would eventually fail to convince the Spanish people that it had really altered its spots.

The momentum for reform in Spain gathered pace as the 1970s went on. It gained a huge stimulus in April 1974 with the peaceful 'revolution of the carnations' in neighbouring Portugal, which overthrew the Caetano régime, the successor of the government of President Salazar, who had matched Franco in style and longevity. The opposition groups in Spain were gaining in strength and confidence, forming anti-government associations to work on common platforms of free elections, political amnesty and freedom of expression.

In June 1974 Carrillo and La Pasionaria addressed their biggest public meeting for decades in Geneva. Thousands of Spanish exiles came from all over Europe to hear the communist veterans speak. Their legend was still potent enough for the Swiss authorities, ever anxious to guard their neutrality, to ban them from speaking to the meeting, to be held in a sports stadium. But the organisers had thought of a way of getting round the ban. They took Carrillo and La Pasionaria to a recording studio where they taped their speeches. When she got on the podium, La Pasionaria was given a great ovation. She then surprised the crowd by announcing: 'Comrades, we have been forbidden from speaking but no one has forbidden us from singing. And I am going to sing a revolutionary song from my youth.' She then proceeded to do so, and earned a great ovation. Her speech and Carrillo's were then delivered on tape. They were of the greatest significance, given the tense times. Carrillo promised that the PCE would respect democracy and would not resort to violence unless violence was used against a democratic government. In her turn, La Pasionaria repeated his pledges, talking of 'a transition from Francoism to democracy without bloody confrontations or violence.' She also devoted a long passage in praise of the new spirit abroad in the Catholic Church, many of whose bishops and clergymen were active in the democratic movement in Spain and whom La Pasionaria had been targeting in her speeches for some years. And she concluded with a sentence spoken 'live', in defiance of the Swiss authorities' ban:

> Goodbye for now, comrades and friends, compatriots, until we meet
> again soon in a democratic Spain, in which you also will have a task to
> fulfil in the building of a new, free and democratic country, raised with the
> enthusiasm and love of all Spaniards.[4]

The Swiss reaction was to ask Carrillo and La Pasionaria to leave the
country forthwith. Carrillo did so but La Pasionaria, calculating
perhaps that the Swiss would not rush to remove an old lady of 79
before the eyes of the world's press, stayed on for several days. She
wanted, she said, to show something of the country to her granddaughter Dolores, who had accompanied her from Moscow. When
she did eventually leave, a customs officer searched her bag and that of
Irene Falcón. When he discovered a photograph of La Pasionaria
among Irene's copious papers, his sour expression turned to one of
delight. 'Is that the lady who sang on television?' he enquired. When
told that it was indeed her, he said he hadn't recognised her, she had
been marvellous and could he keep the picture?[5]

The days of the Franco government were obviously numbered. The
old dictator was in poor health and his hand-picked political successor,
Admiral Luis Carrera Blanco, was audaciously assassinated by ETA in
the middle of Madrid in December 1973. His car was blown up, over
an apartment building and into its courtyard, and with it went the one
man who might have delayed the advance of democracy by a few
years after Franco's departure. But back in Moscow, La Pasionaria
could detect no sign that she would soon be allowed to return home.
Official hostility to the still illegal Communist Party, and to her
personally, remained as deep-seated as ever. She made repeated
requests for a Spanish passport and was continually turned down, in
increasingly terse terms. At her advanced age, she could be forgiven
for wondering if death might catch up with her before her old enemy
Franco, and before she could return home. Her thoughts turned more
and more to the end of her long separation from Spain, but as more
and more political exiles were allowed to return and she was still
denied a passport she grew increasingly depressed about the prospect
of ever going home.

In the event, she did outlast Franco, who was three years her senior.
He died on 20 November 1975, aged 83, after a long-drawn-out
agony, having been kept alive (but little more than that) by every

artificial aid modern medicine could muster. La Pasionaria delivered a sober speech on Radio Pirenaica which was notably lacking in the vitriol she had traditionally reserved for the departed Caudillo:

> As if awakening from a horrible nightmare, our people have heard of the death of Franco . . .
>
> Franco is dead, but eternal Spain, the Spain of democracy and freedom, the Spain which gave life to a whole world, lives on in its marvellous people . . . and Spain . . . begins to open new paths, overcoming not a few difficulties, but sure of re-establishing in our country the fact of Spaniards living together, which was not possible under Francoism.
>
> Dawn is breaking over Spain, and that dawn is today, breaking with the shadows of the past. It is the dawn of a Spain in which the people will be the main actor . . . In these emotional moments, my first thoughts go to our prisoners, to all those political prisoners, who must immediately be released; and this must be the principal preoccupation of all those who fight for and wish for the re-establishment of a democratic régime in Spain.[6]

Two weeks later La Pasionaria was 80. The anniversary would have been celebrated with customary splendour in any event but coming so soon after Franco's death it had a renewed symbolism for the communist movement. The Italian Communist Party used her birthday as the centrepiece of a grand act of solidarity in Rome with the Spanish Communist Party, and the cause of democratic reform in Spain. Far from being the outcast of old, forced to wear a wig and disguise, she was now accorded a welcome befitting her status as the grand dame of the communist movement. She was welcomed by the Mayor of Rome (a Christian Democrat) and presented with the medal of the city. Then it was on to the indoor Palace of Sport to be greeted by a crowd of 30,000 people, chanting 'Dolores a Madrid, si, si, si', and 'Free Spain'. This was the heyday of Eurocommunism, the attempt to blend Marxism with the Western democratic tradition, and the Italians were in the forefront of it. The atmosphere was one of euphoria and celebration. On the platform with La Pasionaria were two old friends who had both fought in the Spanish Civil War, Luigi Longo, President of the Italian Communist Party (PCI), and Pietro Nenni, leader of the Italian Socialist Party. After the PCI's general secretary Enrico Berlinguer and Santiago Carrillo had spoken, La Pasionaria responded with one of her strolls down memory lane, invoking the ghosts of past glories and the phantoms of future greatness. Robin Lustig, a young journalist with Reuters, was sent to report on the event. In his dispatch he wrote:

> The 80-year-old Señora Ibárruri told the cheering crowd: 'The bloody Francoist tyranny was never able to stifle the desire for struggle of a people which would not, and which will not, live on its knees.'
>
> The echo of one of her most famous Civil War slogans – 'it is better to die on one's feet than live on one's knees' – brought a deafening roar from the crowd, which included many exiled Spaniards and veterans of the International Brigades who fought on the republican side during the 1936-39 Civil War.
>
> . . . Señora Ibárruri, who spoke with much of the rhetorical power which made her famous during the 1930s, ended her speech by quoting the Archbishop of Madrid, Cardinal Vincente Enrique y Tarancón: 'For Spain to advance along its own road . . . there is a need for the co-operation of all, with respect for all.
>
> 'With all the strength of my communist convictions,' she added, 'I call for a national reconciliation to put an end to the state of dividedness which the Francoist dictatorship imposed on the country, over the bodies of one million dead.
>
> 'I don't say adiós to you but hasta pronto, y a Madrid.
>
> '(See you soon, and in Madrid.)'

Recalling that day 16 years later, Lustig said: 'I remember this liverish figure with an enormous presence. It was like seeing a dinosaur come back to life.'[7]

Back in Moscow, there was more homage for her birthday from the Soviet Communist Party. At a ceremony in the House of Science, attended by hundreds of Soviet dignitaries and Spanish exiles, Boris Ponomarev, whom La Pasionaria had berated in 1968 for the invasion of Czechoslovakia, read out a message of greetings from the central committee. The old lady had been forgiven for stepping out of line (and anyway it had turned out to be a one-off gesture). She was presented with the Order of the October Revolution, which made a complete set of Soviet medals. La Pasionaria rewarded them with a long and familiar speech, pledging herself to continue fighting for the cause to which she had devoted her long life.

Franco's death removed the cork from the bottle in which the forces of reform in Spain were pent up. From now on the momentum for democracy was unstoppable, although it was to pass through many nasty moments. The Communist Party had been admitted to one of the two umbrella movements for democratic reform, the Junta

Democrática (Democratic Union). Its main aim now was to press to be legalised, for the first time since 1939, but there was no sign that this would happen in the near future. The new monarch and the governments of first Carlos Arías Navarro and then Adolfo Suárez, dared not contemplate such a deed for fear of upsetting the already nervous armed forces and precipitating a coup d'état.

Santiago Carillo, still in exile in Cannes, knew the only place to be now was in Madrid. In February 1976 he returned to Spain, illegally, for the first time in 37 years, disguised in a wig, and took charge of the Party organisation within the country. In Moscow, La Pasionaria applied again for a Spanish passport and again was turned down. She took the rebuff badly, as might be expected. For three-and-a-half decades she had waited for this moment and still her hopes were being dashed. Her granddaughter Dolores, who lived with her, recalled that time as being a particularly low ebb for La Pasionaria.

> I think that was one of the worst periods of her life. She was old, surely there could be no more obstacles to her return. She thought she was going to die in the USSR. She became very introverted after Franco's death.[8]

The political scene in Spain was explosive. Prime Minister Arías, a Franco placeman, was holding the ring but little more than that. He was obviously not the man to guide the country towards the democratic constitution and free elections that were increasingly being demanded. In this climate of excitement, intrigue and expectation La Pasionaria found herself experiencing a sort of Indian summer of interest, as the Italian celebration of her birthday had shown. She was regarded as a mythical figure who had been out of the Western limelight for so long that most people probably thought she had passed away with Stalin.

The same sort of process, indeed, was happening to the Spanish Communist Party. It was emerging from the mists of history into the public eye after decades of semi-clandestinity. Its leaders were well known in the Eastern bloc but hardly at all in the West, while within Spain the Party was still viewed with a mixture of fascination and horror. The Party could not demand to be legalised yet remain unknown to the public. So in July 1976 its central committee held an open meeting in Rome, to which the press and representatives of other parties were invited. The venue was the Teatro delli Arti and more than a hundred members of the central committee appeared in public for the first time together. The oldest was La Pasionaria, whom one observer described as playing 'the role of Juno, widow of Jupiter, and queen and mother of Olympus'.[9] But there was a whole generation of new figures too, some of them well-known in Spain whose membership of the Communist Party had hitherto been a secret; the revelation came as a surprise and shock to the Spanish public. It was an important step in demythologising the Party and preparing Spanish public opinion for its re-legalisation.

To La Pasionaria fell the honour of the opening speech. She was notably conciliatory in tone and for once looked to the future rather than dwelling too much on the past. She demanded recognition for the Party, which had, she said, 'maintained a heroic resistance for 40 years and which now emerges as a force to be reckoned with, even if one is not in agreement with all its beliefs. A force without which democracy in Spain cannot be built.' But she repeatedly called for reconciliation among all Spaniards, and once again emphasised the Party's desire to work hard with progressive Catholic forces in the new Spain. 'All the indications are,' she finished, 'that this will be the last Plenum of the central committee which we celebrate outside our country.'

At almost the same time, the man who was to be the architect of Spain's successful transition to democracy, Adolfo Suárez, was sworn in as prime minister, and the pace of reform quickened. But while other opposition political parties were legalised, the communists remained beyond the pale. Suárez gave no sign of giving in on the issue. Indeed, he knew all too well that legalising the Party might be the last straw for the armed forces, already anxious about the reform movement. For them and for the Francoist Right, the communists were still persona non grata. On the ground, the Party would take two steps forward, and one step back. It was openly participating in Democratic Co-ordination (later the Platform of Democratic Organisations – POD), the umbrella beneath which all the principal pro-democracy political movements were now gathered. Negotiations between the Party and the government via intermediaries were going on behind the scenes, and it had two representatives on the ten-strong POD negotiating committee which started talking with Suárez late in 1976. But its leaders were still liable to be arrested, as happened to Carrillo and several of his colleagues, some ten days after he had made his first public appearance inside Spain, when he gave a dramatic press conference, undisguised, and effectively dared the government to take action against him or give him absolute freedom of action.

Suárez's public reaction was to lock him up over Christmas in Madrid's Carabanchel prison. There were large public demonstrations in support of Carrillo: the slogan, chanted and written on banners, was 'Freedom for Santiago – Dolores to Madrid'. Carrillo was freed after eight days and continued to press for the PCE to be legalised before the general election scheduled for June 1977, the country's first free elections since 1936.

The issue was the most delicate one on Suárez's busy agenda, not so much because of the Communist Party's inherent strength as for its symbolic importance. There was a widespread feeling that the readmittance of the communists to the full political process was the touchstone of democracy in the new Spain: despite their record, without them there could be no full democracy and there was also a real danger of pushing them back into illegal, possibly violent, activity. Suárez was almost convinced that the Party had to be legalised but his cabinet was divided and the attitude of the armed forces difficult to gauge: most senior officers opposed the idea but how would they react in practice? Carrillo knew that he had to convince Suárez that the Party's oft-stated commitment to democracy and pluralism was genuine, and he also had to show adherence to the idea of a constitutional monarchy, the chosen framework for democracy. The tension was further heightened in January 1977 when four communist labour lawyers and an assistant were shot dead in their Madrid offices by gunmen presumed to be extreme right-wing activists. The murders shocked Spain and may have achieved the opposite of what their perpetrators intended. The dignified response of the Left and the PCE in particular – they refused to rise to the bait with the sort of violence that the assassins may have been hoping to provoke – impressed the whole country. The minister of the interior, Rodolfo Martín Villa, wrote later of listening on the radio to the huge demonstration-cum-funeral organised by the PCE: 'I knew that the PCE had earned its legalisation that day.'[10]

The Spanish press was now free to interview La Pasionaria without fear of prosecution. At the end of January 1977 the magazine *Cambio 16* reported her in fine fettle but anxious to go home:

> To return to Madrid! It's what I've wanted most for forty years, from the moment I had to leave. I have had all the months and days of forty years to dream that I was walking through the streets of Madrid.
>
> In my house we're always talking of Spain. It's in our conversations, our

feelings, our habits. I look out of the window and there on the balcony are the geraniums of Spain. Now a layer of snow is covering them but they will grow again in the spring.[11]

On the political front, she made clear that the communists would respect the figure of the King and conceded that even under a monarchy there could be democracy. She denied the existence of such a thing as Eurocommunism. For her, each Communist Party developed according to the characteristics of the country it belonged to. And she pleaded again for the PCE to be legalised.[12]

A month later it was the turn of Ismael López-Muñoz, a journalist with *El País*, the most prominent and successful of the new newspapers that had sprung up in the mid-1970s, to visit her in the Spanish Centre in Moscow. She had just spent three weeks in a clinic for a complete check-up to prepare her for the journey home. 'Her physical appearance is magnificent and she shows great vitality,' he wrote. After she had been through her life story with him (it was probably news to *El País*'s young readers), López-Muñoz obtained from her the important admission that the PCE was no longer insisting on the concept of the dictatorship of the proletariat, recognising that it was not appropriate in Spain's current circumstances. She forecast that the PCE would be involved in some form of alliance after the elections, in which she forecast winning 'a large number' of seats. But the Party would behave 'modestly, without bluster'. She finished: 'We do not seek hegemony. We only wish for unity among democratic forces.' It was all part of the PCE's campaign to show itself in the most moderate possible light.[13]

So hysterical was the climate in extreme right-wing circles in Madrid that the neo-fascist newspaper *El Alcázar* confidently reported that La Pasionaria had already returned secretly to Spain. 'It does not offend the dignity of the Suárez government,' the paper editorialised, 'but it does offend the dignity of the Spanish people, of whom she (and Carrillo) were such merciless executioners in the service of Moscow.' The comment was graphic evidence that in some quarters the Civil War was by no means forgotten and certainly not forgiven. The PCE swiftly issued a denial. It was eventually concluded that the mistake had arisen because La Pasionaria had disappeared from her normal haunts during her three-week check-up in Moscow which *El Alcázar* had taken as evidence that she must have returned to Spain.

Adolfo Suárez himself was won over to recognition of the PCE when he finally agreed to meet Carrillo. On 27 February 1977 they met at the house of an intermediary and talked privately for several hours. Martín Villa wrote: 'Now there can be no doubt that, in the conversation which took place there, the seducer Adolfo Suárez was politically seduced by the veteran communist leader.'[14]

While that may have been so, Suárez still had to tread a narrow path between the expectations of the Left and the caution of the Right. Although receiving a setback when the PCE's formal application to be legalised was rejected by the courts, Suárez now had the bit between his teeth. After consulting the cabinet and finding it still divided, he obtained a more favourable ruling from a higher court. With the country and the politicians out of action for Holy Week, when Spain virtually shut down, on 9 April Martín Villa signed the decree which legalised the Communist Party at last and allowed it to put up candidates at the general election. The news was received with consternation on the Right and jubilation on the Left. The navy minister, Admiral Pita da Veiga, resigned but the armed forces as a whole stood firm. Other civilian cabinet ministers threatened to resign too; they had been unaware that Suárez would move so decisively. But in Moscow La Pasionaria was overjoyed by the news. The front page of the communist newspaper *Mundo Obrero* carried photographs of her and Carrillo beneath the headline: 'The PCE legal: A triumph for democracy and reconciliation', in addition to messages from both of them.

La Pasionaria imagined that the last obstacle to her return home had been removed, but she was mistaken. Conservative elements within the government and civil service continued to deny her a passport. Her bitterness knew no bounds. A month passed and finally she announced that she was going to take a flight to Madrid and dare the authorities to arrest her. Shortly afterwards she received a telephone call from the Spanish embassy: her passport was ready and so was Irene Falcón's. They collected them on 12 May and the next day caught an Aeroflot flight to Madrid, after being seen off by a large crowd headed by Mikhail Suslov and Boris Ponomarev, on behalf of the central committee of the Soviet Communist Party. There was a brief stopover in Luxembourg during which the plane was beseiged by dozens of journalists wanting to get a glimpse of the legendary La Pasionaria. Tired and anxious just to get home at last, she declined to see them. Her 38 years of exile – nearly half of her life – were almost over.

CHAPTER SEVENTEEN

RETURN OF THE NATIVE

At Barajas airport, Madrid, a large crowd was waiting to greet La Pasionaria but neither the authorities nor the Communist Party were keen on a massive public homecoming. She was hustled out of the airport in a van belonging to the Spanish national airline Iberia and driven straight off to the apartment the Party had prepared for her and Irene in Sangenjo Street, in the Barrio del Pilar, a new development in the north-west of the city.

The Suárez government and the PCE had a common interest in keeping the old lady on a tight rein. The government did not want to take a chance on her inflaming old passions; the row within the cabinet over the legalisation of the PCE showed how raw nerves still were about the Party. There was also an understandable concern for her security. The Communist Party was, just as understandably, nervous about what La Pasionaria might say once she had found her feet. There was always a chance that a few trenchant statements, say, in defence of the Soviet Union could ruin the Party's careful efforts to build a new image in the run-up to the election.

On her first day back, however, she was the soul of discretion. To the journalists who flocked to her new address, she merely expressed her pleasure at being back in Spain. 'I've come to live in peace and to work in the Party as one works in a normal country,' she said. 'Not to revive old stories.' So sudden had been her return, after such a long wait, that Santiago Carrillo had been caught out on a visit to Seville. He hastened to La Pasionaria's side along with a host of other friends and colleagues from the Party. Then she was off on a drive round Madrid, to revisit some of her old haunts and wallow in the pleasure of coming home.

Reaction to her return was mixed. The newspaper *Arriba* urged her to 'use her moral strength, her prestige, her status of a woman who has suffered so that neither hatred nor anger can flower again here.' The right-wing *ABC* called her 'a ghost from the past, a bitter past which we do not wish to revive.' She had frequently promised that her first journey outside Madrid would be to her native Basque Country and she was as good as her word. On 21 May she travelled to Bilbao, to an emotional welcome, and went on to her native Gallarta, now relatively prosperous and greatly changed from the poverty-stricken village in which she had grown up.

Two days later she made her first speech since returning, to a Communist Party rally in her honour in Bilbao attended by 30,000 people. The poet Blas de Otero read a poem he had composed in her honour. La Pasionaria was clearly tired by her recent exertions and overcome by emotion at her rapturous reception. 'She was visibly moved and unable to contain her tears on several occasions,' reported *ABC*. She invoked the Basque name of her native region which, like the Communist Party, had been banned by Franco: 'Not for a single moment of my life, not during the sorrows and the joys, was the name of Euskadi far from us, but deeply rooted in our heart.' She also praised the Soviet Union. The reference was not lost on other observers, who saw in it a potential timebomb ticking under Santiago Carrillo, sitting beside her on the platform.

Carrillo did not seem to see it that way. He was determined to exploit the legend of La Pasionaria for all that it was worth in the election that was now less than a month away. He proposed that she should stand for a seat in the new Cortes, at the head of the Communist Party's electoral list in Asturias, the tough coalmining region for which she had first been elected 41 years previously to launch her on the meteoric parliamentary career that had effectively ended with the outbreak of the Civil War. Asturias was still a stronghold of the Party but Carrillo's announcement did not go down at all well with the local communists. They expressed their fierce opposition to her candidacy being imposed on them, and with good reason. For them, she was a historical relic who had nothing to offer to the Spain of the 1970s.

It was a direct confrontation between the communist veterans who had lived largely outside Spain for 40 years, and the new generation of communists who had forged their own identity in the face of severe persecution by Franco. But it was a delicate matter. The Asturians used the excuse of her age – she was, after all, now 81. Carrillo would have none of it, and dispatched various other veterans to Asturias to assure them that La Pasionaria was as good as new. She was driven from Euskadi to meet the Asturian Party leaders and initially made a favourable impression on them, describing with relish her visit to Gallarta. Unfortunately, as the day wore on, they heard the same story from her several more times.[1] La Pasionaria was showing every day of her 81 years but it was too late to reverse Carrillo's order; she was to be their chief candidate, whether they liked it or not. (To make matters worse for the Asturian communists, Carrillo imposed another ancient exile, Wenceslao Roces, an 80-year-old who had spent the past 40 years in Mexico, as their candidate for the upper house, the Senate. Although he was elected, he disappeared back to Mexico within a few months, and was replaced by a socialist.)

Despite their misgivings, La Pasionaria was comfortably elected to the Cortes at the general election held on 15 June. From a purely symbolic point of view, Carrillo was undoubtedly right to push her back into parliament. There could be no more ideal symbol of the healing of Spain's wounds than that the fiery orator of the 1936 Cortes should walk through its doors as a deputy to the first democratically elected parliament since that year. At the first session, on 13 July, she was personally greeted by the retiring president of the Cortes, and by the prime minister, Adolfo Suárez, to whom she wished good luck. 'We're going to need it,' he replied with a grin. The minister of the interior, Rodolfo Martín Villa, saw her and the veteran communist poet Rafael Alberti (who had been elected in Cadiz) in the entrance hall. To him, they were, as he put it, 'living history', and assisting them to return had been a task well worth accomplishing.[2] To cap it all, as the oldest member of the Cortes La Pasionaria temporarily became its president (the equivalent of the British Speaker of the House of Commons) because the post was vacant, the previous incumbent having resigned the previous month. It was purely ceremonial, as a new President was swiftly chosen, but the enormous symbolism of her brief appointment was not lost on anyone. For La Pasionaria, it was her crowning moment. Truly the wheel had come full circle.

The symbolism, potent as it was, could not mask the fact that the general election had been a disappointment for the communists. They won only 9.38 per cent of the vote and had 20 deputies. Their campaign had been hurried, because of the delay in winning legal status, but none the less they had hoped for much better: perhaps 20 per cent and 50 deputies, who would have formed a powerful bloc in parliament. Although the election was won by Suárez's centre-right

Union of the Democratic Centre, the clear winner of the left-wing vote was the Socialist Party (PSOE), the communists' old rival, who had kept their distance ever since the break-up of the Popular Front in 1939. The socialists, under their charismatic young leader Felipe González, projected a fresh, youthful yet moderate image which was much more attuned to the popular pulse than Carrillo's brand of communism. They won 29.2 per cent and 118 seats.

Carrillo had run the election campaign the way he wanted, his lists packed with former exiled veterans, and it turned out to be a disappointment. After 40 years of intrigue and self-delusion, the Party had won the allegiance of fewer than one in ten of the Spanish people. It had kept the red flag bravely flying during 40 years of exile and undercover work but the ultimate victory would never now be attained. It had played a dignified – and crucial – role in the restoration of democracy, only for the spoils to go to somebody else. The outlook was not altogether gloomy, however. The communist-dominated and now legal Workers' Commissions were expanding fast and the Party was successfully attracting new recruits: during the next year its membership grew to more than 200,000, making it the largest single Party in the country. But it also became embroiled in a deep internal argument over its future strategy.

The Asturian communists' doubts about La Pasionaria's abilities as a parliamentarian were quickly seen to be entirely justified. Although a regular attender, she did not once speak and made no contribution to the many sessions devoted to formulating a democratic constitution. Indeed, she was often observed to be apparently asleep in her seat, although she denied it. She was, she said, 'thinking'.

The strain of the last few months had taken its toll. In September she went into hospital to have a pacemaker inserted in her heart. In November the unhappiness of the Asturian Communist Party at her imposition on them became public. The regional Party voted to ask her to stand down. She ignored them but continued to have problems with her heart and the following February a new pacemaker was put in.

While she slowly recovered, the Communist Party's wrangling intensified. Carrillo proposed the formal removal of its commitment to 'Leninism' to make it more attractive to the electorate. The change was approved at its IXth Congress in Madrid in April 1978 (incidentally, the first the party had ever held openly inside Spain). This change of direction was opposed by hardliners, particularly in Asturias and

Catalonia, and many members resigned in protest. La Pasionaria was also unhappy with any move that distanced the Party from the Soviet Union and voiced her opposition within the executive committee, although not in public. However, an American journalist who interviewed her later in the year elicited from her a fresh commitment to the dictatorship of the proletariat when the time was right, a complete contradiction to what she had told El País 18 months previously before her return. In truth, the old lady's statements in the interview seemed confused and out of touch and she was frequently corrected by the ubiquitous Irene Falcón, who sat in on the interview. When the journalist tried to get another session with La Pasionaria the next day to clarify matters, she was rebuffed. Irene Falcón told her she could not have another interview and she herself would provide any answers the journalist might require.[3] The message was clear: the Party would not tolerate any further embarrassment.

To the great relief of the Asturians, La Pasionaria announced that she did not wish to stand again for the Cortes when fresh elections were called for February 1979, under the new constitution approved in 1978. Suárez's UCD once again emerged as the major Party, although short of an outright victory, while the socialists, who had looked like winning for much of the campaign, in fact lost a little ground. The communists increased their vote by 300,000 to nearly 2 million, and gained another three deputies for a total of 23. It was a highly respectable performance in the circumstances. La Pasionaria could bow out with honour. She continued to rise at 6 am, doing her exercises, reading and writing before breakfast. As the Party's president, she still had an office in its headquarters and she went there every day, accompanied by the faithful Irene Falcón. She received delegations, attended the odd meeting, gave the occasional interview. She continued to travel, around Spain and to the Eastern bloc. She usually went back to the Soviet Union once a year to see Amaya and her three grandchildren.

More milestones were faithfully celebrated by the Party. In April 1980 the PCE celebrated its 60th anniversary with a big rally in Madrid's principal bull ring at Las Ventas, where she had delivered stirring speeches during the Civil War. Now she shared the platform with Carrillo and Enrico Berlinguer, leader of the Italian Communist Party. The following December she was 85.

In February 1981 came the last spasm of Franco's ultras, who had never accepted the country's transition to democracy: the attempted coup led by the comic-opera figure of a civil guard colonel, Antonio Tejero, who stormed into the Cortes and held the deputies, including all the main political leaders, hostage. Other military units came out in sympathy – the tanks rolled on to the streets in Valencia – but the King stayed firm, broadcasting to the nation on television to denounce the coup, which then collapsed. It was a tense night for people on the Left, who feared a wave of repression as had happened in the wake of Pinochet's coup in Chile in 1973. Many did not return home that night, while others packed bags and passports (and kept them handy for several nights afterwards). But there were many on the Right who were equally appalled by the attempted coup and the spectacle of a few civil guards occupying parliament at gunpoint. A conservative family who were among La Pasionaria's neighbours immediately called on her and offered to take her in and look after her, for it was eminently possible that had the coup been successful soldiers would have come looking for her. It was led by the sort of extreme right-wing Francoists who detested La Pasionaria and would have had no compunction about taking her away and even shooting her. Although she was immensely touched by her neighbours' offer, she decided to sit tight and hope that the coup would fail. Her sangfroid was justified. Spain's new democracy emerged all the stronger for the scare it had received and surmounted.

In July 1980, the writer and journalist Manuel Vicent visited La Pasionaria at the Party's Madrid offices for an article in *El País*. He found her sitting at a big, shiny desk without a single paper on it. He likened her to 'a sacred relic', jealously guarded by the Party, surrounded by devotional objects left by admirers. Her misty eyes would wander off during their conversation to gaze through the window at nothing in particular. She confided that she hoped to live to be 100.[4]

She played no part in the next general election, in October 1982. It was a particularly bitter campaign for the communists. The result, a socialist landslide, showed that the country had moved decisively to the left while simultaneously rejecting the communists out of hand. Their vote sank by more than a million to a humiliating 865,000; they were left with only four deputies, including Carrillo. The decline was largely due to his autocratic rule and failure to modernise the Party. Since the Xth Congress in July 1981 the Party had been riven with dissent and purges, carried out by Carrillo in a style familiar from the 1950s and 1960s. Members were leaving in droves, and the decline accelerated after the election when Carrillo resigned the leadership but secured the job for his protégé Gerardo Iglesias, a little-known ex-miner from Asturias. Another former exile, Ignacio Gallego, resigned in protest and set up his own splinter Communist Party. (That made three, if one counted Enrique Líster's Stalinist faction which the old general still ran.) This latest split, and the factional fighting which continued to rend the Party, prompted La Pasionaria to make virtually her last political gesture, a pathetic and unsuccessful plea for unity at the Party's XIth Congress in 1983. She was deeply upset by the fate of the Party to which she had devoted her life. She did not know it, but the Spanish Party was for once ahead of its time in disintegrating completely. In 1983 neither she nor many other observers could have dreamed that the same thing would happen to the mighty Soviet Communist Party itself within eight years.

La Pasionaria's second volume of memoirs, taking her from the end of the Civil War to the end of her parliamentary career, was published in 1984. Like the first volume, *El Unico Camino*, it left out more than it left in. Irene Falcón collaborated in producing it, and her contribution was doubtless important. For decades she had watched over her famous mistress, administering the details of her life, screening her from the over-inquisitive. It would have been unlike her not to perform this last function when it came to La Pasionaria's version of history.

Irene and La Pasionaria lived quietly together (though they had maintained separate private lives during the years of exile). La Pasionaria had a small circle of friends who visited her regularly. One of the most interesting was a Roman Catholic priest, Father José María de Llanos, who also had the distinction of being a card-carrying member of the Communist Party. This was all the more remarkable because his two brothers had been shot by communists during the Civil War, a fate that Father de Llanos would doubtless have shared had he not been studying for the priesthood in Belgium, where he spent the war years. Returning to Spain after the war, he had worked for many years with immigrant workers in Madrid, and his experience of the poverty in working-class districts of the capital had turned him into a communist sympathiser. He joined the PCE when it was legalised (though he continued his pastoral work as before). It was at a welcome-home party that he met La Pasionaria soon after her return. They became firm friends, and once a week Father de Llanos would visit her at her flat to take coffee with her and Irene. 'She was old and tired and didn't go out much, except to the Party building. But she liked to hear what was going on, so I would tell her what was happening in my district,' he reminisced not long after her death. 'She was a great woman, with the natural charisma of a great lady, despite her poor upbringing. She always wore black, and she didn't talk much. She listened more than she talked, at least with me. She didn't like to speak ill of anyone, though she had many enemies. Her obsession was to talk about the people and justice, and justice for the people, for the little people.'[5]

La Pasionaria's friendship with Father de Llanos (who died in 1992) was one more example of her continuing kinship with the Catholic Church, which was a recurring theme in her life. For all the Spanish hierarchy's image as a deeply conservative force in the land, there were also many 'progressive' priests like Father de Llanos in Spain, working with the poor or on the factory floor. Several such priests, as well as those of a more conservative hue, visited La Pasionaria at her home. So did a local Bishop. 'She was such a figure that they wanted to make up for the calumnies of the past,' was Father de Llanos's opinion.

The last big act of homage to La Pasionaria in her lifetime came in December 1985, to mark her 90th birthday. The Communist Party pulled out all the stops to celebrate the event, as well it might, for it had little else to cheer about. The process of fragmentation had carried on unabated, with Santiago Carrillo still trying to pull the strings behind the shaky leadership of Gerardo Iglesias. The modernisers eventually won the upper hand, forcing Carrillo and his followers off the central committee in 1985; his response, like Líster in 1970, was to set up his own rival party, the 'marxist-revolutionary' Communist Party. That made four Spanish Communist Parties, quite apart from regional variants, fighting over an ever-diminishing slice of the popular vote. It was indicative of its sad position that the main PCE should have to use the 90th birthday of its oldest member as its biggest public event of a bitter year in which it was trying to persuade the Spanish public that it had something new and fresh to offer.

La Pasionaria was now increasingly frail and forgetful, although she still did her physical exercises. Her daughter Amaya and her granddaughter Dolores moved more or less permanently from Moscow to Madrid to look after her. They found a new, more central, apartment in another modern block in the Chamartin district, in Victor de la Serna Street, named after a pro-fascist journalist who was a prominent Franco supporter during and after the Civil War. In post-Franco Spain, such ironies abounded. On 13 September 1989, by now 93 years old, La Pasionaria was admitted to the Ramon y Cajal Hospital, suffering from pneumonia. It was widely thought that the end was near, and the PCE started to make the appropriate arrangements. Eight hundred thousand posters with her face and the legend 'Pasionaria: A Flower of the Twentieth Century' were printed and prepared for distribution. But she rallied and after a month in hospital was well enough to return home on 15 October. It was only a temporary recovery, however. On 7 November, pneumonia was diagnosed again and she was taken back to hospital. A stream of visitors came to wish her well, including Santiago Carrillo. True to her colours to the end, she was bright enough to sing a few bars from an old Asturian revolutionary song for one of them. But in the afternoon of Sunday 12 November, her condition deteriorated. She died peacefully at 7.15 pm, with Amaya, Irene Falcón and three members of the PCE central committee by her bedside. Her granddaughter Dolores arrived soon afterwards, accompanied by Julio Anguita, the latest PCE general secretary. The government sent its chief spokesperson, Rosa Conde, to the hospital to express its sadness at the news and its condolences to La Pasionaria's family.

On the other side of Europe, people were strolling through the huge breaches that had been made in the Berlin Wall two days previously. Throughout Eastern Europe, communist governments were tottering towards collapse. The ordinary people in the countries that had been home to La Pasionaria for 40 years were rejecting the system that she had worshipped, to which she had dedicated her life. The event that had transformed her life was the bolshevik revolution of 1917. The last embers of that fire were now being extinguished in Europe. There could have been no more appropriate time for the grand dame of international communism to leave the stage.

The conservative press initially marked the occasion with little of the rancour La Pasionaria had once inspired. *ABC* commented:

> At the moment in which man confronts the most naked truth of his existence, the only possible attitude is one of respect. This is the first thought we wish to express about the death of Dolores Ibárruri. Respect which grows, confronted with the unbreakable faithfulness to communist ideas which La Pasionaria maintained throughout her life and in the most diverse circumstances.[6]

Although *ABC* next referred to the assassination of Calvo Sotelo in 1936 as 'one of the dark episodes that weigh on Dolores Ibárruri', the generally muted tone would have been unthinkable a few years earlier. This acceptance that there might have been some good after all in La Pasionaria was a further indication of how far Spain had come in shedding the blind hatred between Left and Right which had disfigured so much of its twentieth-century history.

The general reaction in the press was one of nostalgic affection for her, and for what she had symbolised. This was perhaps to be expected. The political stance of the newspapers – *El País, Diario 16, El Mundo, El Independiente* – which had sprung up in the wake of the Franco era was overwhelmingly centrist or moderately left-wing. Their leader writers and columnists treated La Pasionaria sympathetically, although they did not gloss over her political deficiencies. She was treated as a great mother figure, to be respected for standing up to fascism throughout her life. A generation which tended to try to forget that Franco had ever existed had, by contrast, no compunction in lovingly trawling over La Pasionaria's great days in the Civil War and hailing her as a tragic heroine whose return to Spain was a symbol of national reconciliation.

Her body lay in state for three days at the headquarters of the PCE (more irony – it was in Holy Trinity Street) during which some 70,000 people from all over Spain filed past the open coffin to pay their last respects. They included dignitaries like Adolfo Suárez, the former prime minister who had allowed her back into the country, and many luminaries from the Left. But most of them were ordinary people, by no means all communists, who felt that she had cared about them during the hard times. There was a surprising number of young people, for whom she was a figure from the history books. Several said they regarded her as a sort of grandmother. Most touching of all were the disabled Civil War veterans, some in wheelchairs, propelling themselves past the coffin and saluting it with the communist clenched fist.

The size of the crowds who attended the funeral ceremonies, on Thursday 16 November, surprised most observers, perhaps because so many people regarded La Pasionaria as having passed away many years previously. The coffin, draped in the red flag, was slowly borne in a Mercedes hearse through streets packed with mourners, some waving red flags themselves, others chanting slogans from the transition era, like 'Sí, sí, sí, Dolores está aquí'. (Yes, yes, yes, Dolores is here.) Behind the vehicle walked Amaya, the young Dolores and Irene Falcón, and a host of PCE worthies. It took the cortège an hour and a half to reach the Plaza de Colón (Columbus Square), where the main farewell ceremony was held. The square too was packed solid. Ana Belén, a folk singer, sang a song; then, touchingly, Rafael Alberti, the poet who had known La Pasionaria since 1932 and left Spain for exile on the same day, a frail yet dignified figure with flowing white hair, recited one of the many poems he had written about her in their long lives. This was the one he had composed for her 80th birthday party, celebrated in Rome:

> Who does not love her?
> She is not sister, nor girlfriend, nor comrade
> But something else – the working class.
> Mother in the morning sun,
> Soul of our reconquest,
> The open sea, hope,
> The highest revolution,
> She is the Communist Party.

Julio Anguita delivered the address, finishing: 'Sleep, comrade Ibárruri. Repose, comrade Pasionaria. Rest, president. Dream sweetly, mother Dolores.' Then the final emotional moment: a recording of the voice of La Pasionaria herself, speaking to the crowd which had gathered to cheer her on 8 December 1985, the day before her 90th birthday, thanking them for coming and then breaking into a little song. When her voice had died away, the crowd sang the 'Internationale', many with the clenched fist salute. They were not just burying La Pasionaria; they were burying the dream of Red Spain. The actual funeral took place privately at the Almudena cemetery. Fittingly, La Pasionaria's body was laid to rest next to the tomb of Pablo Iglesias, the father of Spanish socialism, who died in 1925.

On the right-wing, there was something of a reaction against the scale of La Pasionaria's funerary ceremonies. There were accusations that the Communist Party had manipulated them for its electoral ends, and more seriously that the tidal wave of eulogies was a deliberate perversion of history, a typical piece of communist rewriting. Pro-Franco historians and writers, like Ricardo de la Cierva, broke their silence to revive long-dormant controversies centring on her. The accusation that she had issued a death threat against Calvo Sotelo in the Cortes in June 1936 was dragged up again, although no new evidence was produced against her. It was clear that the Franco diehards would never forgive La Pasionaria, although it was overwhelmingly evident that she had lost every battle except the last: to be welcomed back into the bosom of the vast majority of her compatriots.

One afternoon in Madrid in May 1991, after I had finished work for the day in the archives of the Spanish Communist Party at its headquarters, where I was researching this book, I walked down the street and went down into the Diego de León Metro station. My eye was caught by a poster on which a graffiti artist had scribbled something. I stopped to look. The message, in bright red ink, read: 'It is better to die on your feet than to live on your knees.'

NOTES AND SOURCES

For bibliographical details see Select Bibliography.

Introduction

1 Ernest Hemingway, *For Whom the Bell Tolls*, ch. 32.
2 Ibid.

1 A Basque Childhood

1 An article in *Le Gringoire*, an extreme right-wing French magazine, 19.9.1936, quoted in *Diario 16*, 13.5.1983, said: 'Pasionaria, although of the Spanish race, is however a person of dubious background. Formerly a nun, she married a monk who had hung up his cassock: thus her great hatred of religious people. She has made herself famous for having hurled herself on an unfortunate priest in the street, cutting his jugular with her teeth.'
2 Raymond Carr, *Spain, 1808–1975*, p. 391.
3 Dolores Ibárruri, *They Shall Not Pass (El Unico Camino)*, pp. 23–4.
4 Video, *Dolores Una Vida, Una Lucha*, produced by José Luis G. Sánchez and Andrés Linares (Marx Memorial Library, London).
5 Ibárruri, op. cit., p. 43.
6 *El País*, 25.7.1981.
7 *Diario 16*, 13.5.1984.
8 *El Mundo*, 18–19.11.1989.
9 Ibárruri, op. cit., pp. 49–50.
10 *Diario 16*, 13.5.1981.
11 *Mundo Obrero*, 18.3.1936.
12 *El Mundo*, 18–19.11.1989.
13 Sebastián Zapiraín, interview, November 1990.
14 Ibárruri, op. cit., p. 44.
15 *Diario 16*, 13.5.1983.

16 Hugh Thomas, *The Spanish Civil War*, Penguin edn, p. 39.
17 Gerald Brenan, *The Spanish Labyrinth*, p. 219.
18 *Mundo Obrero*, 18.5.1936.
19 *Pasionaria* (pamphlet), Partido Comunista de España, 1938.

2 Dolores becomes La Pasionaria

1 *Pueblo*, Interview with Julián Ruiz, 8.11.1972.
2 Ibid.
3 Ibid.
4 *Diario 16*, 13.5.1981. (Apparently, Julián had been reported as claiming in a newspaper interview that they had married after she had her first child. I have not traced this interview and it may be that Julián, by then an old man, was misquoted.)
5 Dolores Ibárruri, *They Shall Not Pass*, p. 59.
6 *Diario 16*, 13.5.1983.
7 Ibárruri, op. cit., p. 60.
8 Ibid.
9 Ibid., p. 62.
10 Tomás Tueros, interview, November 1990.
11 Ibárruri, op. cit., p. 64.
12 El Campesino (Valentín González), *Listen, Comrades*, p. 3.
13 Ibárruri, op. cit., p. 66–7.
14 Her first newspaper by-line was simply 'Pasionaria' (with no prefix) and although abroad she was generally referred to as La Pasionaria, in Spain she was frequently just known as Pasionaria.

3 Tragic Years

1 Hugh Thomas, *The Spanish Civil War*, Penguin edn, p. 40.
2 *El País*, 25.7.1981.
3 Dolores Ibárruri, *They Shall Not Pass*, p. 76.
4 Ibid. pp. 80–1.
5 Sebastián Zapiraín, interview, November 1990.
6 Ibid.
7 Amaya Ruiz Sergueieva, interview, 21 May 1991.
8 Ibid.
9 Ibid.
10 *Pasionaria, Memoria Gráfica*, p. 24.

4 A New Life

1 Archives of Communist Party of Soviet Union, Moscow, 494–1–477, pp 8–9.
2 Dolores Ibárruri, *They Shall Not Pass*, p. 105.
3 Ibárruri, op cit., p.98
4 Amaya Ruiz Sergueieva, interview, 21 May 1991.
5 Angel Ruiz Ayúcar, *El Partido Comunista, 37 Años de Clandestinidad*, p. 23.
6 Irene Falcón, interview, November 1990.
7 Ibárruri, op. cit., p. 128.
8 Ibid., pp. 135–8.
9 Ruiz Ayúcar, op. cit., p. 26.

5 The Road to Civil War

1 Amaya Ruiz Ibárruri, interview, May 1991.
2 Santiago Alvarez, interview, November 1990.
3 Amaya Ruiz Ibárruri, interview, May 1991.
4 Ibid.
5 Olga Lepeshinskaya, interview, July 1991.
6 Dolores Ibárruri, *They Shall Not Pass*, pp. 138–48.
7 Ibid., pp. 148–9.
8 *Mundo Obrero*, 3.1.1936.
9 Ibid., 25.1.1936.
10 The Spanish Falange (Falange Española) was a right-wing anti-liberal, anti-marxist political movement which had many characteristics in common with fascism. It was founded by José Antonio Primo de Rivera in October 1933 and soon merged with another similar organisation, the National-Sindicalist Offensive Unions (Juntas de Ofensiva Nacional-Sindicalista – JONS). Although José Antonio (as he was always known), a romantic figure idolised by his supporters, disowned terrorism, the Falange's enthusiastic young bloods were to some extent shock troops of the Right during the years immediately preceding the Civil War, committing acts of terror, murder, sabotage and arson. José Antonio was executed by the republicans in November 1936, at the age of only 33. The Falange, by then numbering some 100,000 members, was effectively taken over by Franco in 1937 and merged into his Movement (Movimiento) which maintained most of the Falange's pro-Catholic, nationalistic ideals during Franco's long dictatorship.

11 Ibid., 21.2.1936.
12 Ibárruri, op. cit., pp. 165–8.
13 *Mundo Obrero*, 24.2.1936.
14 Ibid., 29.2.1936.
15 Ibid., 7.3.1936.
16 Letters in the Archivo Histórico Nacional, (AHN), Sección Guerra Civil, Salamanca.
17 *Mundo Obrero*, 17.2.1936.
18 Ibid., 7.3.1936.
19 Ibárruri, op. cit., pp. 174–5.
20 *Mundo Obrero*, 11.2.1936.
21 Santiago Carrillo, *Mañana España*, p. 130.
22 AHN, Sección Madrid, Leg 432 (3.272).
23 Carrillo, op. cit., pp. 130–4.
24 *Mundo Obrero*, 15.2.1936.
25 Irene Falcón, interview, September 1990.
26 *ABC*, 17.6.1936.
27 *Mundo Obrero*, 17.6.1936.
28 *ABC* 17.6.1936.
29 Ibárruri, op. cit., pp. 179–80.
30 *ABC*, 5.8.77.
31 Ibárruri, op. cit., p. 180.
32 Irene Falcón, interview, November 1990.
33 Hugh Thomas, *The Spanish Civil War*, Penguin edn, p. 207.
34 *Epoca*, 27.11.1989.
35 *ABC*, 14.11.1989.
36 *Diario 16*, 19.11.1989.
37 Video, 'Dolores Una Vida, Una Lucha', produced by José Luis G. Sánchez and Andrés Linares. (Marx Memorial Library, London).

6 Civil War

1 Bill Alexander, interview 1990.
2 Alvarez, *Memorias*, II, p. 23.
3 *El Sol*, 19 July 1936.
4 Alvarez, op. cit., II, p. 28.
5 William Forrest, interview, November 1990.
6 Enrique Castro Delgado, *Hombres Made in Moscu*, pp. 237–41.
7 Enrique Líster, *Memorias de un Luchador*, p. 82.
8 *Mundo Obrero*, 24.7.1936.

9 *Heraldo de Madrid*, 23.7.1936.
10 *Mundo Obrero*, 28.7.1936.
11 Dolores Ibárruri, *They Shall Not Pass*, pp. 209–10.
12 Santiago Alvarez, interview, November 1990.
13 Ronald Fraser, *Blood of Spain*, p. 292.
14 *Heraldo de Madrid*, 24.8.1936.
15 Franz Borkenau, *The Spanish Cockpit*, pp. 120–1.
16 Ibárruri, op. cit., pp. 222–6.
17 *Mundo Obrero*, 3.9.1936.
18 Santiago Alvarez, interview, November 1990.
19 *Mundo Obrero*, 24.9.1936.
20 Ibid., 15.10.1936.
21 Geoffrey Cox, *Defence of Madrid*, pp. 15–17.
22 Antonio Candela, *Adventures of an Innocent*, pp. 56–7.
23 *Heraldo de Madrid*, 15.10.1936.
24 Alvarez, op. cit., II, pp. 75–6.
25 Forrest, interview, November 1990.
26 *Mundo Obrero*, 4.11.1936.
27 Ibid., 9.11.1936.
28 Ibid.
29 Alvarez, op. cit., II, p. 101.
30 Fraser, *op. cit.*, pp. 266–7.
31 *Heraldo de Madrid*, 1.11.1936.
32 *Daily Worker*, 1.1.1937.
33 *Heraldo de Madrid*, 20.1.1937.
34 Ibárruri, op. cit., p. 298.

7 The Communists in Power

1 David Cattell, *Communism and the Spanish Civil War*, p. 97.
2 Alvarez, *Memorias*, II, p. 157.
3 *Mundo Obrero*, 19.3.1937.
4 Walter Krivitsky, *I was Stalin's Agent*, p. 100.
5 Dolores Ibárruri, *They Shall Not Pass*, p. 281.
6 Jesús Hernández, *Yo Fuí Un Ministro de Stalin*, p. 92.
7 Ibid., pp. 128–48.
8 Ibárruri, op. cit., p. 285.
9 George Orwell, *Homage to Catalonia*, Penguin edition 1989 p. 230.
10 Ibid., p. 247

8 La Pasionaria in Love

1 John Tisa, *Recalling the Good Fight*, p. 194 et seq.
2 Philip Toynbee, *The Distant Drum*, p. 158.
3 Enrique Castro Delgado, *Hombres Made in Moscu*, p. 234.
4 Santiago Alvarez, interview, November 1990.
5 Jesús Hernández, *Yo Fuí Un Ministro de Stalin* p. 130.
6 Ibid.
7 Santiago Alvárez, interview, November 1990.
8 Enrique Líster: *Así destruyó Carrillo el PCE*, p. 95.
9 El Campesino, *Listen Comrades*, p. 68.
10 *Nuevo Diario*, 7.11.1972.
11 *Pueblo*, 8.11.1972.
12 Ibid., 29.4.1977.

9 Mother of Battles

1 J. Fyrth with S. Alexander (Eds) *Women's Voices from the Spanish Civil War*, pp. 251–2.
2 Stella Volkenstein, interview, July 1991.
3 *Mundo Obrero*, 19.7.1937.
4 Ibid.
5 David Cattell, *Communism and the Spanish Civil War*, p. 180.
6 *Mundo Obrero*, 23.7.1937.
7 Alvarez, *Memorias*, II, p. 310.
8 Ibid., p. 316.
9 *Mundo Obrero*, 30.7.1937.
10 Antonio Candela, *Adventures of an Innocent*, p. 97.
11 Dolores Ibárruri, *They Shall Not Pass*, p. 296.
12 *Heraldo de Madrid*, 31.1.1937.
13 *Rusia de Hoy*, August 1937.
14 Cattell, op. cit., p. 188.
15 *Heraldo de Madrid*, 1.12.1937.
16 Cattell, op. cit., p. 193.
17 *Heraldo de Madrid*, 31.12.1937.
18 Cattell, op. cit., p. xx.
19 Jesús Hernández, *Yo Fuí Un Ministro de Stalin*, p. 235 et seq.
20 *Mundo Obrero*, 7.1.1938.
21 Enrique Castro Delgado, *Hombres Made in Moscu*, pp. 297–307.
22 Hugh Thomas, *Cuba*, p. 1287.
23 *Mediodía* (Havana), 21.2.1938.

24 *Pasionaria, Memoria Gráfica*, p. 77.
25 John Tisa, *Recalling The Good Fight*, p. 188.

10 Goodbye to Spain

1 Palmiro Togliatti: *Escritos sobre la Guerra de España*, p. 255.
2 Dolores Ibárruri, *They Shall Not Pass*, p. 324.
3 Ibid., p. 325.
4 Ibid., p. 325–6.
5 Togliatti, op. cit., p. 275.
6 Ibárruri, op. cit., pp. 328–30.
7 Ibid., 335–6.
8 Enrique Castro Delgado, *Hombres Made in Moscu*, p. 650.
9 Togliatti, op. cit., p. 275.
10 Ibid., p. 289.
11 Rafael Alberti, interview, November 1990.
12 Irene Falcón, interview, November 1990.

11 The Retreat to Moscow

1 Dolores Ibárruri, *Memorias de Pasionaria* (*Memoirs*, II), p. 26.
2 El Campesino, *Listen Comrades*, pp. 66–71.
3 Ibid., pp. 95–6.
4 Ibid., pp. 98–203.
5 Gregorio Morán, *Miseria y Grandeza del Partido Comunista de España 1939–1985*, p. 32.
6 Ibárruri, op. cit., II, pp. 53–4.
7 Santiago Alvarez, interview, November 1990.
8 Spanish Communist Party (PCE) archives, File 28/1.
9 Lord Citrine, *Two Careers*, pp. 106–7.
10 Ibárruri, op. cit., II, p. 63.
11 Ibid., p. 65.
12 El Campesino, *Comunista en España*, p. 85.
13 Ruiz Ayúcar, *El Partido Comunista*, p. 68.
14 *Madrid magazine*, 13.8.1971.
15 Ibárruri, op. cit., p. 64.
16 Ibárruri, op. cit., II, pp. 65–6.
17 Ibid., p. 66.

12 Coups and Débâcles

1 Public Record Office, FO 371/c1750.
2 Gregorio Morán, *Miseria y Grandeza del Partido Comunista de España*, p. 76.

13 The Guerrilla Dream

1 Dolores Ibárruri, *Memorias de Pasionaria*, p. 89.
2 Ian Gibson, *Paracuellos – Cómo Fue*, p. 235.
3 Ibárruri, op. cit., p. 56.
4 All the papers quoted in this episode are from the PRO, FO371/16234.
5 PRO, FO371/Z1546.
6 PRO, FO371/Z3643.
7 In Spain, children take the name of both father and mother, but are usually known only by the first (the father's): thus La Pasionaria's full name was Dolores Ibárruri Gómez, which is how she correctly identified herself when she applied for her British travel documents. In Cairo British Intelligence referred to her incorrectly as 'Madame Gómez'. This misunderstanding may have been the reason for the tone of the embassy's telegram to London.
8 PRO, FO371/Z4379.
9 Ibárruri, *Memorias de Pasionaria*, pp. 90–92.
10 Enrique Líster, *Así Destruyó Carrillo el PCE*, p. 29.
11 Amaya Ruiz Ibárruri, interview, May 1991.
12 Jorge Semprún, *Autobiográfía de Federico Sánchez*, p. 18.
13 Ibid., p. 7.
14 Ibid.
15 See Daniel, 5:25.
16 Ibid. p. 71–72.
17 Ibid.
18 Gregorio Morán, *Miseria y Grandeza del Partido Comunista de España*, p. 134–136.
19 Líster, *Así Destruyó Carrillo el PCE*, pp. 73–93.
20 Jorge Semprún, *Communism in Spain in the Franco Era*, pp. 91–92.

14 Antón's Downfall

1 Gregorio Morán, *Miseria y Grandeza del Partido Comunista de España* pp. 190–207.

2 Dolores Ibárruri, *Memorias de Pasionaria* (*Memoirs*, II), p. 149.
3 Anastasio Monge Barredo, interview, July 1991.
4 Fernando Claudín, *Santiago Carrillo, Crónica de un Secretario General*, pp. 107–8.
5 Jorge Semprún, *Autobiografía de Federico Sánchez*, pp. 181–4.

15 La Pensionaria

1 Líster, *Así Destruyó Carrillo el PCE*, pp. 115–16.
2 Ruiz Ayúcar, *El Partido Comunista* p. 287.
3 Dolores Ibárruri, *Memorias de Pasionaria* (*Memoirs*, II), p. 149.
4 Gregorio Morán, *Miseria y Grandeza del Partido Comunista de España* p. 262.
5 Ibid., pp. 264–5.
6 Fernando Claudín, *Santiago Carrillo*, pp. 109–10.
7 Ibid., p. 117.
8 Líster, op. cit., p. 124.
9 Ibárruri, op. cit., II, pp. 139–41.
10 Morán, op. cit., pp. 306–7.
11 Fernando Claudín, *The Communist Movement – from Comintern to Cominform*, pp. 7–8.
12 Morán, op. cit., p. 319.
13 Ibid., p. 321.
14 Claudín, *Santiago Carrillo*, p. 136.
15 Ibid., p. 138.
16 Alvarez: Interview, November 1990.
17 Ibárruri, op. cit., II, pp. 153–4.
18 Ibid., p. 153.
19 *ABC*, 20.8.1960
20 *Ya*, 5.12.1962.
21 *Pasionaria, Memoria Gráfica*, p. 121.
22 Her granddaughter Dolores, born in 1960, lived with her from being quite young, and her grandson Fiodor was often there too. When Amaya's marriage broke up in 1968/9 she moved in with La Pasionaria, and the third grandchild, Rubén, joined them in 1975.
23 Dolores Sergueieva Ruiz, interview, May 1991.
24 Ibid.
25 Morán, op. cit., p. 389.
26 Ibid., p. 404.
27 Ibárruri, op. cit., II, p. 174.
28 Stella Volkenstein, interview, July 1991.

16 The End of Exile

1 Jorge Semprún, *Autobiográfía de Federico Sánchez*, p. 282.
2 Ibárruri, *Memorias de Pasionaria* (*Memoirs*, II), p. 184.
3 Gregorio Moran, *Miseria y Grandeza del Partido Comunista de España*. p. 471.
4 Ibárruri, op. cit., II p. 199.
5 Ibid., p. 200.
6 Ibid., p. 201.
7 Robin Lustig, 7.1.1992.
8 Dolores Sergueieva Ruiz, interview, 24 September 1990.
9 Morán, op. cit., p. 518.
10 Rodolfo Martín Villa, *Al Servicio del Estado*, p. 62.
11 *Cambio 16*, 30.1.1977.
12 Ibid.
13 *El País*, 20.3.1977.
14 Martín Villa, op. cit., p. 62.

17 Return of the Native

1 Gregorio Morán, *Miseria y Grandeza del Partido Comunista de España*. p. 564.
2 Rodolfo Martín Villa, *Al Servicio del Estado*, p. 164.
3 David Gilmour, *The Transformation of Spain*, p. 205. *ABC*, 8.9.1978.
4 *El País*, 25.7.1981.
5 Father José María de Llanos, interview, September 1990.
6 *ABC*, 13.11.1989.

SELECT BIBLIOGRAPHY

Alvarez, Santiago, *Memorias*, I–IV, Edicios do Castro, La Coruña: I, *Recuerdos de Infancia y de Juventud (1920–1936)*, 1985; II, *La Guerra Civil de 1936/1939*, 1986; III, *La Lucha Continua (1939–1945)*, 1988; IV, *Mas Fuertes que la Tortura y la Pena de Muerte*, 1990—*Los Comisarios Politicos en el Ejercito Popular de la República*, Edicios do Castro, La Coruña, 1989.

Ayúcar Ruiz, Angel, *El Partido Comunista, 37 Años de Clandestinidad*, Editorial San Martín, Madrid, 1976.

Beevor, Anthony, *The Spanish Civil War*, Orbis, London, 1982.

Bolloten, Burnett, *The Grand Camouflage: The Spanish Civil War and Revolution, 1936–39*, Pall Mall Press, London, 1968.

Borkenau, Franz, *The Spanish Cockpit*, reprinted, University of Michigan Press, 1963.

Brenan, Gerald, *The Spanish Labyrinth*, Cambridge University Press, 1943, repr. 1990.

Campesino, El (Valentín González), *Listen Comrades: Life and Death in the Soviet Union*, William Heinemann, London 1952.

Comunista en España y Anti-Stalinista en La URSS, reissued Ediciones Jucar, Madrid, 1977.

Candela, Antonio, *Adventures of an Innocent in the Spanish Civil War*, United Writers, Penzance, Cornwall, 1989.

Carr, Raymond, *Spain 1808–1975*, Oxford University Press, 2nd edn, 1982.

Carrillo, Santiago, *Mañana España: Conversaciones con Regis Debray y Max Gallo*, Madrid, 1976.

Castro Delgado, Enrique, *Hombres Made in Moscú*, Luis de Caralt, Barcelona, 1963.

Cattell, David, *Communism and the Spanish Civil War*, University of California Press, Berkeley and Los Angeles, 1955.

Citrine, Lord, *Two Careers*, Hutchinson, London, 1963.

Claudín, Fernando, *The Communist Movement: From Comintern to Cominform*, Peregrine Books, London, 1975.
—*Santiago Carrillo, Crónica de un Secretario General*, Editorial Planeta, Barcelona, 1983.
Cox, Geoffrey, *Defence of Madrid*, Gollancz, London, 1937.
Fraser, Ronald, *Blood of Spain – The Experience of Civil War 1936–1939*, Allen Lane, London, 1979; Pelican Books, London 1988.
Fyrth, Jim, with Alexander, Sally (Eds), *Women's Voices From The Spanish Civil War*, Lawrence & Wishart, London 1991.
Gibson, Ian, *Paracuellos: Cómo Fué*, Argos Vergara, Barcelona, 1983.
Gilmour, David, *The Transformation of Spain*, Quartet Books, London, 1985.
Graham, Robert, *Spain: Change of a Nation*, Michael Joseph, London, 1984.
Hemingway, Ernest, *For Whom The Bell Tolls*, Penguin, Harmondsworth, 1990.
Hernández, Jesús, *Yo Fuí un Ministro de Stalin*, G. del Toro, Madrid, 1974.
Ibárruri, Dolores, *They Shall Not Pass: The autobiography of La Pasionaria*, Lawrence & Wishart, London 1966.
—*Memorias de Pasionaria 1939–1977*, Editorial Planeta, Barcelona, 1984.
Jackson, Gabriel, *The Spanish Republic and the Civil War 1931–1939*, Princeton University Press, 1965.
Khrushchev, Nikita, *Khrushchev Remembers*, Little, Brown, New York, 1970.
Krivitsky, Walter, *I was Stalin's Agent*, Hamish Hamilton, London, 1939.
Lange, Peter and Vannicelli, Maurizio (Eds), *The Communist Parties of Italy, France and Spain: Postwar Change and Continuity*, George Allen & Unwin, London, 1981.
Líster, Enrique, *Memorias de un Luchador*, Madrid, 1977.
—*Así destruyó Carrillo el PCE*, Editorial Planeta, Barcelona, 1983.
Low, Mary and Brea, Juan, *Red Spanish Notebook*, reprinted City Lights Books, San Francisco, 1979.
Martín Villa, Rodolfo, *Al Servicio del Estado*, Editorial Planeta, Barcelona, 1984.
Morán, Gregorio, *Miseria y Grandeza del Partido Comunista de España 1939–1985*, Editorial Planeta, Barcelona, 1986.
Pasionaria, Partido Comunista de España, Madrid, 1938.

Pasionaria, Memoria Gráfica, Partido Comunista de España, Madrid 1985.

Pettifer, James (Ed.), *Cockburn in Spain*, Lawrence & Wishart, London, 1986.

Preston, Paul, *The Spanish Civil War*, Weidenfeld & Nicolson, London, 1986.

Prieto, Indalecio: *Entresijos de la Guerra de España*, Editorial Bases, Buenos Aires, 1954.

Rubio Cabeza, Manuel, *Diccionario de la Guerra Civil Española*, Vols 1 & 2, Editorial Planeta, Barcelona, 1987.

Semprún, Jorge, *Autobiografía de Federico Sánchez*, Editorial Planeta, Barcelona, 1977. (Translated into English as *Communism in Spain in the Franco Era*, Harvester Press, Brighton, 1980.)

Thomas, Hugh, *Cuba, or The Pursuit of Freedom*, Eyre & Spottiswoode, London, 1971.

—*The Spanish Civil War*, Hamish Hamilton/Penguin, London, 3rd edn, 1977.

Tisa, John, *Recalling The Good Fight: An Autobiography of the Spanish Civil War*, Bergin & Garvey, Massachusetts, 1985.

Togliatti, Palmiro, *Escritos sobre la Guerra de España*, Barcelona, 1980.

Toynbee, Philip (Ed), *The Distant Drum*, Sidgwick & Jackson, London, 1963.

INDEX

Sergueiev, General Artiom, 162, 165

Sergueieva, Dolores (grand-daughter 'Lola'), 17, 18, 162, 183, 184, 196, 199, 212, 213, 215, 225

Sergueiev, Fiodor (grandson), 162, 183, 225

Sergueiev, Rubén (grandson), 162, 225

Sirval, Luis de, 57

Slansky, Rudolf, 39, 161

Socialist Party of Spain, 6, 9, 10, 16, 18, 21, 24, 48, 82, 131, 208, 209

Solis, Oscar Perez, 133

Somorrostro (first home after marriage), 20, 21, 25, 30, 31, 32, 35, 37, 93, 94

Soria, Castille, 12

Sotelo, José Calvo, 55, 56, 57, 58
    alleged death threat by La Pasionaria, 58–9, 215
    assassination, 58, 59, 63, 214

Soviet Communist Party, 2, 3
    becomes increasingly conservative under Brezhnev, 188
    homage on La Pasionaria's 80th birthday, 198
    role in Spanish Civil War, 62, 81–8
    Stalin denounced at XX Congress (1956), 169–70, 171, 172

Soviet Union
    Hungarian uprising, 175–6, 188
    invasion of Czechoslovakia, 3, 188–90, 192
    Nazi conflict, 123–4, 126–7, 129–33
    La Pasionaria: children

evacuated to, 44–6; exile in, 2, 3, 4, 92, 117, 119–44, 155–203

Spanish exiles, 93–4, 116–17, 119–25, 126–7, 129–30, 131–4, 136, 162–4, 165, 180, 188, 190

split with China, 180–1

Spanish-American war of 1898, 7

Spanish Communist Workers Party (PCOE), 25

speechmaking by La Pasionaria, 29–30, 148, 149, 150, 165, 176, 180–1, 185, 186, 190, 194, 195–6, 197–8, 200, 206
    addresses Plenum in Bucharest (1956), 174
    alleged death threat to Calvo Sotelo, 58–9
    Civil War speeches and broadcasts, 64–5, 67, 82–3, 96–7, 98, 100, 101, 102–3, 107; appeal to America and Europe, 68; during siege of Madrid, 73–80; mass rally in Valencia, 70
    Cortes speeches (1936), 55–60
    début in elections of 1931, 29
    farewell speech at VI Party Congress, 179
    goodbye to International Brigades in Barcelona, 108–10, 111
    Paris Velodrome speeches, 30, 72, 107–8
    Toulouse anti-American speech (1947), 150–1

Spender, Stephen, 95

Stakhanov, A.G., 97

Stalin, Joseph, 34, 36, 37, 38, 43, 81, 83, 87, 92, 97, 99, 108,